AMERICAN IMMIGRATION AFTER 1996

KATHLEEN R. ARNOLD

AMERICAN IMMIGRATION AFTER 1996

The Shifting Ground of Political Inclusion

The Pennsylvania State University Press
University Park, Pennsylvania

Portions of chapter 2 were previously published in
"Enemy Invaders! Mexican Immigrants and U.S. Wars Against
Them," *Borderlands* 6, no. 3 (December 2007),
http://www.borderlands.net.au/.

Chapter 4 is an expanded version of a paper first published
as "Economic Prerogative and Its Political Consequences,"
Constellations 18, no. 4 (2011).

Library of Congress Cataloging-in-Publication Data

Arnold, Kathleen R., 1966–
American immigration after 1996 : the shifting ground
of political inclusion / Kathleen R. Arnold.
    p.   cm.
Includes bibliographical references and index.
Summary: "Examines the underlying complexities of immigration
in the United States and the relationship between globalization
of the economy and issues of political sovereignty"—Provided by publisher.
    ISBN 978-0-271-04889-5 (cloth : alk. paper)
    ISBN 978-0-271-04890-1 (pbk. : alk. paper)
    1. United States—Emigration and immigration.
    2. Immigrants—United States—Social conditions.
    3. Immigrants—Civil rights—United States.
    I. Title.

JV6465.A76 2011
304.8'73—dc22
2011008010

The Pennsylvania State University Press is a member of the
Association of American University Presses.

It is the policy of The Pennsylvania State University Press to
use acid-free paper. Publications on uncoated stock satisfy
the minimum requirements of American National Standard
for Information Sciences—Permanence of Paper for Printed
Library Material, ANSI Z39.48–1992.

For DAD AND GAYAN;

THANKS FOR YOUR SUPPORT AND LOVE

Contents

Acknowledgments

Although I was particularly motivated to write these chapters during the widespread backlash against immigration between 2006 and 2008, this book was also inspired by my personal experiences with immigration (living and working abroad), as well as by numerous experiences with immigrants as friends and coworkers in the United States. My ideas on immigration were also greatly aided when I first taught a course on immigration at Harvard University. I would like to thank the students of those seminars—particularly the first one I taught—for their enthusiasm and suggestions. The anonymous committee that oversaw and chose the course was also very helpful and suggested some works that are crucial to my discussion in this book. Although I now work in relative isolation, the discussions I had with Nicholas Xenos about the course and my earlier work on immigration were invaluable, as always. I continue to teach a similar course on immigration and have learned quite a lot from my students in Texas. In addition, audiences and panels at conferences where I presented these chapters—including the Western Political Science Association Meetings of 2008 and 2009 and the Lonestar Theory Workshop of 2009—were also very helpful.

I want to thank Sandy Thatcher, who is truly a great editor. Sandy is open to new approaches and interdisciplinary work, and I am grateful for his suggestions and enthusiasm for this project. I would also like to thank James Martel, Sheila Croucher, and a third, anonymous reviewer for their engagement with my arguments and their very constructive comments. In addition, my friend Karuna Mantena gave me critical feedback on the chapter on guest workers and the maquila program at a crucial time—I really appreciate the help. Finally, I would like to thank *Borderlands* for permission to reprint an earlier version of chapter 2 and *Constellations* for permission to reprint parts of chapter 4. Any errors in this book are my own.

On a personal level, I would like to thank my friends Jonathan Bernstein, Joshua Dienstag, Ashley Díaz, Patricia Jaramillo, Amy Jasperson, Karuna Mantena (again), and Kimberly Sims, as well as my mother, Kathy, for their support during a difficult period. My daughter, Hannah, continues to make single motherhood joyful and exiting. I am dedicating this book to my father, Tony, and his wife, Gayan, whose support for my work and personal life I truly appreciate.

Introduction

In the two years preceding the 2008 presidential election, immigration became a hot topic of public discussion for the first time since the mid-1990s.[1] In light of the events of September 11, 2001, it has generally been taken for granted that there is an "immigration problem," and concern has largely been directed at unauthorized entrants, mostly from Mexico.[2] Although the perception that there is a serious immigration problem is nothing new, the issue took on new momentum in this brief time period.[3] In 2006, for example, arrests of immigrants nationwide doubled;[4] President George W. Bush succeeded in doubling the number of Border Patrol agents and increased National Guard presence on the southern border;[5] and different states and municipalities began to crack down on immigrants in various ways, including English-only laws,[6] the increased use of E-Verify (a program that verifies a potential employee's citizenship), expedited deportation, as well as increased numbers of deportations.[7] The self-evidence with which it has been asserted that immigration, and particularly unauthorized entry, constituted major problems meant that there was a backlash with little recognition of this fact.[8] This has been the case even though today's backlash is reminiscent of those during other periods in American history, drawing on the same stereotypes and worries. But perhaps because the United States is facing a new problem—terrorism and the accompanying "war on terror"—today's measures are viewed not as reactionary, but rather as "responsible" and getting "serious" about immigration.[9] As in other recent time periods,[10] however, the "problem" is narrowly construed.

It seems that the debates on immigration in the new millennium have left people in two camps. On the one hand, proponents of immigration argue that the United States should continue to allow immigrants to enter because they are necessary for the workforce. This group is bipartisan and sees immigration as necessary for the low-tier labor market and to maintain American international economic competitiveness. On the other, there are those who would significantly decrease immigration, build a wall between the United States and Mexico, and increase scrutiny of any remaining immigrants to the United States. For example, one proposal from 2005 included making unauthorized entry a felony, making the provision of aid to any unauthorized entrant a felony, expedited deportation, prohibiting states to grant sanctuary to suspected illegals,[11] and, most notably, increasing surveillance of all entrants, augmenting law enforcement, and building the aforementioned wall.[12] While the first group appears to be more humane toward immigrants and tolerant of their presence, their proposals for the guest-worker program, for example, show that they are much closer to the second group in their desire for surveillance, easier deportation procedures, and weak labor standards that lead to worker exploitation.[13] Alternatively, the second group's concerns are seemingly limited to worries about national security, but their calls for increased surveillance, a wall, and other measures that militarize the southern border ensure that those who work here do so in unfree conditions. In effect, these proposals are really two sides of the same coin, with the only real difference being how many immigrants can enter legally.[14] What these debates tell us is that old stereotypes about immigrants are being redeployed in a time of "war": a war without borders, which has not been officially declared, and yet is being used to justify the suspension of civil rights and the Geneva Conventions. The wars on terror, drugs, and narco-terrorism allow for new power dynamics that will ensure that immigrants' rights and political needs cannot be met by the nation-state.

The continued merging of immigration policy with anti-terror provisions has led to increased arrests of immigrants, harsh treatment of unauthorized entrants, and charges of racial profiling. In one recent case, the interpreter Erik Camayd-Freixas noted that the treatment of 297 undocumented workers in Postville, Iowa, by ICE (U.S. Immigration and Customs Enforcement) officials went far beyond the "crimes" these individuals committed. Camayd-Freixas contends that "according to its new paradigm, the agency [ICE] fancies that it can conflate the diverse aspects of its operations and pretend that immigration enforcement is really part and parcel of the 'war on terror.' This way, statistics in the former translate as evidence of success in the latter. Thus, the Postville charges—document fraud and identity theft—treat every illegal alien as a potential terrorist, and with the same rigor."[15] Nevertheless, because the United States hopes to maintain international economic competitiveness, it also views the same immigrants as crucial to the functioning of its economy. As immigrants are viewed and treated both as a threat to national security and as an exploitable group of workers, their political status becomes increasingly undecidable, leaving them vulnerable in a new way.

Although the United States receives an incredibly diverse group of immigrants and asylum claimants, the perception of an immigration "problem" is mainly focused on Mexicans and Mexican Americans.[16] For this reason, I will also concentrate almost exclusively on this group in this book—not to illuminate its particular characteristics, but to consider why it is the most controversial group in this country at this particular moment in history. On the one hand, this group is now the nation's largest minority and is the main source of both legal and illegal immigration to the United States. It also has deep historical and cultural ties to the United States because of a shared border. For these reasons, the attention paid to this group is logical. On the other, Mexicans and Mexican Americans are arguably viewed as controversial because of the range of stereotypes about them—from poor education, to poor work habits, to high fertility rates, to their supposed desire to milk the United States for its benefits. They are most often low-tier workers and less educated than some other immigrant groups, and they are now considered the heart of such U.S. problems as overcrowded health facilities and "stolen" jobs. Indeed, the conditions of this group and the stereotypes about them have a striking resemblance to discriminatory rhetoric and actions against poor Irish immigrants from the mid-nineteenth century to the early twentieth century.[17] Both groups have been charged with stealing jobs, being parasites, overcrowding housing, having too many children, burdening public welfare, and lacking restraint. But these feelings and stereotypes have far more to do with U.S. political and economic issues than with issues in the particular immigrant community. Essentially, they symbolize all the United States' present concerns: the loss of a social safety net, a crisis in health care, a faltering economy, and the threat of terrorism.

In particular, it is alleged that Mexicans do not assimilate, that they want to use the United States for services or to send remittances home but are not loyal to this country, and that they are a major drain on welfare. But in the context of the war on terror (and related wars), Mexicans' presence is viewed as not merely an economic threat but also a sovereign one—this is a key difference from the perception of the Irish in the mid-1800s.[18] One reason for this is that the border today is far tighter than it was in the nineteenth century, and therefore unauthorized entry has a very different political meaning than it did in the past.[19] Particularly since the 1990s, both the government and vigilante groups have increasingly militarized the border.[20] Nevertheless, the United States' desire to remain competitive in the international market ensures that Mexicans are never denied access to this country. Rather, the goal is to facilitate economic exploitability through increased surveillance and control.

Although there is a significant amount of literature on immigration—issuing from the backlash against immigration in the 1990s[21] and the second backlash resulting from the events of September 11, 2001—there are fewer political-theoretical interpretations of these debates[22] and little recognition of the effect of these "wars" on immigrants. Rather, much of the conventional political literature rests on preconceived notions or unexamined assumptions about the objects of study. Samuel Huntington's article "The Hispanic Challenge," his subsequent book *Who Are We? The Challenge to America's National Identity*,[23] and the spate of responses to his arguments (from popular responses in newspapers to the series of articles examining his premises in *Perspectives on Politics* in 2006 and 2007) are examples of how political scientists take for granted terms like assimilation, national identity, economic participation, legality, and political loyalty.[24] For instance, Huntington contends that Mexicans' Catholicism is a hindrance to their economic progress. Not only does he not explore this assumption (which rests on the notion of Protestantism's superiority), but in fact many of his critics misunderstand his point or simply try to disprove him. For example, one author simply notes that it is true Latinos have not converted to Protestantism, rather than challenging the preconception that only certain religious values will make an individual fit for U.S. citizenship.[25] Further, all parties involved seem to think that these matters can be settled empirically even though they involve highly arbitrary, qualitative terms (e.g., measuring loyalty by examining a survey question regarding feelings about the U.S. flag).[26]

In this book, I examine the monolithic images that can be found in public policy, opinion, and recent debates (all of which Michel Foucault would broadly term "discourse"), rather than looking at the target populations (Mexicans, as well as individuals from Central and South America, the Caribbean, and those of Arab/Middle Eastern/Islamic descent or belief) in terms of their culture and their "assimilability." In the spirit of Bonnie Honig, Saskia Sassen, and Yasemin Soysal,[27] I believe that host countries are not passive agents in immigration patterns, simply receiving immigrants and formulating policy on their goodwill or lack thereof. Further, I do not think immigrants simply come to this country because of the deficiencies of their home country per se, or for purely individual reasons. In conventional lines of argument, questions of assimilation, work conditions, political status, and loyalty are viewed in terms of the immigrant groups' background and beliefs. Rather, it is more fruitful to consider the "linkages" or "bridges" that the United States has built to foster these migration processes (as Saskia Sassen has called for), what norms of assimilation can tell us about American national self-understanding, and how requisites of the nation-state as well as global capital inform political status and produce a situation far more complicated than mainstream U.S. public debate and policy provide for.[28]

More specifically, I believe that few conventional analyses of immigration have fully accounted for the linkage between the globalization of the economy and issues of sovereignty.[29] This is particularly true in political accounts of immigration[30] and less true of scholars whose work is interdisciplinary (though these ideas are not reflected in mainstream debates or in the media). Since the end of the Cold War and the increasing predominance of neoliberalism, the connection between a more global economy and sovereignty is more significant than in the past—that is, as sovereign matters have increasingly become intertwined with economic ones. Issues of immigration crystallize both sets of concerns and shed light on the status of citizenship, democracy, and the meaning of assimilation. Unlike some authors who claim that the increasing globalization of the economy means that the sovereign state is weakening,[31] I believe that the U.S. government is increasing its deployments of sovereignty—particularly prerogative power—at the same time that borders are challenged by global capital and global terror. Immigration is a significant area in which sovereignty has been strengthened, despite the rhetoric of a loss of control over the border.[32] Prerogative power is the legal suspension of the law during times of emergency, natural disaster, or when the law is outdated.[33] As low-tier immigrant workers are hired and yet denied the rights and protections afforded citizens, a "free" market is established alongside an increasingly unfree labor force. Indeed, there is a symbiotic relationship among the increasing militarization of the border, Patriot Act provisions that suspend some civil and human rights, the greater surveillance of all immigrants, and the greater exploitation of immigrants who work in low-tier, informal conditions (e.g., in sweatshops, deregulated factories and meat-processing plants, and maquiladoras). But this does not mean that the traditional nation-state is the only source of power or legitimacy;[34] rather, transnational areas and identities are becoming the norm alongside the transmogrification of state power (rather than its increasing absence). It is for this reason that U.S. policies and mainstream debates, including conventional scholarly analyses, are too narrow and outdated.

As discussed above, recent proposals for immigration policy reform have suggested that there are only two possible solutions to the alleged problem of immigration and unauthorized entry: either enlarge the guest-worker program or militarize the southern border even more, make punishments and fines for illegal entry (or aiding illegal entry) even harsher, and work to stem or halt the flow of the Mexican "invasion."[35] The first solution has been presented as more humanitarian and democratic, but both sets of proposals issue from mutually informing notions of immigrants—either as exploitable labor or as potential security threats. In this way, they are binary modes of operation that reinforce rather than challenge the connection between sovereign power and the demands of global capital. Further, neither solution accounts for increasingly transnational processes of labor relations, political identities, and geographical areas that defy the logic of the nation-state (e.g., free zones). The transnational status of many Mexicans and Mexican Americans is particularly relevant to this discussion.[36]

What makes these workers' political status ambivalent and thus precarious is the politically undecidable character of their lives. The status of Mexican immigrants today is transnational in at least three ways: First, there is a great deal of crossing the southern border, accompanied by mixed allegiances.[37] Transnational families are those "whose core members are located in at least two nation-states."[38] These arrangements reflect border enforcement at the individual level, which comes at the expense of family or community: "Transnational households signify segregation."[39] Second, the border area is truly transnational because of the agreement that established the Border Industrialization Program (BIP) in 1964, which created a free zone on the Mexican border, allowing "foreign manufacturers to assemble goods without having to abide by existing import-export duties and regulations."[40] Significantly, employment and factory regulations are lax in this area. Third, the United States' historical ambivalence about Mexicans places them in a paradoxical position—valued and degraded, crucial to the U.S. economy and yet waging a war on it, upholding family values and yet destroying social welfare institutions and producing too many babies. These ambivalent spaces allow for hybrid identities (e.g., Chicano/a identity),[41] hybrid political formations,[42] and some financial gains, but they also constitute a precarious political space that is increasingly marked by a war mentality and violence.[43]

Throughout the book, I consider the theories of Michel Foucault and Giorgio Agamben together.[44] In each chapter, I explicate how I use their theories, but here I will briefly sketch how their ideas are relevant to this subject. Two of the main Foucaultian concepts I use throughout the book are bio-power[45] and disciplinary power.[46] These concepts indicate the historical transformation of political power, broadly defined, with the growth of science and industrialization. Among other things, disciplinary power involves the increasing subjection of individuals to social, political, and economic norms that they are expected to internalize. It marks a turn from traditional institutional forms to more systematic arrangements in prisons, schools, and the workplace, based on stricter schedules, the "optimization of [the body's] capabilities,"[47] and self-surveillance, leading to "usefulness and docility."[48] Although some have argued that disciplinary power is no longer relevant to today's "flexible" work structure,[49] I believe that this term is still pertinent to immigrant workers' conditions both within the United States and on the southern border; in particular, I am concerned about how these conditions have a disciplinary effect on low-tier conditions for all workers.

Bio-power emerged later, when scientific analysis began to conceive of individuals as a species and when the control of public health became possible. Bio-power involves the increasing concern of politics with biological matters, including issues of reproduction, disease control, demographics, and migration. More insidiously, this sort of power can lead not only to the "optimization of life" but also the use of bio-political norms to determine what counts as human and subhuman. For this reason, as notions of race became more "scientific" in the twentieth century and Western governments were increasingly oriented toward bio-politics, racial divisions and genocide have become the logical extensions of this concern with the population as a species. Although Foucault briefly discusses state-sponsored racism in his analysis of bio-power, in chapter 3 I explore this link in more depth and more specifically than he does. I argue that older racial images and stereotypes of Mexicans and Mexican Americans now have bio-political meaning; that is, for this population race has become an issue of sovereignty in ways that were not true in the past.[50] Combined with an even more prevalent concern about immigrant women's reproduction and "anchor babies," these immigrants are not merely "other" but are conceived as threats to U.S. sovereignty.[51]

Further, the case of Mexican workers in the United States and on the border shows how the intersection of disciplinary power and bio-power can produce a subject that is economically necessary yet also often treated as a potential enemy. In Agamben's terms, the economic and political conditions of many of these workers approach that of bare or biological life.[52] Simply put, bare life is individual life stripped of its citizenship and "humanity." For this to be possible, first the term "humanity" must be almost meaningless outside the status of citizenship, thus rendering human rights ineffective in a world still defined by the nation-state.[53] Second, this implies that humanity itself has no biological referent, that it is constantly being defined and redefined, even though discourse indicates otherwise (i.e., it is naturalized). To Agamben, bare life is subject to prerogative power (again, the legal suspension of the law); thus it is the object of political power but has a highly ambivalent political status.

In terms of how I use the concept of bare life in this book, I am clearly not discussing a group of American-born citizens who have been stripped of their citizenship. But nor am I discussing a group—particularly individuals of Mexican descent—who have clearly been outsiders, even though they have recently been constructed this way. In fact, the unique history of Mexicans and Mexican Americans shows a narrative that challenges any inside/outside binary. For example, the Treaty of Guadalupe Hidalgo (1848) is a case of borders crossing people as portions of the Southwest went from being Mexican to American territory. In the twentieth century, two mass deportations indeed stripped Americans of their citizenship: the first such effort was called "repatriation" while the second utilized an ethnic slur as the title of an operation to disenfranchise hundreds of thousands of individuals.[54] Parts of the United States have often bled into Mexico, and this blurring of boundaries is most evident today in the Border Industrial Program (also known as the maquila program). Although other immigrant groups do not have the same history, many do have established ties to the United States both here and in their country of origin, even though these links have been de-emphasized in policy and public debates. These examples defy the inside/outside logic of terms like "citizen" and "foreigner," and suggest a more undecidable status. It is this undecidability or ambivalence in Agamben's concept of bare life that I want to draw on in the pages that follow.[55]

The term "bare life" has also been very controversial.[56] First, Agamben has developed this concept using the concentration camp as the paradigm of the extreme limit of bio-power. Although he has been careful to state that the concentration camp is the *extreme* manifestation of this sort of power, each declaration by him or others that a group is being treated as bare life has elicited such responses as "but they are not in a concentration camp" or "this is not Nazi Germany." The point is not to call all uses of the suspension of the law Nazi, nor to call all individuals subject to prerogative power victims of fascism, but rather to highlight the significant rightlessness (broadly conceived) of the stateless in democracies.[57] They occupy a space that is highly indeterminate but still political. Significantly, this does not mean a legal void, but often a second set of laws that somehow make the subject of these laws inferior to citizens; this is an important proviso in my own use of the term "prerogative power."[58] He is also trying to show how the power mechanisms at work in the Nazi regime are not foreign or wholly anomalous to the development of modern Western political power, but rather the most dangerous manifestation of the use of prerogative power in a democracy that declares a state of emergency. I do not want to suggest that my use of Agamben's work then equates the plight of immigrants with the victims of fascism. Instead, I find his work suggestive in terms of the statelessness that is often the result of uprooting policies and norms. Like his emphasis on camps, I want to explore how politico-economic policies and practices in effect denationalize parts of national territory[59] and render individuals stateless. In particular, I suggest the effects that the *threat* of deportation has on the lives of ordinary foreigners, as well as the broader perception that immigrants are no longer just potential lawbreakers but potential terrorists as well.[60] Rather than focus on detention centers, however, I examine at greater length how the guest-worker system as well as the Border Industrial Program are geopolitical spaces that suspend workers' rights during the length of their work contract.

A second problem is the possible conflation of the term "bare life" with "enemy." To Agamben, these two expressions should be kept distinct, even if at times they are one and the same.[61] Following Agamben, I draw on both terms, focusing on "bare life" first and then discussing how this term can be related to "enemy" in the context of the wars on terror and drugs. What I want to emphasize is that current power dynamics lead to the suspension of the law, but this does not mean that all individual entrants are treated the same way. Instead, given the current political and economic dynamics, controversial immigrants face a range of power mechanisms, the extreme point of which is detention or deportation.

I should also note that I use the term "prerogative power" (a term Agamben almost never uses), which I feel is more precise than the terms "sovereign power" or "sovereignty." Sovereignty is in fact important when considering U.S. immigration: immigration is regulated by "Congress's plenary, or

absolute power to regulate immigration as part of its authority over foreign relations, in the same realm as declaring war and making treaties."[62]
The term "prerogative" is a particular deployment of this sovereign power,
indicating the act of suspending the law and establishing a less determinate
political status of the subjects of this power; this term has special meaning
in the context of the United States' continued engagement in the war on
terror and the current economic crisis of 2010. What is remarkable about
prerogative power is that it is exercised internationally and domestically,
and with increasing regularity and permanence. But I do not mean presidential prerogative or the prerogative power of a governor alone, but also a
form of power wielded by a variety of governmental institutions and agents
under nondemocratic auspices and aimed at noncitizens.[63] I also argue that
vigilante groups can uphold this sort of power through physical threats and
racial profiling. Roxanne Doty calls this a form of "statecraft from below."[64]
Thus I conceive of this power as being deployed not vertically but in a
weblike network (influenced by Foucault, but also challenging his distinction between sovereignty and, respectively, bio-power, disciplinary power,
and governmentality).[65] Additionally, it is important to note that as power
becomes more dispersed and deterritorialized, it becomes more porous.
Hence it should not be confused with older conceptions of prerogative as
absolute or totalizing. The terms "prerogative" and "bare life" indicate that
their objects—the stateless or enemies—are in a legal limbo, and that this
limbo is not anomalous but rather produced by U.S. political power today.
These distinctions will be made clearer throughout the book.

   In sum, there are four factors crucial to my argument: (1) the growth
of U.S. domestic wars and the state of emergency (i.e., the increased predominance of prerogative power), (2) the ambivalent political status of many
recent Mexican immigrants and workers on the border, (3) a public debate
that presents the (Mexican) immigration issue in polarized and simplistic
terms, and (4) neoliberal demands for cheap, "flexible" labor to ensure that
the U.S. economy is internationally competitive.

   I begin examining these issues by considering assimilation norms in the
United States today. As many have recognized, assimilation norms in the
past were rigid, ethnocentric, and class biased, and demanded a wholesale public disavowal of one's identity, language, and traditions. Mainstream
authors argue that this was replaced by a discourse of difference—whether it
is multiculturalism, post-modernism, or post-structuralism—in the 1980s and
1990s, and that today a more sensible and democratic model of assimilation

has returned. This return of assimilation, as Rogers Brubaker argues, corrects the excesses of the *différance* camp.[66] If racism is accounted for and assimilation is viewed as a mutual interaction between immigrants and host country, Brubaker contends (along with others) that this is a welcome return of the canonical model. I dispute this view but find that it does unmask the preconceptions of a great number of immigrant researchers,[67] who often unquestioningly accept the categories of the normative model of assimilation, derived from the Chicago School. These preconceptions are closely linked to stereotypes and conventional wisdom, reaffirming the status quo rather than challenging it. For example, why do these scholars take it for granted that economic success should be a criterion of democratic citizenship? Or that language acquisition is truly an issue in the United States *and* that it measures one's fitness for citizenship? At the very least, these presuppositions must be questioned and their relationship to democracy considered. Although it is often argued that the categories of assimilation—wealth, skills, and language—are merely instrumental to citizenship, many of these authors slip into conceptualizing these categories as enacting or performing citizenship functions. For example, language in particular is not treated as a mere instrument to naturalizing in the United States, but is considered the litmus test of whether an immigrant is loyal to the country.[68]

Assimilation debates also say very little about the immigrants themselves but quite a lot about "us," the host country. As mainstream academics write about the subject, they obscure just as much as they explain. In particular, the focus on economic assimilation overemphasizes the economic viewpoint, obfuscating other facets of an individual's life.[69] But it also places the focus on the immigrant, with the assumption that she or he left home due to poverty, overpopulation, or poor job opportunities, among other things. Challenging these views, Saskia Sassen has convincingly shown that the political, economic, cultural, and military links that the host country formed with the sending country are crucial to understanding why certain groups move to a specific country. Nevertheless, the focus is nearly always on the immigrant individual or group and not the host country.[70] Researchers of immigration who rely on conventional views also tend to neglect the interdisciplinary nature of this specific issue. I mean this in a special sense: the subjects of immigrants and immigration necessarily fall into domestic politics and international relations, thus splitting the conceptual "border" that often marks how these subjects are investigated. To put it differently, analyzing citizenship involves not only democratic theory but also an analysis of the nation-state. Interestingly, many authors presuppose the nation-state as a naturalized and singular homeland, a monolithic entity, without discussing this preconception.[71] Linda Bosniak has also remarked on this, noting that citizenship scholars tend to ignore the "growing (though uneven) permeability of national borders," leading to an "insular framework" that "treat[s] the national society as the total universe of analytical and moral concern."[72] For this reason, they stay firmly in the intellectual terrain that was set when assimilation norms were intolerant and openly biased. While there are excellent accounts of assimilation that are far more complex and interdisciplinary, these accounts do not seem to have influenced policy, media portrayals of assimilation, public debate, or conventional views of immigration in mainstream academic work.[73]

Finally, today's expectations of assimilation shed light on the status of democracy and citizenship in the United States. Indeed, I believe that the concept of assimilation unites all other concerns about immigrants—it is an "umbrella" issue, bringing together all anxieties about immigrants and guiding public reaction, public policy, and mainstream scholarly work. Demands for assimilation today reflect sovereign concerns and economic requisites, as I have argued above, but they also demonstrate that U.S. citizenship and democracy are based on notions of conformity and consensus rather than debate, diversity, and the right to dissent. Mainstream and right-wing reactions to the mass protests on behalf of immigrants in April 2006 are evidence of this; the protests were portrayed as illegal, traitorous, and evidence of immigrants'—particularly Mexicans'—unassimilability.[74] What is more, they demonstrate that economic issues are tightly linked to sovereign ones as illegal entrants are increasingly treated as threatening to national security and as potential terrorists.[75] What I suggest in chapter 1 is, first, that the scholarly norms of assimilation that find the most resonance in immigration policy and public debates are also the most conventional ones; and second, that not only are the U.S. norms of assimilation impossible to meet for the bulk of immigrants, but they also suggest the limitations of current democratic conceptions and processes.

In the second chapter, I explore aspects of gender, race, and class in public discourse and policy, and link these to sovereign interests. In particular, public discourse and policy demonstrate binary modes of operation concerning work and the work ethic: Mexicans steal jobs but also welfare; Mexicans depress wages but are also apathetic; Mexicans are taking over the job market but are lazy. These binary modes not only are mutually reinforcing but also can be linked to other binary modes of operation regarding gender and fertility: Mexicans are models of family values but have too many children; they are models of religious faith, but this belief system leads to their lack of restraint regarding birth control. Mexican women are models of sacrifice but they also burden the educational and medical systems as a result of their profligacy; they are viewed as irresponsible and as drains on the economy, but they are also clearly viewed as vehicles of assimilation, responsible for taming their wilder male counterparts. Mexican men are ideal laborers but are also portrayed as hypersexual, out-of-control, potential rapists (e.g., in the documentary *POV: Farmingville*).[76] But these binary modes of operation are more significant for what they say about American national self-understanding, notions of race and ethnicity, and gender than about the Mexicans themselves. These meanings in turn have important implications for the status of U.S. democracy today.

In the third chapter, I argue that just as civil society groups can foster democracy, we forget an important lesson from Tocqueville, who also warned about the linkage between tyranny of the majority and the increasing centralization of government: that civil society can also serve a far more negative role, which can ultimately lead to censorship, conformity, and an expansion of the central government at the expense of truly democratic processes. Applied to contemporary immigration politics, I examine the role of anti-immigration groups like Ranch Rescue, American Patrol, and the Minutemen. I find that although they follow the rule of law, they use individual rights to create a warlike atmosphere and facilitate the suspension of law.[77] In this way, although these groups often position themselves against the government, they uphold the state of emergency and the suspension of law that the government actively seeks in order to foster its wars on terror, drugs, and narco-terrorism. This book challenges conventional notions of assimilation and immigrants, not to mention drawing attention to the connection between conventional presuppositions about immigrants and the status of democracy today.

In the following chapter, I examine the guest-worker program for low-tier workers and the BIP (aka the maquila program). I argue that the power dynamics of these two programs are ideal forms both of neoliberal policies and of sovereign power, as they seek to control the movements of workers while creating "free" conditions for their employers. Although these zones have been rhetorically construed as purely economic and therefore absent of politics and the political, I contend that the deterritorialization and rightlessness they effect work with sovereign power to create a more exploitable and controllable population. These two programs, which are outside the norms of citizenship and immigration law, are aimed at controlling illegal entry (a problem of sovereignty) and ensuring U.S. competitiveness in the global market (an economic problem that relies on the intervention of the state). For these reasons, they have an important role in structuring policy goals toward all immigrants as well as affecting the conditions of low-tier work in less formal sectors. That is, they are ideal types for the treatment of all low-tier workers in this country and on the border, influencing the political and economic status of immigrants who are not participants in either program.

As I discussed above, I draw on Giorgio Agamben's work on sovereignty to explain how the suspension of law problematizes conventional and scholarly assumptions about assimilation and the immigrant experience. I expand this argument in chapter 4 to discuss how the suspension of economic laws and the increasing inequality of the labor contract effectively leave these workers stateless. That is, they are stateless by virtue of working in a denationalized territory, being subject to a different set of laws, marked by the suspension of normal law and policing, and laboring in conditions that are not considered healthy or normal for full citizens. The Border Industrial Program, which has been a partnership of the U.S. and Mexican governments, has effectively created such a space on the U.S. southern border.[78] The unsolved murders of more than three hundred women in this area over the past ten years are evidence that the disciplinary power of the factories is also shaped by bio-power as theorized by Agamben. These women have been murdered with impunity, based on their status as workers (these have been called the "maquila murders") and as women (most of the women have been raped and disfigured before their murders).

Correspondingly, the U.S. guest-worker program and other service programs that bring in workers to the United States are also marked by abuse and conditions that do not allow workers to unionize or negotiate wages and working conditions. These workers are tied to one employer and have no political or legal rights. Additionally, they usually owe recruiters a fee for their placement.[79] Their lack of mobility, inability to change employers, and suspension of nearly all political rights lead to a contemporary form of indentured servitude. Low-tier workers outside the guest-worker program are often subject to the same conditions and with just as little recourse if an unauthorized entrant, even if they are freer in other ways. Saskia Sassen has argued that informal workplaces and conditions today have analogues in the formal sector; I would like to suggest that the guest-worker program has a similar effect on low-tier work in the same sector (e.g., agricultural).[80] For this reason, I believe that the conditions of this program not only are undemocratic for these particular workers but also have a negative effect on the dynamics and expectations of low-tier immigrant workers in general.[81] In turn, economic conditions (e.g., flexibility and deregulation) cannot be divorced from political ones. These two programs open up spaces of deterritorialized territory that can lead to the abandonment or over-policing of workers; this space is where sovereign aims are carried out, rather than in the more limited space of domestic politics, the rule of law, and citizenship. Importantly, both programs have been responses to crises—which is why they both bypass normal regulations on labor, the environment, safety, housing, and citizenship—and yet have been relatively long lasting.

I conclude this book by reflecting on how immigration norms and policies, public debate, and informal politics elucidate the status of U.S. democracy and citizenship. I also consider the question of whether today's wars—on terror and drugs—will continue to shape immigration policy to such a degree. Some may diagnose the mood in the contemporary United States as one akin to the post-Vietnam era, when citizens were disgusted with presidential excess and a proxy war with dire costs in lives and dollars; therefore, such commenters expect that these more abstract wars will soon end. But I do not think that change will come so rapidly; the push for a free market has ironically entailed greater uses of prerogative power and hence a more warlike atmosphere. Unless the linkage between these two dynamics is recognized, the United States will continue to fight enemies abroad and within, while economically exploiting the latter. Moreover, state and municipal governments have adopted many of the repressive measures initiated at the federal level and are continuing this trend unabated. As I have argued elsewhere, cosmopolitan visions of the future are the appropriate solutions for dealing with processes that are not only domestic but also markedly transnational and hybrid. For example, because domestic efforts to hold the police and Mexican government accountable for investigating the maquiladora murders have failed, a transnational group of human rights advocates (including professors and NGOs) filed a suit in international court against the Mexican government.[82] It is at this level that the most disenfranchised individuals—immigrant women of color, indigenous groups, the least skilled workers—may be able to carve out an adequate political status that has historically been denied them at the domestic level. But human rights norms, practices, and institutions must undergo radical change in order to establish democracy for individuals at the international level. Statelessness must be moved from the conceptual margins to the ideational center to critique not only existing immigration policies, practices, and rhetoric but also a political status that moves between and in the margins of nation-states. With Agamben I argue that the stateless are not just emblematic of the most pressing immigration issues today, but also provide insight into identifying cosmopolitan practices that will broaden democratic agency.[83] Although quite a bit of transformation and innovation is necessary, hopefully my arguments (particularly in the conclusion) will show the urgency of this task.

In sum, I want to introduce a sort of critical theory of conventional assumptions regarding immigration, which are predominant not only in everyday discourse but also in much academic work on the subject. In this regard, I want to highlight relationships between global capital and sovereignty, domestic politics, and transnational or international politics, and the centrality of the nation-state in these conventional understandings, all of which is often unacknowledged. Although I do not aim to add to the literature on race, class, and gender per se, I do want to examine the important connection between sovereignty and race, class, and gender. The significance of race and gender to sovereign concerns today demonstrates the degree to which racism and sexism are not merely cultural forms. Nor can they merely be reformed through altered legislation. Recognizing the use of racial and gendered stereotypes to mobilize a politics of fear, to argue that immigrants do not assimilate, and to suggest that they are stealing "our" jobs and invading the country is to recognize the connection between biopower, disciplinary power, and sovereignty. The global economy's use and abuse of immigrant men and women has similar foundations that articulate with[84] sovereign concerns. Conventional notions of assimilation, work, and immigrant worthiness for American citizenship must be reconsidered in light of this analysis. Indeed, these categories say far more about U.S. citizenship and politics than they do about any particular immigrant group. In essence, I hope to open a new set of debates that recognizes the linkages among the many factors affecting immigrants' lives and the contemporary forms of political belonging in the United States today.

— 1 —

CONTEMPORARY ASSIMILATION IN THE UNITED STATES

In this chapter, I explore presuppositions about assimilation norms expressed in recent literature, public policy, and public debate. This discussion will be schematic, ignoring the complexities of some authors' arguments, but will point to largely unexamined preconceptions in all these areas. The literature I am broadly referring to includes the work of conservatives like Lawrence Auster, Samuel Huntington, Peter Skerry, and George Borjas; moderates like Rogers Brubaker, Victor Nee, and Richard Alba; and accounts that still rely on conventional categories but can be classified as either alternative or more progressive, such as those of Alejandro Portes and Rubén Rumbaut. These scholarly accounts have many differences but are well within the discourse of the general public, students of immigration, and mainstream political debates.[1] In contrast, truly alternative accounts, like those of Saskia Sassen and Yasemin Soysal, may have received high scholarly praise but certainly stand outside conventional understandings of the immigration debates, both public and academic.[2] These two authors look at integration or assimilation (words that are used interchangeably in the literature but arguably mean different things)[3] not only in terms of a domestic, liberal, "social contract" framework, but also in terms of dynamics of the nation-state, including how the strengthening of borders and concepts of the nation have shaped the immigrant experience in the post–World War II era. Rather than taking the nation-state for granted, they examine how the logic of the nation-state plays an important role in assimilation norms and yet how this primacy is obscured in the more conventional accounts. Even more important, they both consider how nation-states' power is challenged by global capital and increased migration flows, on the one hand, and how the nation-state has increasingly closed its borders to poorer migrants since the mid-1990s, thereby strengthening state sovereignty.[4] Both authors contend that nongovernmental organizations and human rights institutions mediate between domestic and international spheres, allowing for new types of citizenship. Sassen and Soysal are not the only commentators to analyze the issue in a complex and interdisciplinary manner, but what is notable among the authors who do examine this issue in a more multifaceted way is their own recognition that these efforts do not reflect the norm. Rather, the conventional literature on immigration and assimilation gives a different picture of the immigration process and its political possibilities.

Rogers Brubaker argues that assimilation in the United States was once conceived around a core set of values that were coercive and "Anglo-conformist." By the 1960s these ideas were discredited, and by the 1980s notions of difference (a "differentialist turn") became popular.[5] Brubaker is referring to the increasing use of multicultural perspectives and post-structuralism as well as (what he argues are) immigrant studies that focused solely on the value of ethnic communities but ignored what happened to individuals who left those communities. By the 1990s, these ideas were justly attacked and today, he claims, we are experiencing a "return" of assimilation norms minus their coercive and ethnocentric character. To Brubaker, today's assimilation norms are not as "organic," Anglo-centric, or coercive as they have been in the past; rather, they allow for mutual interaction and respect for other cultures, traditions, habits, and even languages.

To Brubaker, Richard Alba and Victor Nee's work is an example of this more benign and fair-minded model of assimilation. Nee and Alba argue that "as a state-imposed normative program aimed at eradicating minority cultures, assimilation has been justifiably repudiated. But as a social process that occurs spontaneously and often unintendedly in the course of interaction between majority and minority groups, assimilation remains a key concept for the study of intergroup relations."[6] Their *intentions* are certainly not prejudiced (e.g., racist or class based), and their main argument is that controversial immigrants are assimilating, despite the perception that they are not. But they do argue that the canonical model of assimilation, developed by the Chicago School, still largely holds (if factors like length of time, generational change, and race are accounted for).[7] Their more conservative counterparts, such as Huntington and Borjas, often interpret the same conceptual categories and data sets but draw far more negative interpretations.

Although I will be ignoring certain nuances in these authors' work, I would like to suggest that a lack of critical analysis of the key categories of assimilation (whether canonical or more benign) results in a coercive or "violent" set of assimilation norms for some immigrant groups, leading to an uprooted political status.[8] To put it differently, the linkage of residence, language acquisition, socioeconomic status, race or ethnicity, and religious beliefs (among other categories) to citizenship is missing how the normative deployment of these categories can automatically exclude or marginalize certain groups, even when they do naturalize. For instance, most studies largely downplay the context of reception[9] and instead focus on the ethnic group, asking whether its culture will allow for assimilation.[10] This obscures how, for example, immigration policy can affect each immigrant group differently, permitting a relatively easy assimilation process for some and a much more difficult path for others (racism and sexism are other factors that should be assessed in the context of reception). Further, these investigations overlook the degree to which national identity, national security, and the needs of global capital inform current U.S. understandings of assimilation, thereby ignoring their undemocratic character. Finally, they also obscure the undemocratic or unfree character of low-wage, deregulated, "flexible work" and broader economic trends (such as trade agreements like NAFTA) that shape the demand for low-skilled workers.

The canonical model of assimilation gives the impression that it is a peaceful process (it is voluntary and rational), neutral (all immigrants are subject to the same norms), universal (it is the same course that other immigrants have followed in the past), individually driven (even if "ethnic" context is taken into account), and a clear path to citizenship.[11] This model is also premised on the idea of individual action, mirroring the "action" of the social contract as the foundation for democratic citizenship.[12] Additionally, there is a distinction made between "new" and "old" immigrants—old immigrant groups are said to have assimilated rapidly, overcoming various prejudices and hardships (like racism and discrimination) to integrate into mainstream, "nonethnic" institutions, neighborhoods, and groups.[13] In contrast, it is argued today by more conservative scholars that new immigrants are too backward (in terms of skills, education, and rural affiliation) and unmotivated to assimilate. They are "stagnant"[14] and will pass this on to the second generation. For this reason, authors and policy makers contend that we must limit "labor" immigration and admit more professionals ("human capital" immigrants).[15]

Finally, almost every aspect of immigration is viewed in economic terms.[16] Immigrants are thought to migrate here because of overpopulation, starvation, and low wages in their home countries.[17] Immigrant assimilation is viewed in economic terms (though racism, sexism, and xenophobia also inform conventional views), and even typologies in progressive literature on immigration are based on economic classes.[18] Additionally, policy making and sovereign decision making are determined by economic categories. For all these reasons, citizenship is unproblematically and uncritically linked to economic attainment. Indeed, economic success seemingly takes precedence over all other concerns about immigrants.[19]

Recent reactions to immigrants belie the peaceful and individual image of assimilation norms and can properly be called a backlash, as discourse has been increasingly hostile and warlike. Immigration has been conceived of as a major problem, an invasion, and a source of degradation, whether it be at the level of culture, language, employment conditions, or politics. Moreover, these reactions are mainly targeted at poorer, working-class Mexicans, which suggests that status rather than action determines how the host country views the assimilation process. Historically, "controversial" immigrant groups are usually among the poorest, lowest skilled, and least educated, and any efforts they have made to assimilate are broadly viewed as insufficient.[20] Considering public and political discourse and policy that embrace negative images of these immigrants, launching an assault on them in numerous ways, the canonical model of assimilation appears to be a smoke screen for a more coercive and hierarchical set of norms. In turn, this coercion is meaningful in defining not only the political status of immigrants but also citizenship and democracy within the United States. If assimilation norms are actually uprooting (maintaining people as alien) rather than rooted (establishing them as citizens), and are premised on status (race, gender, class, ethnicity) rather than action or performance, one can ask if democratic citizenship in the United States today is not also uprooted and founded on static, exclusive categories rather than action, dialogue, and autonomy.

I would like to suggest first that the terms of assimilation must be questioned in and of themselves, and that the somewhat peaceful account of assimilation in the liberal-capitalist model, predicated on both individual will and cultural background, masks a more coercive set of beliefs and expectations. This coercive set of beliefs can be traced to the concerns of the nation-state and the primacy of that institution over and above multiple loyalties and identities. Further, U.S. norms of assimilation suggest that the "nation" (not just the "people," but how the notion of "people" is racialized, gendered, and so on) matters more than the "state" (i.e., democratic processes such as discussion, dissent, education); and this, in turn, challenges the degree to which U.S. citizenship is truly democratic. This argument follows Hannah Arendt's critique of the historical tendency of the nation-state to privilege the nation at the expense of the state. In relation to this idea, I contend that national self-understanding and issues of sovereignty must be taken into account when investigating liberal democratic analyses of assimilation. Against Arendt (or conventional interpretations of Arendt), however, I do not believe that the state as the sole object of patriotic devotion, citizenship loyalty, and source of all political values is the answer.[21] Instead, issues of assimilation put into question the static norms of U.S. citizenship and democracy today—post-national citizenship is not only necessary for democratic processes, but also a reflection of lived daily reality. But I will investigate this possibility only briefly in this chapter; my chief aim is to look at conventional categories of assimilation in a new and critical way.

Assimilation = Economic Attainment

Although various authors rely on the canonical model of assimilation, based on the Chicago School studies of the early twentieth century, they have also accounted for contemporary dynamics to ensure that the model is more flexible, up-to-date, and perhaps fair.[22] Significantly, they claim that assimilation today no longer involves a core set of values on which to "measure" immigrant integration.[23] Even if this last point is true (and I do not believe it is), the authors have not asked why the categories themselves—acculturation, language, residence (spatial assimilation), and socioeconomic attainment— are democratic in nature, and whether they *should* be the foundations of citizenship. One of the key puzzles in examining assimilation is whether these categories are instrumental to citizenship, are equated with citizenship itself, or serve a more complex performative function in which they enact unfulfilled national ideals. I will argue this last point in my analysis of economic attainment here and English-only laws below. In this section, I will explore what is taken to be the most important element of assimilation: socioeconomic attainment.

Alba and Nee argue that socioeconomic attainment "is of paramount significance because parity of life chances with natives is a critical indicator of the decline of ethnic boundaries, and for the reason that entry into the occupational and economic mainstream has undoubtedly provided many ethnics with a motive for social . . . assimilation."[24] Brubaker also contends that acknowledging the importance of socioeconomic matters is an important shift in studying assimilation.[25] Similarly, George Borjas argues that immigrants must move from ethnic to mainstream (nonethnic) employment because they will earn more, thus establishing the foundation for better assimilation.[26] These authors believe that labor relations and entry into the mainstream job market are not coercive because they can involve a two-way process, with each party being influenced by the cultures and practices of the other.[27] But it is not clear how this is possible in moving from the ethnic to the mainstream job market. If the most crucial element of assimilation in fact entails a one-way process, then socioeconomic attainment is conceived of statically and does not quite allow for the mutuality of a cultural exchange that they idealize. Moreover, these authors recognize that conditions in today's economy are shaped by neoliberal policies, a "flexible" job market that exploits the poor, and polarized incomes, and yet they indicate that linear movement is possible and preferable.[28]

Thus, on the one hand, they recognize that neoliberal policies leave many of the poorest immigrants who come to the United States without a means for social or economic mobility, not to mention security. On the other, they not only hierarchize immigrants by discussing "labor" immigrants and "human capital" immigrants, but this division is the foundational concept in their model, applied to all other categories.[29] In fact, this tendency to see immigrants in economic terms above all others is prevalent even in alternative accounts like those of Portes and Rumbaut. In an otherwise insightful analysis, Portes and Rumbaut introduce *Immigrant America* by creating a typology of immigrant groups based on labor categories.[30] Although Brubaker argues that this emphasis on the economic can allow authors to critique the marginalization or ghettoization of immigrants, it is not clear that this is happening in conventional scholarly articles or public policy. After all, this would involve critiquing neoliberalism and capitalism more broadly, not to mention examining sexist and racist labor relations. Rather, this hierarchy of labor and human capital has been replicated in works of Samuel Huntington and public policy proposals (the point system proposed in 2007) that reward education and skills and attempt to limit or exclude the allegedly less educated or less skilled.[31] It should also be noted that in an economy guided by neoliberal principles and "flexible" conditions, for a working-class immigrant from Mexico to follow the path of socioeconomic attainment could lead to poverty and exploitation—not citizenship.[32] To put it differently, by following this course of assimilation fully, one could cut off rather than facilitate possibilities of democratic agency.[33]

It can also be asked why the term "ethnic" pertains only to immigrant hiring networks but not to those for the native born. By presenting the "mainstream" job market as nonethnic, this literature effaces its own origin and biases. Just as authors have investigated gender- or race-neutral language, policies, and employment,[34] it is legitimate to question whether the insistence on mainstream employment is that far away from basing an assimilation model on a core set of values.[35] It is also hypocritical in that Americans have "ethnic" businesses along the Mexican border and that a key part of attracting this business has been the promise that workers could return home to Texas each night rather than having to live in Mexico themselves.[36] Instead of labeling this a marginal business venture or a threat to Mexican culture, this partnership of American business, the U.S. Treasury, and the Mexican government is deemed good business and a financially responsible mode of interaction with Mexicans.

The economic viewpoint also says both too much about immigrants and not enough. First, when most authors and policy makers argue that people come to the United States for purely economic reasons, they frame this justification in terms of the immigrant's home country and not the U.S. demand for labor. This view also ignores the linkages that have been formed between the United States and other countries—including foreign direct investment, regional trade agreements, cultural ties, and military interventions—that spur migrations in the first place.[37] This line of reasoning also conceptually privileges class above all other identities, which then obscures gender, racial, ethnic, and religious identities and how they intersect.[38] Rather than explain why this privileging takes place, most authors simply take it for granted that economic assimilation matters most.[39]

Finally, at its most basic level, it is not clear why class should matter when judging whether people will be good citizens.[40] One could argue that economic independence will allow for other modes of assimilation, such as learning English, and it is true (according to some studies)[41] that poorer people learn the language more slowly. Other countries have solved this issue by providing language classes at government expense. At its base, this argument does not justify the direct linkage between economic class and citizenship. What is more, the dominance of the economic viewpoint in understanding nearly every other aspect of assimilation demonstrates that it is not merely a *precondition* for citizenship but rather conflated with democratic actions and liberal citizenship. This analysis suggests that assimilation norms are far more rigid and tied to previous norms than many would argue. I would now like to develop this idea further by arguing that the subject of immigration itself is an ambivalent one, and that most theorists miss the elements of the nation-state that inform conventional understandings of assimilation.

Assimilation Norms and the Nation-State

Consider the following images: Mexican immigrants, both legal and illegal, carrying the Mexican flag down the street in the demonstrations against the immigration bills proposed in spring 2006; overcrowded housing in "ethnic enclaves"; immigrants speaking Spanish in public and on the job; day laborers waiting on street corners or outside Home Depot for work. All these images have been used to argue that Mexican immigrants, unlike other immigrants, cannot assimilate to the United States economically, politically, or culturally. Further, these examples are not only evidence of inability to assimilate, but they also represent lawlessness (because it is assumed they are illegal), a threat to sovereignty, and opposition to democratic processes. It is charged that the Mexican flag displaces the American one,[42] that ethnic enclaves bring "Third World" conditions to more civilized neighborhoods and drive property values down,[43] that speaking Spanish automatically excludes proficiency in English,[44] that immigrant organizations must work outside the "system" rather than reflecting the organizational processes that every other immigrant group has followed,[45] and that day laborers usurp public space and steal jobs.

These reactions are not merely private but have led to the increased number of grassroots anti-immigration groups,[46] calls for more punitive legislation, condemnation of legislation deemed too "soft" on immigrants and "illegals,"[47] and constant attacks on immigrants (mostly Mexicans) in the right-wing media.[48] Why are these images so threatening in a democracy?

And is it possible to claim that assimilation norms are peaceful, consensual, and individually willed when mainstream reactions to controversial immigrant groups are so radically intolerant? I believe that this intolerance stems, in part, from the uncritical—and yet unacknowledged—acceptance of the primacy of the nation-state.

Because assimilation norms have been developed on a domestic citizenship model, the premises that are based on notions of sovereignty, international action, and the logic of national security are ignored in conventional accounts of assimilation. This speaks to the conceptual (and scholarly) division between the "welfare" state and the "warfare" state (or domestic versus international politics).[49] Nevertheless, it is important to recognize how norms of assimilation as a result of not only the development of liberal democracy but also the development of the nation-state. In fact, classic divisions of domestic and international, welfare and warfare, friend and enemy, are woven together in expectations about controversial immigrant groups, sometimes contradicting one another and at other times working together. Concerns about national security, the integrity of the border (which have increased over time), racial and cultural purity, and loyalty have been paramount in the treatment of controversial immigrant groups. These dynamics have been reinforced by attitudes toward such groups since September 11, 2001. Because the relationship between the domestic and international spheres has been conceptualized as opposite by political scientists, politicians, and the public, it is fraught with unresolved tensions. But these tensions are further complicated by the way demands for a singular devotion to the nation-state effect a sort of violence, uprooting citizens and others who become their objects. By violence, I mean radical displacement, political exclusion, the cutting off of democratic processes, and, at times, the suspension of law or legal norms. The particular focus on Mexicans today exemplifies the intermingling of citizenship norms with a war mentality (i.e., violence); further, assimilation means legality while what is perceived to be incomplete or failed assimilation is directly tied to illegality and invasion.

The belief that controversial immigrant groups are not assimilating has its intellectual and emotional roots first in the idea that the modern nation-state must be the sole object of patriotic devotion. Thus bilingualism, foreign flags, ethnic enclaves, and ethnic entrepreneurship (among other examples) are viewed as threatening because they represent dual loyalties. True assimilation can be achieved only when the identity of the host country (broadly conceived) replaces that of the immigrant's original home. Hypothetically, this assimilation is most complete when an immigrant will die for his or her new country.[50]

A corollary of this primacy is the belief that all individuals necessarily and naturally belong to one nation-state. This ignores shifting borders, the history of the nation-state that contradicts any notion of a "natural" or "true" home, the plight of the stateless, and the reality of multiple loyalties. In the case of the most controversial immigrant group—Mexicans—who are called invaders, illegals, and so on, it obfuscates how the United States and Mexico have developed together, each influenced by the other's language, culture, architecture, and habits, and each sharing a border that has shifted and alternated between openness and tight surveillance. Mexicans living and working on the U.S. border, growing up with two cultures, learning that this border has shifted and re-shifted, are most threatening to conservative immigration scholars.[51] One could guess this is because these individuals defy the logic of the nation-state, not showing absolute loyalty or devotion to either Mexico or the United States—they are somewhere in between.[52] The demands of the nation-state are inextricably tied to assimilation because immigration is not just a domestic matter, or even a matter of citizenship alone—immigration brings together the foreign and domestic, citizen and alien, and therefore involves matters of sovereignty in relation to domestic, "democratic" politics.

Nicholas Xenos's essay "A Patria to Die For" illustrates these tensions and helps us understand why, for example, a liberal democracy is politically intolerant of bilingualism, dual loyalties, and multiple political affinities. In this essay, Xenos explores patriotism in the modern nation-state, remarking on its abstract nature and intolerance for multiple loyalties. In the aftermath of 9/11, Xenos remarks that dissent was increasingly viewed as threatening—as with the Bush Doctrine abroad and its domestic corollary, "You're either for us or against us"—and various media outlets and intellectuals were accused of insufficient loyalty. Xenos argues that this intolerant patriotism is a symptom of the logic of the nation-state, noting that the nation-state is not merely an abstraction but also a force that undercuts democratic possibilities and processes. Current debates about cosmopolitanism manifest this monolithic conception of patriotism, and many authors argue that unless the sole object of devotion is the nation-state, no one will be willing to die for it.[53] Xenos's critique of this unitary focus is relevant both to mainstream reactions to controversial immigrants today as well as to the conclusions I reach about post-national citizenship.

Xenos begins his essay by discussing the film *Saving Private Ryan* to introduce the themes related to dying for one's country. Death, as he notes, is ennobled by images of the United States, the family, and the sacred.[54] The Ryan family has already suffered the loss of three of their sons and this loss is linked to Abraham Lincoln's idea that dying for the United States is a "sacrifice" on the "altar of freedom." These images of the battlefield, dying for one's country, and higher causes are contrasted with the domestic sphere and the world of women. This contrast is sharpened when the wrong Private Ryan is found and he wants to go home rather than staying and fighting. The real Private Ryan makes the distinction between true nobility and courage, on the one hand, and the urge to go home—although two men have died trying to find him, he will not leave the battlefield. Xenos argues that what this represents is the contrast between the biological family and the national family—a distinction at the heart of the development of the modern nation-state. One family replaces another, and while an individual's true family may serve as inspiration to fight for the national family, only by leaving one's original family can this be done. It is this *replacement* of the biological family, or even one's "home" country, for the American national family that is required today of immigrants. But loyalty to one's country (and thus fitness for citizenship) was not always conceived in such an abstract and monolithic fashion.

Xenos notes that the movie rests on an assumption passed down from Horace—that it is sweet to die for one's country. Watching a friend die from gas poisoning in World War I, the poet Wilfred Owen argues that this is a lie and that anyone who had seen what he had would not think it so sweet to die for one's country. Nevertheless, the modern usage of Horace's idea is complicated by the fact that when he was writing it, people did not think of the patria and loyalty in the same terms we do today. Xenos discusses Cicero's ideas to make this point. Today, dying for one's homeland means transcending the family and home, and therefore sacrificing oneself for a concept that is much more abstract. In the past, people felt loyalty to at least two entities: a home place by birth and a homeland by law; as Cicero suggests, there are "two *patriae*: one of location and nature and one of citizenship; one encompassing the other; one to return to for leisure and reflection and one to die for."[55] Translations of Cicero have projected our modern conceptions on these two loyalties, implying that there is an unproblematic shift from the home to legal belonging. What Xenos wants us to see is that in Cicero, there is a comparison between home and homeland, but that devotion to the latter entails a different mind-set. Citizenship involves a much larger group of people and thus is different from the relationships among family. Cicero does not compare the public altar (what we would call the nation today) to the household—rather, this relationship is *reconstituted*.[56] It is this second, more abstract identity that can offer citizenship.

The Romans themselves struggled with origin myths precisely because no one could really be called a native of the region. The struggle for Romans to find a fitting genesis story was important in establishing its power over its empire as well as in stirring up patriotic sentiments. This self-conception came at a price for the lands that the Romans conquered. The need to find roots resulted in uprooting others and made the nation an object of idolatry or blind faith, as Xenos argues, referring to Simone Weil's work. To put it differently, the idolatry of the state is vital to understanding nationalism, and the Romans' lack of roots explains the need for a story about their roots.[57] Like the Romans, citizens of modern nation-states are uprooted because of both the abstraction of the nation-state as well as the consequences of capitalism and secularism. In turn, the uprooted uproot others, forcing them to give up identities and relationships they have actually experienced for a more abstract notion of belonging. This has direct relevance to today's assimilation norms and helps explain why any manifestation of multiple loyalties inspires such strong, negative reactions.

One of Xenos's main points in this discussion is to highlight that while patriotism is thousands of years old, nationalism is something new. In the past, patriotism was more fluid and permitted multiple loyalties.[58] Today, there is less flexibility in the object of attachment and nationalism is geo-graphically circumscribed. This is true even when authors on the Left try to replace an unhealthy, irrational nationalism with a more democratic and rational form of patriotism.[59] For example, in the late 1990s, Rich-ard Rorty began a discussion about patriotism among those who consider themselves on the Left. He argued that such individuals need to affirm a need for collective identity and patriotism rather than just criticizing these concepts. Martha Nussbaum responded by contending that what we really need is a cosmopolitan politics, opening ourselves to more universal ide-als rather than the narrow, more parochial attitudes taken with patriotism. Although Xenos understands Nussbaum's impulse to call for a cosmopolitan politics, he finds that it is not so different from the patriotism advocated by Rorty. Nonetheless, he argues that those who criticized Nussbaum's idea of cosmopolitanism as being too abstract do not consider how abstract the nation-state and nationalism already are. By accepting the nation-state as the sole object of attachment, we have already moved one step away from local, lived relationships and multiple attachments, and toward something essentially imaginary and unitary.[60]

Added to this debate was the question of whether anyone would be willing to die for his or her country if a cosmopolitan politics was adopted. Xenos discusses Anthony Appiah's attempt at resolving the two sides of the debate by advocating cosmopolitan patriotism. What Xenos finds valuable in this discussion is not Appiah's reliance on the nation-state as the ultimate object of devotion but the different levels of devotion that his father experienced in Africa. Appiah's father lived in the Asante region in a town called Kumasi, the nation-state of Ghana, and on the African continent. What Appiah introduces is the different levels of devotion that are possible when discussing patriotism. So one key question is why we think that national identity and the nation-state are the most appropriate designators of patriotic devotion. Why not our city or our continent or some other identity? Our lived daily reality does not let us see what it is to be American in its totality—rather, we see our neighborhood, city, and the surrounding landscape. People fear that cosmopolitanism will mean that citizens have no attachments and insufficient patriotic feeling in the case of war. But Xenos thinks that these fears exist precisely because we already feel uprooted in many respects.[61]

So, as a reaction to the uprootedness of cosmopolitanism and as a method of reclaiming patriotic feeling on the Left, authors like Rorty and Appiah suggest that we need a "good" form of patriotism. But this impulse evades the issue of uprootedness that is caused by the nation-state and the singular devotion to it. Both "good" and "bad" patriotism rely on the same foundation. Xenos has already critiqued the idea that the nation-state *solves* feelings of homelessness or uprootedness; in fact, it causes them. The second part of this question is why we think dying for the nation-state is the litmus test of good patriotism. If the nation-state is already an abstraction and if capitalism further alienates us from one another, should we really die for these concepts? His answer is no—that this is a nihilistic move, a desire to escape tension but not really to resolve it. Again, he argues that Nussbaum's cosmopolitanism does not elude these difficulties but rather extends them outward.[62] But this is not to say that another version of cosmopolitanism is undesirable. Xenos suggests that a cosmopolitan patriotism with shifting, multiple attachments and identities is more attuned to historical experience and, ultimately, would give more meaning to our political lives.[63] This is an argument I will develop further in the conclusion to this chapter and, in more depth, in the conclusion to this book. Here, I am more interested in connecting Xenos's analysis to U.S. assimilation norms, exposing their undemocratic character.

Today, in seeking to replace "home" with "homeland," U.S. patriotism uproots citizens and makes it easier for Americans to uproot others.[64] This analysis is directly relevant to the today's hysteria about immigrants, and particularly poorer Mexican immigrants. In turn, this concern certainly says something about the model of assimilation that has been taken to be canonical. Bilingualism, the Mexican flag, ethnic neighborhoods and business, and Mexican American organizations have been interpreted as evidence of Mexicans' unwillingness to assimilate by authors like Huntington, Lawrence Auster, Peter Brimelow, and many others. In all these examples, multiple loyalties, affiliations, and identities are radically discounted because one patriotic object of devotion must supersede (or erase) another—if not, the immigrant is not merely disloyal but also taken to be illegal. Xenos's analysis allows us to see how a group that has been a crucial part of American history and contributed to American identity, politics, economics, culture, cuisine, art, and architecture (among many other things) is viewed as alien and threatening. Today, media discourse portrays them as "invaders," criminals, and carriers of disease and disorder The border between the United States and Mexico is frozen in time, naturalized, and its history ignored to produce the binaries of patriotic/traitorous, citizen/enemy, legal/illegal. Xenos's account denaturalizes this history, putting into question any notion of inevitability or self-evidence of a unitary object of patriotic devotion. Put another way, his investigation shows how the uprooted ensure that others are uprooted discursively, politically, and economically.

In particular, Xenos explains why the idea of linguistic assimilation has been a particularly hot topic. This issue evokes especially impassioned responses to subjects such as bilingual education, language on official forms (like ballots and the census), and the question of what language is used to conduct public affairs and commercial business.[65] In this debate, bilingualism is mistaken as the inability or refusal to speak English, and thus is perceived as threatening to Americans' cultural integrity.[66] The demand for English-only laws[67] provides a context for invidious remarks, such as the charge that "Hispanics" want to fight these laws because they "exist off" of bilingualism[68] or simply cannot learn English.[69] But as Robert King points out in "Should English Be the Law?," language is more a symbolic issue than a real one, since by most estimates roughly 94 percent of the population speaks English.[70] Further, native-language retention does not mean that individuals do not or cannot speak English.[71] Thus, although it could be contended that English-language acquisition is important for fulfilling the social contract (e.g., during the swearing-in ceremony for naturalization, as Honig has analyzed),[72] it is not a statistically significant concern. Because it is not a "real" issue, King believes it is a symbol of national identity and that this should not be the case: "The very idea of language as a political force— as something that might threaten to split a country wide apart—is alien to our way of thinking and to our cultural traditions."[73] And until the 1980s, when the English-only movement emerged, he argues, it did not threaten to divide the country. Nonetheless, from that point onward, it has become a highly emotional subject of debate.

This debate particularly unites the concerns of nation-state consolidation and Enlightenment notions of consent and political legitimacy. For example, King notes that linguistic homogeneity became a more significant political concern in the second period of nation-state consolidation, starting with the French Revolution (if one takes the absolutist period to be the first phase[74]). Clearly, the intolerance of bilingualism is tied to the primacy of the nation-state at the expense of multiple loyalties. The United States' "language war" and "culture wars" symbolize the violent logic of assimilation: one must not be bilingual or have dual loyalties but must choose between present and past, rationality and irrationality, civilized and traditional/primitive. In this debate, there is much at stake concerning the nation-state—language not only symbolizes national integrity but also *enacts* the wholeness the nation-state wants to achieve, while bilingualism is a reminder of the constant challenges to this will-to-homogeneity.

Bonnie Honig's analysis of "chosenness" is highly pertinent to these dynamics—she argues that foreignness and foreign figures symbolize and perform chosenness more than any native-born citizen possibly could. That is, foreigners reinforce the superiority of their chosen host country through acts of assimilation and naturalization. In applying Honig's theory of chosenness in considerations of the worthiness of foreigners, it could be argued that English-language acquisition is a clear manifestation of U.S. supremacy.[75] This was particularly important from the 1980s onward when the Cold War was ending and Japan and Germany began to supersede the United States economically. Suddenly, U.S. superpower status was in question on two important levels. At the same time, the demography of major cities began to change due to higher levels of immigration. This was an important time of national redefinition—as discussed in the next section, laws reflected a concern with illegality, the strengthening of borders, and terrorism broadly defined. For these reasons, language is not merely an instrument of assimilation, facilitating communication and employment contracts (for example), but a litmus test of the strength of the nation-state in the face of various challenges (other challenges include the globalization of the economy, military alliances,[76] and greater regional cooperation).[77]

That most authors and policy makers interested in assimilation do not question the category of linguistic assimilation—only whether it should be coerced (through English-only laws or the elimination of bilingual education) or allowed to happen without government intervention—effaces the complexity of this issue as well as its nondemocratic character. If (a) language acquisition has the performative function I believe it does and says more about national sovereignty than being an instrument for greater political participation; (b) policies and policy proposals aim at the gradual replacement of one language for another (often without considering the complexities of language attainment, including age and educational facilities); and (c) controversial groups (because poor, racialized, allegedly uneducated and unskilled) are most often the targets of these debates, it could be concluded that the *norm* of linguistic assimilation involves a violent displacement rather than a mutual, two-way relationship.[78]

Learning English is posed as something that people must be forced to do, and this coercion is viewed as acceptable, placing concerns of national identity over democratic values. For these reasons, legal residence or a green card do not actually make people political equals. Rather, a wholesale public disavowal of one's language, identity, and loyalties is required before equality is bestowed. English-only laws do not just create linguistic and racial hierarchies, they also ignore "intersectionality" as theorized by Kimberlé Crenshaw.[79] As she has argued, English-only policies in a battered women's shelter led to the exclusion of a Mexican woman who was living on the streets with her son after repeated death threats by her husband (in fact, she did speak some English). In this case, language policies were violent on both a symbolic and a very real level. Crenshaw's appeal to consider not just ethnicity or race in formulating policy, but also gender and class, destabilizes the fixed boundaries of race and ethnicity that Samuel Huntington,

Francis Fukuyama, and others have presupposed in their writings about immigration.

Another related issue is illegal immigration. The figure of the illegal immigrant is paramount in configuring Mexican immigrants in such narrow ways, and public policy establishes the illegal/legal binary such that it reinforces the suspicion that *all* Mexicans and Mexican Americans could be illegal. The nation-state as our sole object of devotion today also entails the belief that everyone has a homeland. The rigidity of this belief system is evidenced in the plight of refugees and the stateless, who are often in political and legal limbo. As Hannah Arendt has famously argued, human rights norms are guaranteed by one's homeland, the nation-state, and thus human rights are denied to those who need them most.[80] The increasingly sharp division between legal and illegal reflects this same logic, which is why public officials, the media, and the public ignore the complexity of immigrants' lives, insisting that they must be one or the other. There is no gray area of legality, no understanding of how laws in fact produce this binary. Correspondingly, this reasoning also leads to the claim that immigrants are unwilling to assimilate. In turn, their innate inability to assimilate while they are "invading the country" means that they are enemies and not merely culturally backward. The language of invasion—"stealing" jobs, "draining" welfare, medical, and educational institutions, "flooding" the border, refusing to assimilate—demonstrates that sovereign concerns are central to American notions of citizenship.

While conventional treatments of assimilation place the burden of change and integration on the immigrant, portraying this as a peaceful and democratic process that makes the immigrant worthy of U.S. citizenship, an examination of assimilation norms and history reveals a more violent process—at least for groups perceived as racial others, economically backward, and unskilled. The legal context of reception explains how groups that are racially profiled or treated as inherently illegal cannot be seen as assimilating in many respects.

Assessing the Context of Reception: Assimilation and Backlash

In *The Limits of Citizenship: Migrants and Postnational Membership in Europe*, Yasemin Soysal investigates the integration of Turkish migrants in several European countries. Her compelling thesis, reaffirmed by Saskia Sassen's work, is that the context of reception matters in how immigrants assimilate.[81] Hence, rather than investigating Islam or Turkish culture to understand how these groups have fared, she examined the laws of each country and argues that the actions of each immigrant group reflect the type of political organization they are in.[82] For example, in Sweden (a corporatist state), migrants are given quite a lot of government funding and support, including help with employment placement and social services. They have consultative roles in the government and are given aid for a multitude of needs. In stark contrast, countries that she labels "liberal" have an individualistic model of assimilation, little government support, and few federal organizations; these countries include Switzerland, the United Kingdom, and the United States. In such countries, she argues, Turkish immigrants have mobilized differently than in corporatist states. What her model suggests is that the context of reception matters more than individual immigrants' backgrounds, and that immigrant groups in each country share far more in common in their efforts to integrate than do the same ethnic groups in different countries.

Soysal did not investigate cultural dynamics such as racism or sexism, which I believe would have strengthened her thesis rather than detracting from it. An obvious example would be Great Britain, which progressively stripped "nonwhite" former subjects of their political rights from the postwar period through the 1980s. Combined with Britain's weak antiracism laws and organizations, as well as its blatant societal racism, certain groups' efforts to work and live there would never be viewed as true assimilation.[83] In contrast to authors like Soysal and Sassen, mainstream studies of assimilation tend to downplay or neglect the context of reception—from punitive laws to racism—at the expense of controversial immigrant groups.[84] This obscuring of dynamics in the host country also allows assimilation norms to appear rational, democratic, and peaceful.

As discussed above, authors like Brubaker, Alba, and Nee claim that theories of difference and attacks on assimilation went too far and that a "return" of a more benign form of assimilation is possible. I would first like to challenge the idea that assimilation norms were ever truly benevolent or so oriented toward multiculturalism that assimilation was discouraged and notions of separatism and ethnic pride flourished. In fact, Alba and Nee go as far as arguing that many interlocutors suggested dispensing with the notion of assimilation altogether and that this critique was dominant.[85] It is true that a strong critique of universalism emerged at one point, but their argument ignores the dominant ideas of the time in academia, policy making, and public debate.[86] Following Soysal's method of examining how host-country policies affect immigrant groups, I will examine the two key periods in question: the 1980s and the 1990s (in addition, I briefly consider a third time period: post-9/11).[87]

From Nathan Glazer, George Borjas, Peter Brimelow, and Francis Fukuyama in the late 1980s and 1990s to Lawrence Auster, Dinesh D'Souza, Charles Murray, Richard Herrnstein, Samuel Huntington, and many others more recently, there has been a continuous devaluation of the ideas of difference and multiculturalism. This change was significantly linked to minority and immigrant "refusal" to "assimilate."[88] In comparison to many authors of alterity/difference theories, *these* conservative authors were publishing in far more accessible periodicals and arguably reflected policy making and conventional wisdom much more than their ideological adversaries. This is evident in policy making, public discourse, and the formation of popular anti-immigration groups.[89]

To revise Alba, Nee, and Brubaker's theses, I would argue that the 1980s was the beginning of a backlash against "new" immigrants entering the United States because of the 1965 Immigration Act. This reaction occurred in the context of economic restructuring, the end of the Cold War, and the growing predominance of neoliberal policies. The 1990s crystallized a growing number of concerns and tensions that the general public felt, and public policy increasingly became hostile to the poor, and especially poor immigrants[90]—through the criminalization of the homeless, cuts in welfare and public housing, the dismantling of affirmative action, the war on drugs, and the beginning of the war on terror.[91] Proposition 187 (1994) in California, although ruled unconstitutional, is considered a significant example of public anti-immigrant sentiment at this time.[92] Work conditions also became more exploitative and insecure—in fact, Sassen argues that this is why "labor immigrants" still found work even as the native born were losing jobs and job security.[93] In this milieu, anti-immigration sentiment did not abate, but rather it deepened. The events of September 11, 2001, combined with neoliberal governance and the continuation of a risk economy, only exacerbated this hostile atmosphere, leading to open antipathy toward Mexicans and Mexican Americans (among others) today. I will briefly examine these two time periods, as well as the consequences of 9/11, to argue that this backlash is evidence of a far more hostile context of reception (and, in turn, set of assimilation norms) than Brubaker, Alba, or Nee would suggest—particularly if Mexicans and Mexican Americans are the groups being examined.

First, the passage of the 1986 Immigration Reform and Control Act was an indication that the backlash against immigrants was far more predominant than the multicultural strand of academic thought.[94] This act was passed because of "public outcry about the growth of the foreign population," in addition to media pressure[95] and disquiet about the growing number of undocumented individuals coming over the border. Hence it reflected a concern with sovereignty and regaining control of U.S. borders. Up until this time, the law allowed for gray areas in individuals' legal status; the 1986 act made immigrants both more and less legal, eradicating this ambiguity.[96]

The 1986 IRCA, which affected only individuals already in the United States, had three important parts, dealing with the legal status of foreigners' residence, including amnesty for some undocumented workers; providing for sanctions against employers who repeatedly hired unauthorized immigrants; and expanding the guest-worker program, which would provide cheap labor for agribusiness. The amnesty legalized some residents' status individually, but it also facilitated more rapid deportation of other foreigners, making immigrants either more legal or less legal than they had been. Alternatively, the expansion of the guest-worker program ensured a temporary labor supply that could be subject to strict surveillance. The combination of these three provisions would seemingly allow for more legal immigration while stemming the tide of unauthorized residency.

Finally, the employer sanctions were intended to reduce illegal hiring. But this provision did not have any enforcement power as employers could only be sanctioned for *knowingly* hiring unauthorized immigrants and were not required to verify the authenticity of documents. Further, the businesses involved have far more power than do individual guest workers, and so their influence could not easily be broken. Hence today any risks incurred in entering illegally, or overstaying a visa, fall on the individual worker rather than the employer. This reinforces the notion that it is "they" who are criminal rather than the employers who hire them, despite evidence of heavy recruiting and tacit government encouragement of this recruitment.[97]

The amnesty provision was also ineffectual, in that it was conceived of individually and thus families and communities were broken apart, with some members becoming legal and others being threatened with deportation. For the next four years, what appeared to be an act of generosity led to a significantly more hostile political context for immigrants whose status had been ill defined. The government took steps to rectify this issue in the 1990 Immigration Act,[98] but the amnesty was viewed as "punitive" and "family-busting."[99] The general consequences were families and communities split along lines of legality, and a more criminalized population overall. The point is that the image authors like Brubaker, Alba, and Nee wish to advance—that this was a period celebrating difference and ethnic communities at the expense of notions of mainstream assimilation—is believable only if one ignores the legal context of reception that controversial immigrant groups would experience, not to mention nativist articles by authors such as Nathan Glazer and many others.[100] In truth, the context of reception was a rather hostile one, and assimilation norms, when combined with the negative effects of this law, served to marginalize groups and ensure that the categories of assimilation—hard work, suburban residence, language acquisition—were valid only for elite groups who migrated to the United States. To put it differently, these laws ensured that for some immigrants the obstacles to naturalization would be much greater, and they created a discursive subject—the illegal alien—that has become quite threatening.[101]

By the 1990s, there was "a historically unparalleled level of official and public concern about the U.S. government's ability—or the lack thereof—to police the U.S.-Mexico boundary and to prevent unauthorized or 'illegal' immigration from Mexico."[102] Measures like Proposition 187 in California and Operation Gatekeeper became the logical consequence of an increasingly hostile environment toward immigrants, and particularly "labor" immigrants from Mexico. It is evident in legislation from the 1986 act to the proposals of 2006 and 2007 that the backlash against controversial immigrant groups has continued to this day. The renewal of the Patriot Act and the passage of the nation's "toughest bill" on immigration in Arizona are more recent examples of these trends.[103] The "return of assimilation" cannot be divorced from this historical and political context.

A second example is the 1996 passage of the Antiterrorism and Effective Death Penalty Act and the Illegal Immigration Reform and Immigrant Responsibility Act. These laws initiated the official war on terror[104] and strengthened the legal/illegal binary. As a district court judge and immigration researcher have remarked, "These laws . . . contained a wide range of exceptionally harsh mechanisms aimed at noncitizens, many of whom are legal permanent residents of the United States. Judicial review of certain types of deportation orders has been completely eliminated. Thousands of noncitizens seeking to enter the country are summarily excluded by INS agents operating with virtually unreviewable discretion."[105] These proceedings were often conducted with secret evidence, and more than 150,000 immigrants were permanently detained each year because their countries did not have deportation agreements with the United States.[106] Mark Dow remarks that "the new laws 'eliminated the INS's discretion to release certain aliens' and required that it detain large numbers of legal resident aliens without setting a bond. The laws also mandated increased detention of asylum seekers and, through a process known as expedited removal, gave low-level immigration inspectors wide authority to return asylum seekers encountered at airports."[107] Because of this, the average daily numbers of detainees tripled by 2001.

The Patriot Act reinforced these provisions, allowing for greater surveillance of immigrants and open racial profiling. The groups who have been most affected by stricter laws and easier deportation have been Mexicans, Haitians, Jamaicans, and Cape Verdeans.[108] Further, although anti-terror measures did affect Arab Americans and Middle Eastern immigrants significantly, they affected Mexicans even more (in fact, they became the most deported group).[109] The events of September 11, 2001, silenced debates on immigration directly after the attacks, but these issues have recently emerged to produce the alarmist discourse at the end of the first decade of the twenty-first century.[110]

The issue of illegality, which has been made more possible because of the legislation discussed above, is one of the most significant in debating the assimilability of different groups.[111] Although the criminal activity attributed to immigrants is importantly of a civil rather than violent sort, the implication is that this act of lawbreaking will lead to numerous other criminal acts.[112] If immigrants enter the country illegally, the argument goes, what will stop them from committing other, more serious crimes?[113] In this way, they are viewed as inherently criminal, and the laws that made legality that much more difficult are not taken into account. Political acts normally associated with assimilation—such as community organizing, efforts to unionize, and formation of cultural or self-help groups—are correspondingly viewed in a negative light. For example, ethnic networks are labeled ethnic enclaves and political organizing is interpreted as ungratefulness and undermining the law.[114] These sentiments are exacerbated in a time when dissent, protest, and unionization are, overall, decreasingly tolerated.

As Saskia Sassen points out, law-and-order policies characterized by punitive measures and high levels of surveillance merely increase the vulnerability and exploitability of poorer immigrants, and they do not recognize the bridges or linkages that the United States forges with countries like

Mexico.[115] Further, one could hypothesize that these dynamics, in combination with the increased number of anti-immigration groups,[116] the discourse of right-wing pundits (who claim that Mexicans are sexual predators, disease carriers, and colonizers of the Southwest), and fearmongering of certain politicians,[117] have led to a context of reception that is hostile to all immigrants, but Mexicans in particular. In turn, this context of reception will both determine how immigrants act and shape their possibilities. But if certain groups are always already suspected of illegality, job stealing, welfare abuse, and so on, their efforts at assimilation will necessarily be viewed as inadequate or suspicious. The few who "make it" will be considered exceptions.

Other categories of assimilation—including racial assimilation, gendered expectations, and residential assimilation—must also be considered in terms of the context of reception. Alba and Nee discuss the idea of residential assimilation, proposing at least three views of it: first, moving to the suburbs demonstrates "acculturation and social mobility"; second, it can mean that more successful minorities are leaving less successful members behind and are therefore "desegregating" urban neighborhoods; finally, they consider the idea that an ethnic neighborhood affirms "ethnic distinctiveness."[118] Although the authors attempt to refashion an old category of assimilation, they do not question the presupposition that a move to the suburbs means assimilation in some way. They ignore real estate discrimination, transportation issues (particularly from poor urban areas to the suburbs),[119] and racial profiling of the police. In a telling reversal, it is implied that minorities must be the ones to enact desegregation, not the host society. It must also be added that the focus on the suburbs is arguably a relic of the manufacturing age, when capital intensity and the middle class were dominant. In today's service economy, "global cities," as Saskia Sassen has theorized, may have far more resources and economic (not to mention political) opportunities than the suburbs.[120] More broadly, it must be asked why residence equals good or bad citizenship. This connection has the same classist (and, by extension, racial and gendered) presuppositions as the linkage between citizenship and economic success.

The racial and gendered context of reception should also be considered when analyzing an immigrant's assimilation. I will discuss both of these categories in more detail in chapter 3, but it is worth pointing out that although gender is not a classic category of assimilation, gendered assumptions play an important role in scholarly literature. This is true in two ways: First, the immigration experience is described in gender-neutral language that rests on unacknowledged assumptions about gender roles. Second, there are numerous references to immigrant women and yet no context is given, and thus their status, practices, and identity appear to be static. For example, stereotypes about Arab and Muslim women tend to regard ethnic and cultural practices as inherent qualities that cannot be changed. Controversial immigrant women have also historically been accused of reproducing too frequently—as Mexicans are today—and both mainstream and conservative critics uncritically accept the term "anchor baby."[121]

Indeed, concerns about reproduction appear frequently in scholarly literature, particularly in more conservative arguments about assimilation. For example, allegedly high Mexican fertility rates are a significant concern in Samuel Huntington's articles, while that of Puerto Ricans (who are citizens, though treated as foreigners) is of greater concern to Francis Fukuyama.[122] Both of these authors' worries are tied to economic, cultural, and sovereign issues, particularly the idea that "they" will soon outnumber "us." Assimilation then means lower fertility rates and reproductive decisions that mirror white women's choices (although all this is idealized—all women are viewed as needing surveillance and policing of their reproductive choices). Because these normative expectations appear frequently but are not viewed as "gender assimilation," authors can appeal to popular stereotypes without providing empirical evidence. Moreover, they ignore the context of reception, which includes mixed messages for all women about birth control, abortions, and premarital sex, not to mention how the poor are especially targeted by these mixed messages.[123] They also ignore the fact that when women are given access to health care and education (let alone reproductive rights), the reproductive rates of all women are roughly equal in the United States.[124] The idea of "racial assimilation" is discussed more openly but fraught with similar conceptual difficulties.

Like other contemporary authors of assimilation theories, Alba and Nee examine the role of race in assimilation. In part, they are responding to the claim that immigrants who have entered the United States because of the 1965 Immigration Act (the law in which racial barriers were eliminated) are too racially different and thus cannot possibly assimilate.[125] This argument is supposed to reinforce the idea that racial immigrants of the past overcame racism and assimilated while new immigrants cannot possibly do the same.[126] In seeming contrast, Alba and Nee argue that there is no reason why Asians and light-skinned Latinos should not be able to "assimilate" racially.[127] This, of course, reinforces the important connection between race and political inclusion: only the light-skinned will be eligible for citizenship. The authors dispute the fact that earlier groups were viewed as nonracial, and contend that immigrants today may have some hope of acceptance and reduced discrimination over time. Drawing on Tamotsu Shibutani and Kian Kwan's theory of social distance, they acknowledge that how a person is treated in society depends not on how the individual defines him- or herself, but on how society defines this person; perceived "differences give rise to social distances."[128] Upon acknowledging this problem, however, they conclude that the canonical model of assimilation is still the best; this is only possible if they think that the category of racial assimilation is "neutral" or nonethnic.[129] This purported neutrality is challenged by their observations about skin color. Beyond this observation, the idea of racial assimilation assumes that some action or actions on the part of the immigrant group will either allow them to be accepted or not. The emphasis continues to be on immigrant action even though societal prejudices arguably predetermine how assimilation will be judged (taking a job will be stealing a job; taking welfare will be a form of dependence, not need; engaging in informal politics will be a sign of disloyalty and traitorousness rather than democratic and American; etc.).

Related to this, it is interesting how critics recognize the continued significance of race in the United States but, rather than portraying it as part of the context of reception, categorize it in terms of individual choice and will.[130] For example, Peter Skerry argues that because Mexicans' racial status is ambivalent, they can choose whether to emphasize their racial identity (he recommends that they not focus on this in political organizing). Ignoring racial profiling, housing discrimination, employment discrimination, and hate crimes, Skerry places all the power over how others define Mexicans in their hands alone.[131] Mary Waters also discusses (and problematizes) the "choice" that West Indian immigrants can make by emphasizing their immigrant identity over affiliation with U.S. African Americans.

She demonstrates that over time, most immigrants of color have no choice in how they are perceived, and she gives shocking examples of how racism is experienced by different economic classes of West Indians.[132] Similarly, from real estate discrimination to job discrimination to racial profiling to unequal sentencing, there is little evidence that working-class and poorer Mexican Americans can simply shed their racial identity that easily.[133] Skerry and other authors' decision to emphasize immigrant choice in defining race merely reinforces the myth that assimilation norms are peaceful, consensual, and like a social contract: if the immigrant tries hard enough, he or she will assimilate. But what if race "colors" perceptions of immigrants' efforts to assimilate? Again, taking jobs is then viewed as "stealing" jobs, political action is traitorous or ungrateful, and waiting for day labor work is invading public space, harassing women, and children and compromising public safety.[134] This uncritical mode of academic discourse essentially reinforces racial hierarchies in considerations of citizenship and revives racism, albeit in a new form.[135]

On a more practical note, assimilation American-style can lead to diabetes, obesity, and inferior prenatal care. It can also lead to higher high school dropout rates, poorer grades, and disciplinary problems. And, as Portes and Rumbaut point out, when it has been coerced, assimilation can pit one generation against another.[136] This leads to not only the denigration of traditional cultures, languages, and customs but also intergenerational conflict. In turn, these failures reinforce nativist fears that immigrants will fail to succeed.

Conclusion I: Assimilation Norms Are Coercive

In 2004, *Foreign Policy* published Samuel Huntington's article "The Hispanic Challenge," preceding his book on the same theme. Although some mocked him, arguing that he had finally "lost it,"[137] Huntington's essay was not a departure from the literature on assimilation except in its naked acceptance of the idea of an American creed, its explicit targeting of a specific group (Mexicans), and his open preoccupations with national sovereignty in his argument that Mexicans are staging a purposeful invasion of the Southwest because they feel the land is owed to them. But the responses to this article, including an entire issue of *Perspectives on Politics* dedicated to Huntington's assertions, challenged his ideas but within the same categories. One example is Susan Eckstein's reaction to Huntington in which she agrees that "Hispanics"[138] largely have not converted to Protestantism, accepting that religion and citizenship are tied together (and leaving the separation of church and state in the dustbin of history).[139] A second example is Richard Alba's response to Huntington's claim that Mexicans will continue to flood the borders of the United States—Alba contends that there is significant evidence that Mexican labor immigration will begin to abate by 2020, resulting in a potential decline in labor immigration.[140] He does not question the presupposition that manual laborers make bad citizens, but wants to reassure his readers that these interlopers will soon be gone. More generally, Huntington's fears of a Reconquista, as well as his class biases, are not questioned but "assimilated" into other scholars' work, even if these scholars are attempting to prove him wrong on some level.

For all the reasons stated above, although assimilation norms are alleged to have changed from their Anglo-conformist past, I would argue that conventional assimilation norms still involve Anglo-conformism to a great degree. This model's normative expectations are called "straight-line" assimilation[141] because developmentally the process is viewed as progressive and gradually exclusive of older identities, habits, and ties. The expectation is that "symbolic ethnicity" will progressively replace deeper ties to and practices of the "old" culture and language. Symbolic ethnicity is "the manifestation of individualistic expressions of ethno cultural affinities like the observance of certain holidays and the consumption of ethnic cuisine."[142] That is, an individual's former cultural ties should be deployed in superficial ways that do not threaten public space, express dissent, or undermine American national unity.

As discussed above, Brubaker claims that "the new theorists of assimilation do not simply replicate the old, pre-1965 approaches. The older work—even work as sophisticated as Gordon's—was analytically and normatively Anglo-conformist. It posited, endorsed, and expected assimilation towards an unproblematically conceived white Protestant 'core culture.'"[143] This may be true in some scholarly literature, but in public opinion, policy making, and even mainstream scholarly literature, the "old," straight-line account has certainly been the norm since the 1990s.[144]

These norms, in turn, cannot be divorced from American expectations of citizenship, which are based not only on static and hierarchical notions of national identity but also on a monolithic and ultimately undemocratic notion of political loyalty. To put it differently, democratic norms and expectations about citizenship and political obligation have allied themselves more with concerns of the nation rather than the state as such. This is not to idealize the state, but rather to argue that national concerns are then interwoven with what is taken to be democratic: the social contract, notions of consent, the rule of law, and what counts as political participation.

Conclusion II: Post-national Citizenship

Assimilation norms in the United States convey far more about expectations about American citizenship, notions of democracy (or lack thereof), and societal values than about any particular immigrant group. This is not to say that immigrants are entirely powerless, but rather that no one immigrant group can enter a country and alter its institutions, laws, mores, and beliefs in the same way that a host country can affect an individual immigrant. A significant reason this is true is the prevalence of the dominant logic of the nation-state, which permeates all considerations, from legal reasoning about citizenship, to defining immigration policy, to determining human rights norms. Further, this viewpoint ensures that groups whose status is not one or the other—who are in some sense stateless—will not be tolerated on any level. As Simone Weil has argued, the modern nation-state uproots its own citizens through demanding devotion to a meaningless and abstract symbol.[145] In turn, its intolerance of multiple loyalties uproots not only its own citizens but also those who wish to naturalize.

Hannah Arendt would hold that these undemocratic and uprooted tendencies are symptomatic of privileging the nation over the state—that is, the idea of cultural and demographic integrity (even as she shows that this integrity is artificial)—with the result that national identity is confused with democracy and the rule of law. In *Democracy and the Foreigner*, Honig similarly argues that throughout U.S. history, democracy and Americans' reaction to foreigners have been viewed in national terms.[146] The way I interpret this is that Americans have typically cared more about the national body—the "who" of the nation—than the "what": democratic processes, enacting positive democratic rights, and political community, which involve a more substantive notion of rights, group activity, and political community. Because more importance is placed on national self-conceptions, foreigners either serve as a "supplement" to the nation or as a threat to it.[147] The American version of democracy is limited by these dynamics, and Honig argues that "democracy is unexpanded and untested by the insistence that others become 'us' or go back whence they came. Often the punitive insistence itself plays a (never acknowledged) role in producing the very tendencies it excoriates—withdrawalism, recalcitrant particularism, separatism."[148] Hence the political majority has concerned itself more with what immigrants represent in our own cultural and political terms than with seeing the immigrants in all their complexity. There has been a political tendency to privilege national projects over truly democratic ones that could be postnational, plural, and allow for a multiplicity of loyalties and identities.

I would reaffirm these points without advocating a return to a better nation-state as the solution. Weil, Arendt, Honig, and Xenos show how the historical development of this conceptual privileging cannot simply be undone: the state part of this equation is no more democratic as long as rigid boundaries, policing of foreigners (rather than the allocation of positive duties and obligations), and issues of national security define sovereignty. The economic logic that increasingly dominates sovereign decision making, made possible by the increasing prevalence of neoliberalism, further precludes democratic agency, as it depends on the nation-state for law-and-order policies and criminalizing the poor even as it "deterritorializes national territory."[149] Neoliberal policies tend to strengthen individual rights at the expense of the collective, business interests over individual freedoms, and substitute a material ethos for a more justice-oriented politics. The logical consequence of this power dynamic is that status matters more than political agency, democratic collaboration, and the positive enactment of one's rights. In fact, if one is a member of a controversial immigrant group, following the prescribed path of assimilation will be viewed as stealing, disloyalty, parasitism, and invasion.

Because assimilation falls into an academically gray area—between citizenship and foreignness, domestic relations and international relations, democratic or citizenship theory and human rights—the undecidability with which these concepts are deployed obfuscate the undemocratic and uprooting aspects of U.S. assimilation and citizenship. Sovereignty, border politics, and national security concerns are not merely functioning to police foreigners before they become citizens but are foundational to assimilation norms and citizenship. These dynamics ensure that these "citizens" are often still uprooted in many important respects. The effects of recent laws to criminalize Mexicans and make them the most deported group only reinforce this uprootedness.

In order to formulate a solution to these issues, the most obvious changes must include first a transformation of intellectual focus, examining the context of reception broadly conceived. Outdated laws based on stereotypical assumptions must be questioned in terms of how they limit immigrants' political agency and foster xenophobia among American-born citizens. And the economic lens through which immigrants are viewed, thanks to the predominance of neoliberalism, must at least be seen for what it is: historically specific, reductive, and polarizing. Finally, and perhaps most important, the primacy of the nation-state must be questioned (one could call this the "architectonic" issue). Merely to democratize the debate on assimilation would not really change the exclusionary logic of the nation-state that is foundational to any understanding of citizenship. A post-national conception of citizenship is far more democratic than reforming something that is uprooting at its conceptual core. But as Xenos has argued, this cannot be a form of cosmopolitanism that simplistically moves outward from the (national) self, but rather one that permits genuinely different forms of loyalty. In many respects, cosmopolitanism is already a reality—people hold multiple loyalties and affiliations that operate on multiple, shifting levels. Accepting these realities can allow for democratic collaboration and "a complex mesh of overlapping political authorities and loyalties,"[150] paradoxically ensuring that more people are rooted and letting go of a singular object of devotion that has caused so much uprootedness: the nation-state. I will elaborate on these ideas in the conclusion to this book.

— 2 —

ENEMY INVADERS!

Mexican Immigrants and U.S. Wars Against Them

Although U.S. assimilation norms have been historically intolerant of groups who are also the most politically and economically vulnerable, issues of national security, sovereignty, and war time measures today interact with these norms to produce a progressively more hostile context of reception for controversial immigration groups.[1] In this chapter and the next, I investigate how poorer Mexican immigrant workers have been increasingly, constructed as threats to American national sovereignty, and thus more as enemies than either "legals" or (criminal) "illegals." Older discourses and stereotypes about Mexican immigrants resonate with recent national security concerns and the sovereign decision making found in U.S. border patrols, the Bureau of Citizenship and Immigration Services, Immigration and Customs Enforcement, and policies related to the wars on terror and drugs.[2]

But stereotypes, labels, and conventional perspectives of this controversial group, like the gendered and racial meanings that underpin them, are often contradictory. For example, the Mexican immigrant as hardworking and lazy; as a paradigm of family values and yet the cause of overpopulation; as the exemplar of religious faith but viewed as backward due to his or her religious zeal; or as the ideal worker to support the U.S. economy but also responsible for the lowering of wages and the degradation of work conditions. Often divided along gender lines and racist stereotypes, these oppositions function as binary modes of operation that simultaneously justify hiring preferences for Mexicans in certain industries and their treatment beyond the law—as always potentially criminal.[3] I believe that racist discourse and gender splits make sense of these binary modes. So, for example, gender typing explains how Mexicans can be both lazy (men) and hardworking (women); violent or irrational (men) and yet submissive and apathetic (women); job stealers (men) and burdens on the health care and welfare systems (women). Racism intersects with these gendered stereotypes in reference to perceptions of skill levels, reproductive habits, and the ability to think rationally and in a calculated manner.

In turn, the sexist and racist stereotypes that have historically intersected with the broader generalizations about Mexicans' culture and habits are now being linked to concerns about national sovereignty. The connection between race, gender, and sovereignty may not be entirely new— for example, eugenic concerns informed U.S. immigration policy from the 1920s through the early 1950s—but their dynamic interaction is different from the past given that borders today are both tighter since the 1990s[4] and yet more permeable, because U.S. wars are conducted beyond borders and global economic activity is far more prevalent.[5] For instance, some now view the older stereotype about Mexicans having more children than the average American family as a national security threat.[6] Hence protecting borders includes disciplining men and women through gender and reproductive norms as well as racial norms and profiling.

These norms are evident in public discourse about "anchor babies"[7] and overly high fertility rates, as well that surround hiring preferences and employment conditions. Although gender norms are far more complex and explicit as they relate to women[8]—including their reproductive behavior, status as mothers, and job suitability—these norms are also evident with regard to men. Men are the majority of day laborers and fill approximately 80 percent of agricultural positions among Mexican immigrants, both in the guest-worker program and in more informal labor conditions; they are also stereotyped as hypersexual and predatory. Women continue to fill the majority of service positions and, significantly, they are the majority of maquila workers (part of the Border Industrial Program). Indeed, one of the reasons for establishing this program was to ensure that women did not cross the border and give birth in the United States, thereby establishing citizenship for their children.[9] Thus, this free zone along the U.S.-Mexican border must be viewed as an essential part of understanding border issues, efforts at immigration control, matters of global capital, and U.S.-Mexican relations.[10]

The consequences of the articulation of older racist and gendered stereotypes with sovereign concerns are fairly serious. In essence there is a gendered division of labor connected to and often justified by the intersection of sexism and racism against both groups. While, as I discuss below, Mexicans' racial status is ambivalent, their often denigrated status as racial "other" intersects with sexist stereotypes and expectations to position these immigrants as threatening in a multitude of ways. Once viewed as potentially criminal, the dynamics of this criminality waver between true criminality, in the sense that one is subject to laws of a state and treated as a citizen with rights and privileges, and being a foreign enemy, someone who can be deported, barred from re-entry, or held in a detention cell indefinitely and without legal representation.[11] Hannah Arendt famously argued that breaking the law ironically invokes the privileges of citizens because criminals have an array of rights protecting them. In contrast, the stateless have no right to rights, whether civil or human: "The prolongation of their lives is due to charity and not to right, for no law exists which could force the nations to feed them; their freedom of movement, if they have it at all, gives them no right to residence, which even the jailed criminal enjoys as a matter of course; and their freedom of opinion is a fool's freedom, for nothing they think matters anyhow."[12] The shift to a rhetoric and policy based on terror, combined with the increasing tendency to view Mexicans as *the* problem, places them somewhere in between Arendt's two extremes.[13] Today, Mexican immigrants are increasingly viewed as inherently suspect[14] and therefore as the justifiable objects of prerogative power.[15]

As discussed in the introduction, I draw on Michel Foucault's theory of disciplinary power in relation to Giorgio Agamben's concept of bare life to interrogate the political position of poorer Mexican immigrants. Because Mexican workers are treated as both economically necessary *and* criminal, their status is undecidable. Examples include treating guest workers, domestic workers, and maquiladora workers as beyond normal labor regulations, which means that they are abandoned by the law but also subject to excessive surveillance;[16] the indefinite detainment of illegal entrants;[17] the treatment of the southern border as a military zone; and the rapid deportation of legal residents as a result of the 1996 anti-terror laws.[18] In fact, as I discussed in my previous book, anti-terror laws since 1996 have affected Mexicans and individuals from Central America far more than any other group.[19] In all these examples, the rule of law is used to suspend domestic law.

Indeed, as I preliminarily discussed in the introduction, the space these immigrants occupy approaches that of bare life, Giorgio Agamben's term, which means that certain individuals whose status is viewed as less than human are subjected to the suspension of law. This space of bare life allows for their construction as potential terrorists or denigration to the point that violence against them (including attacks and murders) is often unsolved, and therefore they are not treated as legitimate citizens of either Mexico or the United States. The notion of bare life is appropriate for this subject because it captures the dynamics of economic globalization, the increasing emphasis on material well-being in making sovereign decisions, and the status of those who are subject to prerogative power. As I discuss in the first section, prerogative power is the legitimate suspension of the law during times of emergency. Agamben argues that this state of exception can lead to the suspension of the law for some groups more than others. His concept of bare life is biological life that is not abandoned by the state, but which serves as a negative identity against which citizenship is formulated. The theory is an extension of Foucault's concept of bio-power, the increasing politicization of biological matters in the modern state. The status of these individuals falls between that of citizen, immigrant, and bare life—they are treated as enemies by stealth, subjected to harsh working conditions and policed through the wars on drugs and terror. Agamben's term captures the power dynamics of these "wars" that are waged domestically against individuals criminalized due to their status rather than their conduct. But not every entrant is treated as an enemy; as Arendt indicates in the quote above, their good or bad treatment depends on the whims of immigration agents, border patrol, and judges. The point is that arbitrary treatment is the rule when the subject population has an undecidable political status. The conditions of immigrant detention centers are a testament to this arbitrary treatment.

Further, the combination of these recent policy changes—including domestic wartime provisions in the context of a war that has never been formally declared, and civilian activity (from watch groups to those attacking maquiladora workers)—creates a situation analogous to what Foucault argued about a disciplinary society: a war ostensibly aimed at a very narrow group is in fact affecting a far wider group, and not just internationally (accepted as the proper sphere of war) but also domestically. As Erik Camayd-Freixas charges, "Never before has illegal immigration been criminalized in this fashion. It is no longer enough to deport them: we first have to put them in chains."[20] Mark Dow notes that a branch of the Department of Justice reported "widespread mistreatment of detainees as well as the Bush-Ashcroft policy of failing to distinguish between 'illegal immigrants' and 'terrorists'" in detention centers today.[21] Mexicans are construed as "terrorists" in three different ways: first, directly, by groups who espouse the Reconquista theory that Mexicans are purposely colonizing the United States in order to take the Southwest back; second, directly and indirectly, as the group most affected by anti-terror laws, regardless of whether agencies truly believe they are enemies; third, indirectly, by the increasing conflation of border issues with problems tied to the attacks of September 11 (for example, arguing that Middle Eastern terrorists will cross the southern border and therefore all entrants must be subjected to high degrees of surveillance).

Further, this war is waged not only formally (i.e., institutionally) but also informally (e.g., in economic practices, popular discourse, and civic activity). The dynamics of the war on terror—the simultaneous opening of the border (because the war is without borders) and its closing against security threats—is reinforced by the imperatives of global capital, in which the border is both increasingly fortified against potential immigrant workers and concurrently more open to international business. From another perspective, the opening of the border effected by globalization engenders an often unrecognized counterreaction by the state in the form of prerogative power, which is the legitimate suspension of the law during times of crisis. The articulation of interests of global capital with those of the war on terror then explains how wartime measures can affect a workforce that has hitherto been denigrated but not treated as enemies. Consequently, the power deployed in the war on terror serves a far broader function than perhaps originally intended.[22]

It is important to note that these trends are *not absolute*, but rather they highlight how the opening of the border to global capital and the greater surveillance and control of it with regard to workers strengthens the war dynamic. Hence, although Mexicans and Mexican Americans historically have had an ambivalent status with regard to domestic policies and border crossing, what is new is the increasing tendency to configure them as potential enemies and justify the use of prerogative power against them. Thus, while it has been recognized that the political status of prisoners at Guantánamo Bay creates a class of people who are subject to political decision making outside the law, it is important to note how this legally ambiguous area of U.S. politics also affects the largest group of immigrants to this country.

This should not be surprising—in fact, it is precisely the ambivalent status of poor Mexican workers that makes them the logical object of today's new power dynamics. In turn, these circumstances are dependent on the blurring of territorial boundaries, which occurs on many different levels: the intertwining of economic policies with the aims of war, economic status with that of terrorist, and even the blurring of the exercise of prerogative power as the border is fortified not only by the military, border agents, and police but also by citizens' watch groups. This does not mean that individuals cannot resist—the blurring of national identities, power matrices, and boundaries opens the political terrain for grassroots activism just as much as it can lead to domination.[23] Nonetheless, my examination is aimed at showing how Mexican immigrants are increasingly being configured as invaders and enemies, and thus this investigation will largely be negative.

Bare Life and Prerogative Power:
The Status of Mexican Immigrants Today

The persistent inflow of Hispanic immigrants threatens to divide the United States into two peoples, two cultures, and two languages. Unlike past immigrant groups, Mexicans and other Latinos have not assimilated into mainstream U.S. culture, forming instead their own political and linguistic enclaves—from Los Angeles to Miami—and rejecting the Anglo-Protestant values that built the American dream. The United States ignores this challenge at its peril. . . . Demographically, socially, and culturally, the *reconquista* (re-conquest) of the Southwest United States by Mexican immigrants is well underway.
—Samuel Huntington, "The Hispanic Challenge"

War does not have to consist of armed conflict. War can consist of any hostile course of action undertaken by one country to weaken, harm, and dominate another country. Mexico is waging war on the U.S. through mass immigration illegal and legal, through the assertion of Mexican national claims over the U.S., and through the subversion of its laws and sovereignty, all having the common end of bringing the southwestern part of the U.S. under the control of the expanding Mexican nation, and of increasing Mexico's political and cultural influence over the U.S. as a whole.
—Lawrence Auster, "The Second Mexican War"

These are enemies who are wrecking our economy. . . . This is about national security.
—Chris Simcox, cofounder and head of the Minutemen

[Because of the establishment of the Immigration and Customs Enforcement] the sad specter of 9/11 has come back to haunt illegal workers and their local communities across the U.S.A.

—Erik Camayd-Freixas

The passage of the 1996 Antiterrorism and Effective Death Penalty Act marked the beginning of the war on terror, making Mexicans the most deported group of any immigrants to the United States (Haitians, Cape Verdeans, and Dominicans are also targeted for deportation more than other groups). A key provision in this act allowed for retroactive investigations of legal residents, permitting them to be deported for nonviolent offenses such as drunk driving or writing bad checks, dating back to the 1970s.[24]

This retroactivity is connected to a second novelty: the increased use of detention as a tool of immigration policy since 1996. Both of these developments frame the lives of all immigrants, whether directly targeted or not.[25] While the detention system began in the 1980s, the measures of 1996 created the justifications and legal mechanisms for *mass* detention and deportation.[26] Detainees include unauthorized entrants (e.g., people who crossed the border illegally or those who have overstayed visas), asylum claimants, and those who have been convicted of a "felony"[27] and have served their time.[28] Because of the 1996 provisions, classes of crimes that were considered nonviolent and otherwise "petty" were retroactively used as the basis on which to deport individuals. The arbitrariness and abuses of this system, which I will explain below, were made only more profound by the 2001 passage of the Patriot Act. Because of this legislation, Middle Eastern individuals were increasingly detained (sometimes based on secret evidence) and subject to deportation (again, including secret deportation).[29]

While detainees have loosely defined rights, these are merely regulations and are unenforceable. The consequences of this system, as one detainee put it, are that, "on a good day, when we get a good guard, we can stand life. On a bad day, anything can happen."[30] This includes practices that are very similar to the abuse of prisoners at Abu Ghraib, including forced sex, shoving heads in toilets, threatening detainees' family members, and forcing detainees to hold a squatting position for three hours.[31] These abuses are possible and normal because the majority of detainees have not been charged with any crime and thus their status defies classification: they have no right to a lawyer, and they have very few rights with regard to hearings and appeals. Further, the writ of habeas corpus has been challenged with regard to inmates' rights, and pursuing one's democratic liberties—including media exposure of treatment,[32] reports to Amnesty International, and hunger strikes or sit-ins—are used against an individual in his or her case. The fact that even habeas protection is not guaranteed, combined with the secrecy and judicial independence that characterizes the former INS (now incorporated into the Department of Homeland Security), ensures that most detainees are effectively stateless.[33] When their countries of origin refuse to accept them (or will most likely torture them upon return), these individuals are indeed stateless.[34] In combination with the increase in deportation since 1996 (and strengthened through the Patriot Act), these immigration systems are not merely instruments of immigration control, but also "a powerful tool of discretionary social control, a key feature of the national security state, and a most tangible component of the recurrent episodes of xenophobia that have bedeviled our nation of immigrants."[35] In effect, these policies can instill fear in the entire population of resident foreigners, regardless of whether these individuals will be directly affected by them.

The Patriot Act has also affected Mexicans in terms of surveillance, more rapid deportation, and fewer rights during detainment.[36] Anti-immigration sentiment led to increased arrests in 2006 and higher numbers of deportations, prompting the Mexican government to establish a hotline for immigrants in some areas.[37] Since then, the detention and deportation system has only expanded. The consequence of all this is that post-9/11 concerns have been combined with the perception that the border is being invaded so that illegal crossings are now viewed as potential terrorist threats.[38] For example, an informational article about the progress of the border fence states with great self-evidence the connection between the attacks of 9/11 and the policing of the southern border: "The September 11 terrorist attacks revived the immigration debate and advanced the idea of a border fence. Intelligence officials have said gaps along the Southwestern border could provide opportunities for terrorists to enter the country."[39] Mark Krikorian, executive director of the conservative think tank Center for Immigration Studies, has called this "Israeli-style" fencing, which connotes terror and invasion rather than mere crossing or unauthorized entry.[40]

Increased drug activity has also justified further militarization of the border.[41] Rather than treating this gang activity as distinct from terrorism, a relatively new term is being employed—"narco-terrorism"—which links the war on terror and the war on drugs.[42] Consequently, recent policies and discourse tie ordinary Mexican workers to terrorism, and this has led to the greater surveillance of entrants from Mexico. But this area is also one of great lawlessness: at the same time that a border wall is being constructed, citizens' watch groups harass "illegals" and female maquiladora workers have been murdered or have disappeared in Ciudad Juárez and Chihuahua.[43] In comparison to drug-related murders, these rape-murders have not been investigated adequately and women workers today are still threatened (which I discuss in further detail in chapter 4). In the mainland United States, reports are surfacing of abuses of Latina domestic workers[44] and Latino day laborers.[45] What is apparent in all cases is that these individuals are systematically being treated as beyond the limits of democratic citizenship—through the over-policing of their legal status or their neglect by the law when subjected to economically exploitative conditions, abuse, or violence (with gender divisions reinforcing these dynamics). That is, they are treated as individuals who are outside the normal boundaries of citizenship and therefore beyond everyday legal understanding and rights. Although the Obama administration has decided to minimize the language of war, these policies continue to be expanded.[46]

In relation to these circumstances, I want to connect earlier gendered and racial understandings of Mexican immigrants to bio-political policies and discourse, and to sovereign (as opposed to domestic) concerns. This last distinction is important in understanding that what is new about these complex dynamics is the primacy of the nation-state and the increasing importance of the border since the 1990s. The ambivalent status of Mexican immigrants, their transnational identity and movements, and their position as the most controversial immigrant group today—and in the context of an increasingly fortified border and at least two ongoing "wars"—brings them closer to statelessness or an enemy designation (international classifications) than to citizen or criminal (domestic rubrics).

First, the U.S.-Mexican border had historically been very permeable up until the mid-1990s, when Operation Gatekeeper took effect and the Antiterrorism and Effective Death Penalty Act was passed.[47] The progressive tightness of this border ensures that individual crossers are interpreted as either challenging or upholding sovereignty through their actions; that is, their status has become more black-and-white through these fortifications. For these reasons, they are increasingly viewed as enemy invaders rather than mere entrants, whether legal or illegal. Second, as I discuss in more detail in chapter 4, the needs of global capital combine with these dynamics, rendering low-tier workers effectively stateless for the following possible reasons: their workplace is illegal; they themselves are unauthorized; they are guest workers and therefore are neither citizens nor immigrants; or they are participants in the Border Industrial Program. In all these cases, they operate outside normal laws: they are not protected as citizens by either government, and they cannot be protected by human rights norms in a world that is still anchored in the nation-state. They are over-policed in terms of border crossing, background checks, and attempts to naturalize at the same time that they are abandoned by the law to abusive employers, hazardous conditions, and physical violence.

Further, gendered and racial norms place them below the status of citizens. Their status is bio-political because their race, class, and gender all determine their political identity and treatment as less-than-citizens and thus less-than-humans. As I discussed in the introduction, Michel Foucault introduced the term "bio-power" at the end of the first volume of *The History of Sexuality*, defining it as the rising concern of the political with biological matters. Bio-power increasingly became part of political power when modern medicine made it possible for populations to have a predictable life span, when famines became less frequent, and when economic practices ensured greater stability. Thus there has been a growing politicization of biological matters, including issues of reproduction, sexuality, demography, and public health. Given these changes and the advent of what is now modern medicine, Western politics has increasingly concerned itself with the optimization of life. But as Foucault remarks, governments' growing concern with the optimization of life also led to state-sponsored racism, the "hysterization of women's bodies,"[48] and genocide. That is because this very concept—life, or humanity—is constantly called into question. As the idea of humanity becomes central to political concerns, the control of the population can also include viewing certain groups as a threat to society's well-being:

> The formidable power of death . . . now presents itself as the counterpart of a power that exerts a positive influence on life, that endeavors to administer, optimize, and multiply it, subjecting it to precise controls and comprehensive regulations. Wars are no longer waged in the name of a sovereign who must be defended; they are waged on behalf of the existence of everyone; entire populations are mobilized for the

purpose of wholesale slaughter in the name of life necessity: massacres have become vital.[49]

What counts as life and life worth living today are constantly being evaluated and reevaluated in waging these wars. Preceding this, the development of disciplinary power—the power to mold, adhere to, and internalize societal norms—created a "docile subject" for the purposes of capitalism and the state.[50] Foucault argues that disciplinary power is far more complex than a mere ascetic ethos and is reflected in architecture, surveillance systems, and most modern political institutions.

As Foucault notes, bio-power and disciplinary power have worked together "in the form of concrete arrangements that would help make up the great technologies of power in the nineteenth century."[51] Indeed, bio-power has played a crucial role in the development of capitalism.[52] While bio-power views the body as part of a species (with eugenics at its most extreme point), Foucault's notion of disciplinary power is the view of the "body as machine,"[53] a body that can be subjected to strict rules and hard work in order to form a docile worker who has internalized the norms of the industrial age. Both disciplinary power and bio-power illuminate the status of Mexican immigrants today.

For example, the recent concern about "anchor babies" demonstrates how these two powers are manifested. Although the term has been used in various ways, it is an expression describing a woman or couple entering the country illegally and having a child in the United States, since by U.S. law, the child will automatically become an American citizen.[54] The child then is guaranteed a public school education and all the other benefits conferred on citizens. According to the Wikipedia entry on anchor babies,[55] it is assumed that the parents will then use the child's status to take advantage of the family reunification provisions of the 1965 Immigration Act to become eligible for U.S. citizenship themselves. These recent stereotypical assumptions can be linked to the older ones of Mexican women's hyper-reproduction and, to a lesser degree, Mexican men's hyper-sexuality.[56] But they are not *merely* stereotypes; they make up a significant part of politico-economic discourse and practices. Examples of their significance include: movements in Arizona to search hospital emergency rooms for "illegals" giving birth; managerial practices in the Border Industrial Program to police women's reproductive status (by forcing them to take pregnancy tests and birth-control pills, and firing them if pregnant); academic discourse warning of the perils of anchor babies; general concerns about high fertility rates among Mexicans; and U.S. policy instruments designed to prevent this occurrence (e.g., the Illegal Immigration Reform and Immigrant Responsibility Act of 1996, which cut off welfare benefits to new and illegal immigrants).

"Anchor baby" connotes invasion, public usurpation, and the violation of state sovereignty. Accordingly, these women and children are not viewed as deserving the protections of the state. Applying this term to Michel Foucault's ideas, they represent the hysterization of women's bodies, subject to a process by which "sex . . . by itself constitutes woman's body, ordering it wholly in terms of the functions of reproduction and keeping it in constant agitation through the effects of that very function," correspondingly threatening the state's control of reproduction and the paradigm of responsible motherhood it has constructed.[57] This is a particular subject produced by bio-power, indicative of not only a medicalization of the body but also a "biological-moral responsibility towards children."[58] Nonetheless, as I discuss below, the same women are the ideal global workers, viewed as crucial for electronics assembly, textile and garment industries, and child care and other domestic services. The gendered discourse that undergirds assumptions about having "anchor babies," and jobs for which these women are "naturally" fit, is precisely an example of how disciplinary power interacts with bio-power.

Other examples of this intersection are the rape-murders of hundreds of maquila workers and the toxic chemicals to which these workers are exposed. Both maquila workers and guest workers are subject to disciplinary power, such as long hours with no bathroom breaks, forced overtime, strict adherence to schedules, industry blacklisting if they attempt to unionize or complain, and demands for unreasonably high productivity. They are also exposed to deregulated workplaces, which can include exposure to dangerous pesticides, lack of heat or air conditioning, the absence of potable water, and massive exposure to toxic waste (in the case of maquila workers). The regular abandonment, threats of violence, sexual harassment, and rape-murders of these workers happen with relative impunity because they are neither citizens nor immigrants during the lengths of their contracts.[59] Accordingly, their position as both enemy/invader and indispensable economic unit is one of statelessness, bringing them to the brink of bare life. In turn, the stateless are not political curiosities or outliers, but precisely the exceptions that prove the rule, illustrating the issue that must be solved if democratic politics can actually be practiced.[60]

Sovereign Concerns and the Immigrant Work Ethic

In the context of a more global economy, Mexican immigrants are often lauded for their work ethic, their willingness to take jobs most Americans will not, and even their high birthrates, which are evidence of their family values as well as a guaranteed source of future low-tier workers.[61] Echoing figures all over the political spectrum, including Vicente Fox, Francis Fukuyama, Mario Vargas Llosa, and Richard Rodriguez, Tamar Jacoby remarks, "The problem isn't just that Americans don't want to work out in the fields or up on roofs in the hot sun; employers can't pay them enough to make that kind of job worthwhile for most people."[62] In this way, Mexicans are posited as ideal workers who happily labor for long hours in physically intensive conditions for low pay. Bonnie Honig calls this a strain of xenophilia, which is the positive pair of xenophobia in the binary modes of operation found in conventional views of immigrants. Xenophilia is the idealization of immigrants as "agent[s] of national reenchantment," those who reinvigorate the American dream and enact the choice worthiness of the United States.[63] They uphold traditional gender roles and, as Francis Fukuyama argues, have better family values than Americans themselves.[64] Jacoby's comments represent this idealization.[65]

Mexican immigrants are also criticized for being lazy, having no work ethic, stealing jobs from citizens, and (ironically) for their high birthrates, which will strain educational systems, pollute the environment, and generally overpopulate the country.[66] They are the source of much or all that is wrong with the United States. As Honig's binary of xenophilia/xenophobia suggests, these views appear contradictory but work together because they are premised on the same ideational foundations. To synthesize the views of "liberals" and "conservatives" on immigration: Mexicans are ideal workers yet they are also stealing jobs; their acceptance of low-wage positions without benefits or security serves as a reproach to native-born workers who complain about wages, want to unionize, and rebel against poor job conditions, but this willingness to work is also taken as evidence that Mexicans lack ambition and are culturally "stagnant";[67] their work ethic is ideal but they suffer from "mañana syndrome"; their family values are admirable but they are overpopulating the country; and they are planning on "colonizing" the Southwest, although they are faulted for being lazy and lacking in ambition.[68] These contradictory views are echoed in magazines like the *National Review*, *U.S. News and World Report*, *American Enterprise*, and, more subtly, in *Newsweek*, not to mention by Democrat and Republican politicians. In all these perspectives, economic concerns are closely linked to sovereign ones, including the permeability of the border and the possibility of an invasion.

The recent debates on immigration and the resultant policy proposals are evidence that these two strains of concerns—economic concerns and national security concerns—are increasingly being linked. Indeed, the proposal for a new guest-worker program with more extensive background checks for potential workers, higher levels of surveillance, and the continued denial of basic political rights, workplace safety, employer accountability, and wage bargaining ensures a workforce whose economic utility seemingly increases proportionate to its political immobility and powerlessness.[69]

In fact, it could be argued that it is precisely the contradictory nature of this rhetoric that allows the United States to laud Mexicans as exemplary workers while also policing them and treating them as inherently criminal. What I would like to suggest is that gender divisions in these discourses further enable this mass of contradictions to appear meaningful or coherent on some level, thus allowing these conflicting tendencies to work together. Although gender discourse and identities are highly flexible and fragmented, a certain trend is worth noticing. Since the 1980s, this contradictory set of discourses has often been split along gender lines in hiring for low-tier positions: women are more responsible workers, men are lazy and too easily angered; women have a work ethic because of their dedication to their children, while men do not.[70]

Low-tier work in the United States as well on the border (including the Border Industrial Program) has relied on these gendered assumptions that produce and reinforce splits, valuing women's work and devaluing men's work (even as both groups are marginalized together in a variety of ways).[71] This discourse reflects participation in a consensus that women are perfect employees for the new types and conditions of low-tier work in an increasingly international economy.[72] Leslie Salzinger notes that broadly this meant that "in recent decades, young, Third World women have emerged as transnational capital's paradigmatic workers. Managerial manifestos recast women's 'natural' affinity for the home as a transferable set of skills and dispositions. These then crystallize into 'docility' and 'dexterity'—terms that go on to have autonomous effects as 'labor force requirements' for assembly workers internationally. In this process, men have been redefined as non-workers—lazy, demanding, and unreliable."[73] For these reasons, companies participating in the BIP since 1965 have actively recruited women workers even though the program was designed for former male guest workers in the United States. Within the United States, preferences for women workers are evident in the garment industry, domestic work, social services, and nursing.[74] Patricia Fernández-Kelly similarly notes that the feminization of labor has been a "double-edged sword"—women's dependent status "enables the preservation of an exploitable labor pool within the domestic realm, but it also serves to control men, especially those in the working classes."[75] In a broader context, William Julius Wilson also remarks that the feminization of labor is accompanied by the degradation of male labor in the low-tier sector.[76] Gender stereotyping maps onto the more general stereotypes of Mexican workers, serving to unify seeming opposites.

These trends continue today despite the wave of protests initiated by the "docile" maquila workers since the 1980s. Similar trends have occurred in other areas, remote from the border. For example, Paul Apostolidis's work demonstrates the significance of Mexican women immigrants in attempts to unionize the meatpacking industry in the Northwest,[77] thus challenging the idea that these workers are passive, docile, or overly wedded to traditional gender roles. The result has been a fragmenting of actual hiring practices (e.g., hiring more men than in the past but insisting that women are still the best workers) and gendered meanings (e.g., lauding women's work and disparaging men's work) that vary from factory to factory. Of course, the feminization of labor does not just mean the increased hiring of women, but also the progressive typing of many jobs crucial to the functioning of the global economy as female.[78] The consequences of this resistance do not seem to have decreased actual hiring preferences for Mexican women, but rather to fragment gendered discourses and confuse common assumptions.

Alternatively, it could be hypothesized that with the feminization of labor in certain industries, not to mention the difficulty in obtaining mainstream or formal work for some migrants, male immigrants increasingly resort to day laborer jobs and other types of casual employment. This in turn could reinforce the view that they are shiftless, undependable, or unpredictable in ways that women are not.[79] Hence the binary modes of operation praising Mexican work and contending that it is essential to the U.S. economy at the same time that Mexicans are posited as inherently criminal (or enemy) can be explained by these hiring practices. Gender splits clarify how prerogative power is deployed in two ways toward these political others: it can abandon women workers (by not investigating abuses of and violence toward women) while over-policing Mexican men. Or women can be over-policed at the level of reproduction while male guest workers are legally abandoned to inhuman work conditions. But both groups can be harassed by citizens' watch groups, exploited by employers, and subject to labor conditions that would not be acceptable for native-born citizens. The close relationship between the needs of global capital and the war on terror are thus manifested differently for men and women, though in mutually reinforcing ways that can position them as bare life.

Fears about Mexicans' high fertility further reinforce splits between good and bad, contributor and criminal, and man and woman, which, as I argue below, serve to create the ambivalent politico-economic space in which Mexicans operate. This ambiguous space then allows "criminality" to become an object of sovereign concern. In this way, bio-power cuts across disciplinary power to formulate a potential enemy rather than a citizen. The result is to justify surveillance and extrajudicial treatment of a group that is also, in many ways, treated as a "model minority."

Production and Reproduction

Gendered stereotypes about Mexican reproduction illustrate the linkage between denigrating views of a minority other and concerns about national security. In this case, high birth rates are tied to the notion that Mexicans want to "reconquer" the Southwest; most of the interlocutors who claim that there is a colonization movement argue that it is happening stealthily and through sheer numbers (i.e., population increases). This fear has become increasingly popular; once an idea discussed by Mexican American intellectuals and Chicano/a activists, the American Right has begun to appropriate it in everyday language and discourse. This charge not only constructs a hypersexualized subject "colonizing" the country, but it also betrays how Mexican immigrants are viewed as beings that cannot transcend their biology or their natural urges. In turn, this perspective demonstrates how Mexican subjects are viewed as bare life rather than citizens.

The perception that Mexican couples have numerous babies appears to be directed at Mexicans in general, but these stereotypes can be split along gender lines: immigrant women are viewed as being primarily responsible for family and assimilation, and immigrant men are viewed in sexual terms, practically reiterating verbatim historical arguments about African American men (as well as other denigrated men throughout history). Both views posit immigrant men and women as "present thinking,"[80] consuming resources thoughtlessly, and they ultimately define each subject biologically. For example, in Huntington's article "The Hispanic Challenge," his persistent references to the high fertility rates of Mexicans manifest his fear that "they" will soon outnumber "us."[81] Other authors, and notably some environmental groups, have echoed this worry.[82] This anxiety can further be tied to the broader concern that poor Mexican women are having too many children and are burdening the welfare system, hospitals, and educational systems. These notions place the onus of reproductive decisions, maintaining cultural values, and the overburdening of U.S. resources on women.[83] Hence women and women's bodies are the bearers of the responsibility of assimilation, family values, and traditional gender roles.[84]

Further, Leo Chavez argues that "Latina reproduction and fertility, especially that of Mexican immigrant women, became ground zero in a political war not just of words but also of public policies and laws in post-1965 America. . . . Indeed, anti-immigrant sentiment, especially during the 1980s and 1990s, focused specifically on the reproductive capacities of Mexican immigrant and Mexican-origin (U.S.-born) women."[85] Chavez's research shows that these fears are tied to the construction of Latina—and particularly Mexican—reproduction as pathological and threatening.[86] Ultimately, these concerns are manifested in policies as issues of national security, an area that goes beyond policing to the exercise of sovereignty. In this context, Melissa Wright remarks that the militarization of the border is precisely tied to fears about Mexican women's out-of-control reproduction: "Justifications for this militarization of an officially peaceful border frequently invoked the crisis represented by the immigrant *mexicana*, her pregnancies, her poor children, and their consumption of U.S. social services."[87] In this way, women are not mere economic usurpers but also invaders, enemies, or terrorists (and, accordingly, their status approaches bare life).

As Bonnie Honig notes, it is precisely the values that immigrants are praised for (traditional values, a nuclear family, the reluctance to have an abortion) that are also used against them. Moreover, it is often women who are viewed as the vehicles of assimilation—that is, policies and social disciplining of immigrant women are aimed not solely at women, but also at their more irresponsible or wild counterparts. (Similarly, Honig argues that the French government's prohibition of the veil in public schools not only disciplines girls but also is aimed at controlling Muslim men.) She asks why it is that individuals who are perhaps doubly or triply subject to oppression are simultaneously held responsible for what is broadly conceived of as assimilation.[88] In fact, binary modes of operation can be discerned in the treatment of Mexican women as a group. On the one hand, immigrant women are positioned as law-abiding, morally responsible, and, given traditional gender roles, precisely the group that can reinvigorate American family values. Alternatively, they can be viewed as less educated, less cultured, and too entrenched in Catholic beliefs, exemplified by the fact that they have too many children. This second set of stereotypes is then connected to notions of pathology that threaten the United States' borders, culture, and economic well-being. As Chavez comments, this leads to concerns with sovereignty: "The popular discourse of Latina reproduction is decidedly alarmist in that it becomes part of a discourse of threat and danger to U.S. society and even national security, which is underscored in a post-911 world."[89] That is, historical gender stereotypes are being redeployed today to suggest a national security threat—an invasion—rather than a mere social problem.

With regard to men, these arguments suggest the continued representation of Latino men as hypersexual, predatory, and lacking in self-control.[90] This portrayal of minority men is only alluded to in the work of Francis Fukuyama and Samuel Huntington but is clearly evident in the eugenically oriented texts that emerged in the 1990s (e.g., *The Bell Curve*),[91] public concerns about immigrants' fertility rates, and mainstream reactions to male immigrants. Their sexuality is threatening—when it is not contained, they will overtake or invade "us." Thus as neoconservatives point to immigrant women as models of traditional gender roles and true family values, they also criticize poorer immigrant women for their lack of restraint. Their alleged excess will inevitably burden the health and welfare systems. Not only is attention deflected from U.S. consumption patterns and sexual relations, but Mexican women are discursively figured as inevitable burdens on public welfare. Accordingly, problems endemic to capitalism—overconsumption, overproduction, sweatshop labor, and underground economies—are viewed as deviant and related to "backward" cultures.[92] This global paradigm is clearly reflected in the mainstream treatment of poor immigrant women of color, thus justifying their subordination and the attempt to monitor their fertility rates in aid and welfare programs.[93] To put it differently, these charges discursively posit Mexican women as inextricably bound to their biology and uncontrollable sexuality; in the post-9/11 era, these older dynamics are now viewed as evidence of attempts to colonize or invade the United States through stealth.

Reactions to Mexican and Central American immigrant men are simply the other side of the same coin.[94] For example, in the documentary *POV: Farmingville*,[95] the citizens of a Long Island town charge the mostly male immigrant group that has recently "invaded" their town with stealing jobs, overcrowding housing, driving down property values, and corrupting mainstream values. Beyond their economic and cultural degradation, the fact that these day laborers wait on a street corner for work is interpreted as a gross display of public occupancy, an inability to apply for work privately as others have done. Their visibility in key public places is viewed as rapacious, a violation that will threaten the women and children of the town. If they watch women walk or drive by, their glances are regarded as lascivious in intent. The fact that they have traveled to the town without women partners is even more suspect and they are accused of being Peeping Toms. Repeatedly in this documentary, concern is expressed for the girls and women of the town. Nevertheless, the same townspeople ensure that overcrowded conditions are maintained as they refuse to rent rooms to any of these workers, they strike down a proposal to have a hiring hall so that workers can get off the street, and they throw up obstacles for immigrants' organizations (such as a soccer league whose practices are restricted more than any other group's), thus ensuring that their main activities remain economic, deracinated, and public. As each speaker denies his or her racism ("I'm not racist but . . . "), he or she subscribes to biological notions of inferiority, present thinking, and hypersexuality. It is perhaps for these reasons that the organizers against the laborers accepted funding and support from white supremacist groups. It would appear that their economic fears were only one part of the story. The panic that these groups feel about Mexican day laborers' presence in their town mirrors the panic about women's high fertility rates. An invasion is happening on all levels.

The attempted murder of two workers by white supremacists in Farmingville is paralleled by the hundreds of unsolved murders of maquiladora workers, abuses in the guest-worker system, and the exploitative treatment of domestic workers and day laborers throughout the United States. Regular abuses are possible when a group is viewed as beyond the law (in these cases, abandoned by the law); alternatively, systematic violence is evidence that a group's political status approaches that of bare life. At best, it could be called undecidable life.[96] These discourses and policies make their subjects immediately—rather than proximately or secondarily—biological and pose them as threats to American material and demographic well-being. That is, their biological status reflects their potential treatment as bare life and as enemies. That authors like Samuel Huntington and Francis Fukuyama claim to focus on culture, or that the townspeople of Farmingville assert that their concerns are economic and cultural, obfuscates how these individuals' status is viewed in biological terms.[97]

Again, these examples point to a more general trend in viewing poorer immigrants of color as pollutants to the political body.[98] The binary modes of operation function along the lines of gender, linking economic policy to immigration norms, expectations, and policies. That is, economic concerns are connected to concerns about national security and territorial sovereignty through the medium of gender (and race, as I discuss below). Alternatively, these discourses and policy trends reveal the relationship between bio-political concerns and sovereign ones. In the past, gender and racial typing served other purposes—indentured servitude, slavery, and exploitative labor—but today the construction of the political identity of these immigrants in terms of gender and race leads to a political status approaching that of enemy (or, in Agamben's terms, bare life). Inextricably linked to gender, racial norms are significant to the power dynamics of bare life—a subject of prerogative power.

Race

In many respects, racist norms cannot be isolated from gendered ones. In turn, in the context of a war, these dynamics shore up the construction of Mexicans as invaders or threats to sovereignty. Despite claims to the contrary, popular, institutional, and academic discourse racializes Mexican Americans' identity.[99] Samuel Huntington's article "The Hispanic Challenge" warrants particular attention, as it synthesizes most contemporary anti-immigration arguments.[100] Huntington charges that Mexicans have "mañana syndrome," which includes "mistrust of people outside the family; lack of initiative, self-reliance, and ambition; little use for education; and acceptance of poverty as a virtue necessary for entrance into heaven."[101] Although he purports to make a cultural argument, his contention that these values are irreconcilable with American values, and that Mexican immigration should thus be limited, suggests that Mexicans cannot change. Culture is tacitly linked to fixed characteristics, and this racializes Mexicans' ethnicity.[102] These associations, in turn, are connected to Huntington's contention that Mexicans are staging a purposeful invasion as they reclaim their former homeland (Aztlán), which evidences that his cultural concerns are tied to sovereign ones: worries about the integrity of the United States' southern border and a Mexican takeover. Huntington's xenophobic views are shared by popular right wing pundits like Bill O'Reilly and Lou Dobbs, conservative politicians like Tom Tancredo, Jim Sensenbrenner, and Steve King, AM talk radio shows, and a significant number of average Americans.[103]

To ignore the racial aspects of how Mexicans and Mexican Americans are constructed in popular discourse, the media, and law can be dangerous, as Kimberlé Crenshaw has shown. A focus on gender or ethnicity alone does not accurately capture the consequences of the *intersection* of gender and racialized identity, particularly combined with working-class status, in the experiences of immigrants of color.[104] Even as the notion of race has been scientifically discredited since the 1930s, it remains vital in the popular imagination as well as in pseudoscientific discourse (which argues that DNA and chromosomes show that intelligence is hereditary rather than the product of social circumstances).[105] But the status of those of Mexican, Central American, or Latin American descent is complex because race in the United States has often referred to African Americans, and thus it is believed that there is only one race (i.e., since "whites" do not see themselves as a race).[106] Despite the ambivalent racial status of Mexican Americans, their historical and continued subordination justifies referring to race and racism.[107]

For this reason, interlocutors who claim they are making cultural and economic claims rather than racial ones—from the anti-immigration activists in Farmingville and other areas of the country to elite writers like Huntington or Dinesh D'Souza—must consider the following.[108] First, their arguments are not made in a vacuum, but rather in a complex historical, economic, and political context where their ideas certainly resonate with more openly racist dialogue of the past. This is particularly true when immigrants' characteristics are viewed as static, or when their identities are viewed in biological rather than in ethnic or cultural terms. Second, while it may be true that these discourses are not only racial but also nationalist and class based, this does not take away from the racial elements of each argument. Rather, what occurs is a process of racial signification in which cultural and "ethnic" qualities are analyzed in static terms. Indeed, many of the reactions to Huntington's arguments were that his description of the "mañana syndrome" and his contention that there are *"irreconcilable differ-ences"*[109] between Mexicans and Americans were racist.[110] Thus, not only is culture taken to be rigid or static, but so are these groups, leading us from simple racial thinking to racism when it comes to groups deemed incapable of integration. It is in this sense that an implicit racial hierarchy is affixed to the more openly expressed cultural hierarchy.

Alternatively, when authors or activists rely on a biological notion of ethnicity, this is no different than race. Miles and Brown conceptualize how racialization and ethnicization correlate thus: "We define ethnicisation as a dialectical process by which meaning is attributed to socio-cultural signifiers of human beings, as a result of which individuals may be assigned to a general category of persons which reproduces itself biologically, culturally, and economically. Where biological and/or somatic features (real or imagined) are signified, we speak of racialisation as a specific modality of ethnicisation."[111] This dialectical interaction fits the status of many immigrants of color today, and the racial element of Mexicans' status is confirmed in racial profiling, unequal prison sentences, de facto residential segregation, and employment discrimination. The involvement of white supremacist groups in anti-immigration movements is further evidence of the "racial" status of Mexican Americans.[112] The war on terror exacerbates these racist dynamics by legitimating racial profiling and the increased targeting of Mexican immigrants in arrest sweeps, job raids, and deportations.

Current debates on IQ, especially in the popular book *The Bell Curve* by Richard Herrnstein and Charles Murray, have sought to establish "scientific" proof that these cultural arguments are valid. Latinos have been a particular target of this discourse, and the authors suggest not only that this group has lower average intelligence, but that this "fact" should also be taken into account in immigration policy.[113] Despite charges that these studies are faulty (including not accounting for language proficiency), the authors have recommended a "more eugenically minded—and, hence, restrictive—U.S. immigration policy."[114]

These pseudoscientific arguments have been used to reinforce the panicked discourses about Mexicans and Mexican Americans depressing wages, their alleged inability to speak English, and their hypersexuality, not to mention legitimizing the racial profiling of the wars on terror and drugs. Hence they are not *merely* racially oriented but justify the greater deployment of sovereignty domestically. Moreover, there are economic benefits to sustaining racial hierarchy. In fact, it could be argued that racial rhetoric would be entirely gratuitous if it had not validated policing immigrants, denigrating their labor contributions, and justifying the wars on terror and drugs. To put it differently, this form of biologism relies on old stereotypes that are increasingly used today to position Mexican immigrants as bare life.

Conclusion

Returning to the discussion in chapter 2, the canonical model of assimilation rests on the assumption that the process is voluntary, rational, equally applied to all groups, and individually motivated. The conventional view holds that immigrant workers do jobs no one else will, do not complain, and eventually "succeed" by means of assimilation, accumulation of wealth, and naturalization, but this trajectory is less likely as bio-political concerns become more dominant through the widespread adoption of neoliberal policies. Older stereotypes about Mexican men and women, combined with the legal gray area that many poorer Mexican workers occupy, are being redeployed in the war on terror to create a subject that is highly exploitable and legally vulnerable. Gendered and racial discourse and policies, combined with the "grassroots activism" of vigilante groups and systematic violence on the border, reinforce binary modes of operation and allow for the contradictory situation in which these workers both sustain the low-tier workforce and yet are treated as potential threats to national security.

The prejudices against so-called labor immigrants—that they are backward, low skilled, too traditional, and too family oriented compared to immigrants of the past—reflect not merely nostalgia but also the hold that sexist and racist imagery have on public discourse and policy. Targeting poorer, working-class immigrants who are arguably exploited on both sides of the border maintains their uprootedness, ensuring that their integration is perceived negatively. The fact that deportation can occur more easily today is evidence of their unequal treatment. The way this group—the largest immigrant group to the United States and the nation's largest minority group—is criminalized due to its status as racial, economic, and gendered others demonstrates a crisis of democracy in U.S. institutions, practices, and mores. It is evident that social status rather than political or economic contribution founds the criteria for citizenship, and, in fact, that truly democratic actions like protest, unionization, and instances of micro-resistance on the job are viewed as traitorous and subversive. This is an inversion of democracy: a focus on the nation rather than the state.[115] Neoliberal policies combined with a continued emphasis on the nation-state create a hostile context of reception that dooms this group to failure (on these terms—this does not mean they fail in reality).

Mexican immigrants' construction as potential terrorists illuminates the inadequacy of U.S. conceptions of citizenship and current immigration policy. As I discuss in the prior chapter, rather than viewing those caught in legal gray areas as pathological or anomalous, "statelessness" can be seen as the model for a new citizenship that is without borders and which challenges the logic of bio-power.[116] If "we" begin to treat individuals who occupy politically ambivalent spaces not as deviants or criminals but as the norm, we may begin to envision a post-national citizenship. But there are gains to be made from the odd partnership of a free market and war, and so the incentives for change among elites are sadly too few. In the next chapter, I continue the discussion of sovereign concerns by exploring anti-immigration groups.

— 3 —

ANTI–IMMIGRATION GROUPS AND CIVIL SOCIETY

Pathway to Democracy or Support for Prerogative Power?

In this chapter, I continue evaluating the state of democracy in the United States today by exploring a limited number of anti-immigrant groups, including the Minutemen, Ranch Rescue, Civil Defense League, and FAIR (Federation for American Immigration Reform), in order to interrogate their status as political organizations and supporters of (or detractors from) civil society.[1] That is, I question the role of these groups in fostering democracy and political inclusion, and thus I consider how they affect Mexican immigrants to the United States, whether legal or illegal. In examining this issue, problems that were articulated by the American founders, Montesquieu, Tocqueville, and many others are still relevant: When does a civic or political group foment tyranny of the majority? Are all minority voices represented or given equal weight? How are freedom of association and freedom of speech balanced with competing claims? I conclude first that not only are these anti-immigration groups undemocratic in important ways, but they significantly aid the increased use of prerogative power (i.e., the legitimate suspension of the law for emergency reasons). Today, although anti-immigrant groups position themselves against the government or view themselves as doing what the government has failed to do, they contribute to prerogative spaces that make immigrants' political status a "zone of indistinction," as Giorgio Agamben would say.[2]

Second, the political atmosphere fostered by vigilante groups is evidence that power is not deployed in a vertical (elite/nonelite) fashion. Rather, as Foucault maintains (as does Sheldon Wolin in another way),[3] late modern power is dispersed, local, and both governmental and nongovernmental.[4] When combining these two lines of argumentation, it is interesting to note the symbiotic relationship between "outsider" or vigilante groups and public policy and discourse, even when they are ostensibly opposed to each other. Thus these groups are both undemocratic *and* pro-establishment; in fact, the Minutemen and other vigilante or watch groups reflect the extreme end of the spectrum in today's immigration debates. In these respects, they are indicative of broader historical trends and political dynamics. Because of this complex relationship built on articulation[5] or elective affinity,[6] their role in contemporary politics and grassroots organizing cannot be analyzed in isolation, but rather in terms of how they fit into broader economic, social, and political processes.[7]

Classic liberal arguments about the importance of civic and political groups include the notion that civil society is thought to be an antidote to the relative apathy of liberal citizenship, a possible solution to tyranny of the majority, a check on the usurpation of government power, and an intermediary between the individual citizen and elite political processes (i.e., a corrective to political isolationism).[8] Added to these arguments is the fear that an increasingly materialist lifestyle will undermine any of these democratic possibilities, as citizens retreat into individual isolation, value consumerism and economic activity over political obligation, or view one another more as competitors than compatriots. Although arguments from Hegel, Mill, and Durkheim (among others) cannot simply be lumped together, there are three broad warnings: that minority voices and political status must be protected, that government expansion of power must be checked, and that liberal citizenship—particularly in a capitalist context— is inadequate. The sum of these arguments is that we must be careful in what is figured as democratic and remember that tyranny can arise from different sites of power.

The anti-immigrant groups named above fit many of the criteria of a democratic political group—they may be organized democratically, representative of the local or national community, inclusive in terms of gender, race, and sexual orientation, and argue that they are asserting their constitutional rights. Indeed, many of these groups' names and discourse suggest that their members are more patriotic than the average person, more efficient than the government in protecting law and order, and truly sacrificing themselves on behalf of the nation. They also rely on basic constitutional rights to justify their organization—the rights to assembly, free speech, freedom of conscience, and the right to bear arms—and often appeal to governmental agencies to exercise their claims. But there are at least five concerns about these groups. First, even when following the law (which means that they are not allowed to hold suspects at gunpoint or physically touch them in any way), they are creating an atmosphere of intimidation by carrying weapons, dressing in military clothing, and using surveillance equipment, not to mention detaining individuals.[9] Second, several members of these groups have broken protocol and are now being charged with kidnapping, harassment, illegal border crossing, and carrying concealed weapons, among other things.[10] Third, their rhetoric is by no means neutral, but rather is racialized, gendered, and classist, and leads to distorted and damaging images of Mexicans and Mexican Americans.[11] Fourth, economic concerns are linked to worries about sovereignty, invasion, and cultural degradation. And finally, their discourse is warlike and threatening.

Further, it could be argued that they use the rule of law to effect the suspension of law—for example, in exercising their right to bear arms, they are not merely taking advantage of an individual right but also intimidating and harassing others. Essentially, the warnings that earlier writers issued—about the tyranny of the majority, individualism at the expense of the broader community, and the mistaken notion that economic claims readily translate into political ones—must be heeded. That white supremacist groups have been attracted to their rallies, border patrolling, and other political actions suggests that outsiders also perceive them as affirming a racial hierarchy. Hence, although these groups may follow the rule of law in certain respects, observers like the ACLU's Eleanor Eisenberg worry that anti-immigrant border patrol groups "near the Arizona border are engaging in illegal treatment of immigrants." Further, she argues that "the Minuteman project has created a powder-keg situation with the potential to go beyond harassment and false imprisonment to real violence. We hope that our observer project will continue to shed light on the activities of the Minutemen and will ensure that private citizens do not detain, harass or humiliate others in violation of the law."[12] These groups must be analyzed not just in terms of empty legality or the exercise of individual rights, but also in how they affect

Mexicans and Mexican Americans' daily lives and thus undermine their political status; that is, political community must be considered.

Of course, these groups are operating at a time when the U.S. southern border is being fortified in a number of ways (discussed in the previous chapter), including increased surveillance by the Bureau of Citizenship and Immigration Services, arrest sweeps by Immigration and Customs Enforcement, the placement of National Guard troops in certain key areas, and the building of an "Israeli-style" fence. The political context for this fortification is marked by both change and continuity: again, the deployment of old stereotypes combined with the relatively new requisites of neoliberal economics and an increasingly militarized border.

Sovereignty and Grassroots Anti-immigration Groups

Future generations will inherit a tangle of rancorous, unassimilated, squabbling cultures with no common bond to hold them together, and a certain guarantee of the death of this nation as a harmonious "melting pot."

The result: political, economic, and social mayhem.

Historians will write about how a lax America let its unique and coveted form of government and society sink into a quagmire of mutual acrimony among the various sub-nations that will comprise the new self-destructing America.

—Minuteman Project welcome statement

Today, a range of grassroots activists feel that a war is simultaneously being waged on U.S. sovereignty and its economy by Mexican immigrants, and particularly unauthorized entrants. These organizations range from lobbying groups like FAIR, Save Our State, and the California Coalition for Immigration Reform to vigilante groups like American Patrol, Ranch Rescue, the Civil Homeland Defense Group, and the Minutemen. Although vigilante groups are not new, nor are the stereotypes they draw on, what is a more recent development are their perceptions that illegal entry is akin to an act of terrorism, that taking jobs is not merely employment but constitutes an invasion, and that incursions on the border justify warlike measures. As the Minuteman website states, the rule of law is being destroyed "by the whims of mobs of ILLEGAL aliens who endlessly stream across U.S. borders . . . the result: political, economic, and social mayhem."[13] The act of "stealing jobs" is joined to the act of illegally crossing the border to portray a war waged on the United States by "unassimilated" hordes of Mexicans. In this way, economic and sovereign concerns are joined together, and these, in turn, rest on the presumption that certain cultures are inherently chaotic and disruptive of the social order.[14]

As discussed in the previous chapter, these arguments are strengthened (so to speak) by the repeated claim that Mexicans are not invading just for economic reasons, but also to stage a "Reconquista"[15]—that is, to reclaim the area that some Chicano/a activists call Aztlán. Glenn Spencer, the founder of American Patrol, remarks that "the consul general says Mexico is reconquering California. A Mexican intellectual suggests that anyone who doesn't like Mexicans should leave California. What else do you need to hear? RECONQUISTA IS REAL. . . . EVERY ILLEGAL ALIEN IN OUR NATION MUST BE DEPORTED IMMEDIATELY. . . . IF WE CAN BOMB THE TV STATION IN BELGRADE [Serbia] WE CAN SHUT DOWN [U.S. Spanish-language stations] TELEMUNDO AND UNIVISION."[16] These claims are repeated by mainstream academics, reporters, and politicians, including Rep. Tom Tancredo, the pundit Lou Dobbs, and the late professor Samuel Huntington.[17] According to this argument, Mexican job seekers ultimately want to reconquer the lost lands of the Southwest and reclaim what is theirs. In this way, they must be viewed as a threat to U.S. territorial sovereignty and national well-being.

These worries are manifest in calls to build an "Israeli-style" fence between Mexico and the United States, end immigration, and merge the war on terror and the war on drugs to police the border and fight "narco-terrorism."[18] Evoking Israel in describing the construction of the fence suggests that the United States is facing direct and palpable terrorist threats and warlike behavior. Thus Mexicans are viewed as ideal workers who will labor cheaply, do jobs no one else will, and work harder than most Americans at the same time that they are "terrorists" who stealthily destroy U.S. sovereignty, culture, and economy. As discussed in the previous chapter, we see the intersection of disciplinary concerns—the desire to form individuals into hard workers who internalize societal norms, such that they uphold rather than challenge authority—and bio-political ones that treat Mexicans and Mexican Americans as pollutants to the social body and as enemies rather than criminals. In fact, it could be argued that it is precisely the contradictory nature of this rhetoric that allows Americans to treat Mexicans as exemplary workers (at least for certain jobs) while also treating them as inherently criminal. These are opposites that function as binary modes, reinforcing each other and emanating from the projection of unwanted or undesirable aspects of American culture onto a foreign other.

As I have argued in the previous chapters, immigration policy reduces all Mexican immigrants to a dichotomy of legal and illegal that essentially criminalizes those who fall into any gray area below the legal threshold of citizenship. In this regard, Saskia Sassen has argued in the past that these types of solutions treat immigrants as if their motivations are entirely individual, as if the country itself is passively receiving them, and as if all immigration policy must focus on the border alone.[19] Sassen points out that law-and-order policies characterized by punitive measures and high levels of surveillance merely increase the vulnerability of poorer immigrants and fail to recognize the bridges or linkages that the United States itself has with Mexico.[20] By posing both solutions as the only possible alternatives—treat them as potential enemies and security threats and build barriers along the border, or as exploitable commodities, subjecting them to working conditions that are nonunion, highly exploitative, and deregulated (in terms of safety, including pesticides, machinery, and working and living conditions)—these immigrants' highly ambivalent status remains in place. In this context, the increasing power and popularity of groups like the Minutemen and American Patrol should not be surprising; they are simply responding to these very limited terms of the national immigration debate.

Hence U.S. immigration policies are focused so narrowly on the border[21] that immigrants fall under a legal/illegal binary that doesn't adequately portray (or tolerate) the many gray areas of immigration and foreign residence. In addition, this binary does not account for immigrants' significant contributions to the global economy.[22] This problem is magnified in the case of immigrants who are viewed as racial others, given the U.S. history of racial bias in making immigration law.[23] Further, because the status and identity of many Mexican immigrants and Mexican Americans is transnational,[24] their political status is even more ambivalent.

Just as Alexis de Tocqueville and Emile Durkheim argued that civic groups mediate between individuals and government, thus enacting and protecting democracy, citizens' groups and individual activity also contribute to the treatment of Mexican immigrants as enemies. This treatment is also exemplified in the area that makes up the Border Industrial Program, which in many respects reinforces Mexican and Mexican Americans' status as bare life. First, murders of maquiladora workers in Ciudad Juárez and Chihuahua starkly position women as bare life in a space that is already transnational and subject to the suspension of regular law (in terms of employment and factory regulations). Although the Chihuahuan police have portrayed the three hundred–plus murders and seventy-five or so disappearances in Juárez as the work of a serial killer, most interpreters—from academics to political activists—characterize these as the maquiladora murders, acts committed specifically against young, single, poor women workers.[25] These individuals argue that the murders discipline women who do not follow "proper" codes of femininity on the street and in the factories (e.g., snubbing a man who acts interested). They also contend that the failure of the Mexican police to investigate the murders in a timely or effective fashion reflects the denigrated status of women—perhaps not only on the part of the Mexican authorities but also on the part of their American employers. As I discuss in the next chapter, this combination of circumstances serves to denationalize national territory for women workers, allowing them to be killed with impunity. In this way, "civil society" can be a support for prerogative power and acts of international sovereignty just as much as it hypothetically supports and enacts democracy.

Grassroots groups reflect recent changes in policy, but they have also influenced policy to a significant degree and set the terms of public debate. Their increasing numbers follow the brief history I discussed in the "context of reception" section in chapter 1. In the late 1980s, sovereign matters became increasingly oriented toward the southern border, illegal work, and unauthorized entry.[26] At this time, media and political rhetoric constructed illegal aliens as security threats along the southern border, and the 1986 Immigration Reform and Control Act was one of the first pieces of legislation in recent history to focus on unauthorized entry to a significant degree.[27] The nascent development of vigilante groups at this time reflected these concerns, and likewise these policies most likely empowered these groups. For example, the Ku Klux Klan and other white supremacist organizations began harassing Mexican immigrants and Mexican Americans beginning in the 1980s.[28] Joe Nevins remarks about this increased activity that "some of the groups, like the white supremacist American Spring and the White Aryan Resistance, were openly racist; others, such as Light Up the Border, cast their argument more strictly in anti-immigration and/or national sovereignty terms. In practice, however, the line between these two types of pro-boundary-control groups was often rather blurry."[29] Anti-immigration activity was stepped up even further in the mid-1990s.

As the Cold War ended, the United States' superpower status was in question on two fronts: economically, it began to fall behind Japan and Germany, and militarily, it no longer had a cause to justify leading the world. Americans arguably turned inward as sovereign concerns increasingly became intertwined with economic ones. Neoliberal policies were coupled with the rhetoric of individual responsibility and led to attacks on the poor, the homeless, single mothers, and unauthorized entrants.[30] By the early 1990s, a movement in California arose, led by Glenn Spencer. His group, Voices of Citizens Together, began as a neighborhood watch in reaction to the 1992 riots in Los Angeles. This group, along with others, worked together in Save Our State, which called for "mass deportation of undocumented immigrants" and facilitated the passage of Proposition 187.[31] Briefly, Proposition 187 blocked educational access for undocumented children, barred unauthorized individuals from receiving welfare benefits or public health care, required public institutions to report suspected "illegals," and made the use of forged documents a felony.[32] Additionally, Save Our State also successfully lobbied for changes in bilingual education at the time. Operation Gatekeeper, which began in 1994, fortified certain areas of the border and reinforced the increasingly black-and-white perception of Mexican entrants as legal or illegal. Although Proposition 187 was defeated on constitutional grounds, a version of it passed in Arizona in 2004 (Proposition 200),[33] and Governor Arnold Schwarzenegger of California has consistently tried to pass parts of the failed initiative. Even more groups have been founded since September 11, 2001, and some have gained national prominence. Roxanne Doty notes that "by the fall of 2005, over 40 anti-immigrant citizen border patrol groups had formed since April 2005, many of them far from the actual U.S. / Mexican border."[34] She also remarks that media coverage of these groups exploded after September 11, connecting the war on terror to concerns about the U.S.-Mexican border: "After 9/11, anti-immigrant forces were able to link their agenda to national security by drawing on the fears and uncertainty that resulted from the attacks."[35]

In recent times, Spencer has since emerged as one of the leading anti-immigration activists, flying to various parts of the country to advise local citizens about illegal immigration and work. He is a key figure in the documentary *POV: Farmingville*, discussed in the previous chapter. Spencer relocated to Arizona in 2002 and founded the American Border Patrol.[36] Similar to groups like Ranch Rescue, Texas Border Patrol, and the Minutemen, these organizations have adopted military tactics, conducting various covert operations, dressing in military garb, and using high-tech surveillance equipment. Like other groups, Spencer's tries to patrol the border using video cameras and the Internet, aiming to expose individuals as they cross the border by posting their images online. These groups also try to make citizens' arrests and block attempts at entry altogether. The more prominent organizations have websites, many of them linked to one another, and they have attempted to establish offices throughout the country. Hence their activities are both covert and very public. For example, Spencer, Chris Simcox (cofounder of the Minuteman Project), and Barbara Coe (founder of the California Coalition for Immigration Reform and a prominent spokesperson on behalf of anti-immigration legislation) are frequently interviewed on television and radio. Since 9/11, they have been allied with key political figures like Tom Tancredo and Jim Sensenbrenner, writer-activists like Peter Brimelow (founder of VDare) and Laurence Auster, and think tanks like the Center for Immigration Studies in Washington, D.C. Combined with other anti-immigration groups like FAIR, NumbersUSA, and some offshoots of the Sierra Club, they form a vast, interconnected network that not only reflects the increasing intolerance toward "labor" immigrants, but also itself plays a key role in setting the terms of public debate and policy concerns.

The connection between national politicians and these national and local groups is an important one. This unity serves to homogenize discourse, making the separation between the political Right and Left a matter of degrees, rather than leading to debate or exposing the complexities of immigration. It has also consolidated an unacknowledged backlash: if everyone more or less agrees that there is a problem and that Mexicans constitute the bulk of this problem, the only difference among groups is in how to solve the issue. And, as discussed in the first chapters, the solutions reinforce one another: a guest-worker program is simply combined with increased surveillance. For this reason, most politicians have supported the same measures: both Democrats and Republicans have backed the border fence, the guest-worker program, and tighter immigration controls, including the denigration of immigrant labor and the assumption that professional immigration is superior. Even political leaders who are viewed as more progressive than most—the late Edward Kennedy, Barack Obama, Hillary Clinton, Dianne Feinstein—have supported these measures. For example, the Democratic governor of New Mexico, Bill Richardson, declared the border area a "state of emergency" and deployed his state's National Guard before President Bush did in May 2006.[37] Richardson declared this emergency because of the insecurity of the border, citing not only drug violence but also an increased concern with unauthorized entry after seeing "the trails where these illegal routes take place."[38] In this climate, politicians like Tom Tancredo, Pat Buchanan, and Jim Sensenbrenner who may have seemed extreme before 9/11 now set the terms of the debate on immigration, linking the unauthorized immigrants who engaged in terrorist attacks to Mexicans' unauthorized immigration.[39] Thus vigilante groups are supported explicitly by figures like Tancredo and Sensenbrenner and implicitly by the measures that even "progressive" Democrats are willing to back. Of course, many grassroots groups state that they are more committed and better equipped to address these problems than politicians.

Vigilante groups broadly claim that they are waging a war against Mexicans due to their high fertility rates, their inherent criminality, their desire to reclaim the southwestern portion of the United States (aka Aztlán),[40] their importation of criminal and backward ways (i.e., exploitive conditions are their fault and not a product of capitalism),[41] and because they are conducting an economic war (i.e., by stealing jobs). As stated above, although groups like the Minutemen argue that they are merely a watch group, they have also been charged with racism, kidnapping, and intimidation of citizens; other groups are less careful about hiding their tactics. Finally, although these groups argue that they are filling in the gaps of sovereignty that the U.S. government has left open, there is official tolerance of them, demonstrating that the relationship is perhaps more symbiotic than their discourse would suggest.[42]

Their rhetoric is not just centered on security and border issues but also reproduction, the color of Mexicans' skin, their educational levels, and their job skills. Crossing the border is associated with disease, child molestation, and social pathology.[43] Unauthorized immigrants who enter the country are also accused of stealing, vandalism, and trespassing. Some have argued that grassroots anti-immigration groups are hate groups connected to white supremacists, Confederate groups, and neo-Nazis.[44] While leaders like Spencer deny racism,[45] others are more comfortable with the connection to these more overtly eugenic and discriminatory stances.[46]

Public policy, vigilante activism, and public discourse serve to make the political status of Mexicans and Mexican Americans highly precarious and to reinforce their gendered and racialized status. To vigilante groups, even cultural expressions are evidence of enemy invasion. In this way, government policies and grassroots activism mutually reinforce each other. Oliver

Cromwell Cox noted a similar synthesis of powers in the Jim Crow South in his analysis of lynching.[47] In these dynamics, we must recognize that the logic of the nation-state renders the process of assimilation "violent," as Hannah Arendt noted after World War II.[48] Democracy and the nation-state are often at odds, and sovereign acts become possible when an individual's political status is ambivalent.

Civil Society, "Lynching," and Democracy

Both Bonnie Honig and Sheldon Wolin help explain how the American version of democracy frames mainstream reactions to foreigners, including the formation of vigilante groups such as the Minutemen. Honig's observations about the role of foreignness in American political culture and self-understanding help explicate the highly ambivalent role that immigrants play in the United States, while Sheldon Wolin's critique of liberal citizenship is relevant to understanding how the exercise of democratic rights by vigilante groups can lead to undemocratic ends.[49] Based on these two lines of argumentation, I believe that there is a double standard operating, such that the rights of groups like the Ku Klux Klan are defended while Mexican organizing and protests are seen as traitorous and threatening. Added to these dynamics are those that Tocqueville observed in the early nineteenth century—a love of equality of conditions and an overwhelming concern with material well-being over and above democratic processes, which can strengthen the power of the government, producing conformity, intolerance to difference, and the potential tyranny of both the government and the people.[50] Taken together, these observations can help us interpret the power matrices within which anti-immigration groups operate today.

First, to Honig, the United States has historically viewed immigrants either as corrupting or as contributing to its values, economy, and politics.[51] That is, the immigrants are not seen in their complexity, but either as supplements to or corruptors of the American self-image. Not only does this result in seeing immigrants through a purely American lens, it also reinforces binary modes of operation. Entrepreneurial immigrants who exemplify the American dream also "steal" jobs; those who reinvigorate family values and traditional gender roles are also threatening in their uncontrolled reproduction; and immigrants either "dramatize consent" or undermine it through illegal entry.[52] This dichotomized approach to foreigners "is what happens when [they] are pressed into service on behalf of institutions—capitalism, community, family—that seem incapable of sustaining themselves. The deployment of foreignness as a restorative supplement itself positions foreigners also as the original *cause* of the very institutional illness they are supposed to be curing."[53] To put it differently, this binary perspective serves to "renationalize the state"[54] rather than to perform democratic agency; this, in turn, is because American notions of democracy are inextricably intertwined with national projects.

Not surprisingly, xenophilia toward Mexican immigrants, as well as its xenophobic counterpart, emanates from "our" own political frameworks, beliefs, and expectations.[55] The political majority has concerned itself more with what immigrants represent in American cultural and political terms than in seeing the immigrants in all their complexity. Because of this political tendency to privilege national projects over truly democratic ones—which could be post-national, plural, and allow for a multiplicity of loyalties and identities—immigrants have been subject to the binary modes of operation discussed in previous chapters.

Framing these dynamics is a rather empty conception of citizenship and the exercise of rights. Sheldon Wolin argues that because American citizenship has not been defined sufficiently in the Constitution, nor has democracy itself been given substantive meaning, membership in either the Ku Klux Klan or the NAACP can be treated as a valid exercise of citizenship rights.[56] To put it differently, because there is no ethical content to rights, rights themselves are used instrumentally, regardless of whether the exercise of one's individual rights undermines political community, political inclusion, or the democratic agency of others. To the extent that the group does not break the law, liberal citizenship protects membership in any group, regardless of its aims. Accordingly, groups like the Ku Klux Klan arise because our citizenship is more oriented toward individual rights than group commitments, thus fostering a divisive rather than cohesive politics; because majoritarian politics have traditionally been eschewed in favor of a more passive and materialist notion of political obligation; and because only the democratic means are examined, not the ends.[57] Repressive immigration policies, unequal labor relations, an increasingly unstable job market, and neoliberal politics can reinforce fragmentation and divisiveness. In this context, instances of Mexican American organizing—including unionization, protests, self-help groups, legal defense groups, and ethnic identity organizations—are viewed as acts of separatism, disloyalty, and ungratefulness.

In contrast, the conventional reaction to groups like the Minutemen ranges from blanket approval, with no accounting for their racism or violence, to their portrayal as outlaws and vigilantes. But what is significant is that mainstream concern is focused on whether they are following the rule of law—not if they are fostering democracy, equality, or inclusiveness. This reaction signals what Honig and Wolin have argued: that political reactions to foreigners are most often concerned with national projects, and that citizenship-as-rights is a rather empty conceit in the face of popular tyranny. For these reasons, democratic values become inverted such that mainstream, peaceful Mexican organizations like the Mexican American Legal Defense and Educational Fund (MALDEF) and the League of United Latin American Citizens (LULAC) are viewed as threats to our nation's security[58] and evidence that Mexican Americans are not assimilating and should be deported, while groups like the Minutemen, which at least suggest military action and physical violence, are questioned only for their tactics but not their assumptions. In this way, civic and political groups are judged first for whether their means are legal but not whether their ends are undemocratic, but second for their nationalist and materialist, rather than democratic, substance. Thus peaceful Mexican American groups are viewed as separatist and threatening, and American Patrol, Ranch Rescue, and the Minutemen are merely going too far with their tactics but are not threatening to national security or undermining citizenship in any substantial way.[59]

It is in this framework that earlier notions of civil society should be analyzed. As representative democracies began to replace or undermine absolute monarchies, warnings about the dangers of modern democracy became increasingly prevalent. In particular, two tendencies were noted: the tyranny of the majority, and the increased centralization of the state. According to Alexis de Tocqueville, these two tendencies work together. From one perspective, mass democracy leads to consensus—the notion that all political and moral questions can be answered through sheer numbers supporting a process, issue, or candidate ("For they think it not unreasonable that, all having the same means of knowledge, truth will be found on the side of the majority").[60] Conformity of opinion then leads to political apathy, the absence of debate, the threat of social exile for nonconformity, censorship of the media, and, ultimately, support for increased representation by the government for all needs.[61] That is, love of equality trumps love of democratic activity, and people turn to the government to preserve the former at the expense of the latter.[62] Added to representative democracy and the equation of numerical support with justice, materialism also explains this love of equality over freedom. In this way, "self-interest properly understood"—action in the public sphere tied to self-interest[63]—can devolve into egotistic withdrawal.

To apply these ideas to contemporary power matrices, neoliberal policies have increased the gap in incomes, led to stagnant wages for the working class, resulted in degraded labor conditions and "flexible" labor relations, and decreased the power of unions, all of which ensures that the lower and middle classes demand greater protections from the government as immigrants are viewed as stealing jobs and welfare, depressing wages, and degrading work conditions. At the same time, the wars being conducted abroad and on U.S. soil further legitimize the increasing deployment of sovereign power—a concern with national security—over and above democratic freedoms. Under these conditions, Tocqueville predicted that citizens would mistake conformity and equality of conditions for political equality while allowing the government to increase its power.

According to Tocqueville, these two processes—the greater predominance of the tyranny of the majority as well as the centralization[64] of the federal government—can be checked by civic associations and political organizations.[65] Similarly, John Stuart Mill argued in the *Principles of Political Economy* that these groups are valuable not only in their substantive aims but also in the educational process that draws the individual outside him- or herself.[66] Individuals form communities and make democratic processes possible. The local governance—including New England town meetings, local activism, and community action—that Tocqueville valued in book 1 of *Democracy in America* could thus be replaced in more modern times by religious, civic, professional, and intellectual groups, among others. But what was important to Tocqueville was that civil associations would lead to political ones—that is, civic activity in and of itself was insufficient as a means of preserving or enacting democracy.[67]

Variations on Tocqueville's arguments, which were based on warnings by Montesquieu a century before, are seen again in Mill, Hegel, Durkheim, and, more recently, Robert Putnam and other democratic theorists who argue that community and civil society must be strengthened in the modern state to ensure the following: that there are checks on government power, that there are connections between individual citizens and more elite political processes, that democratic power is not just institutionalized and formal but also local, grassroots, and issuing from "below"; and that individuals in a liberal capitalist state are pulled from their apathy or self-interest into the public realm to enact the positive duties of citizenship.[68] What is presupposed today is the distinction that Tocqueville made—that civil associations would lead to political ones or, more minimally, would build "social capital." But unlike more contemporary commentators, Tocqueville's warning about tyranny of the majority must be taken into account—not all civic and political associations are democratic. This is particularly true when they act as a partner to government power—whether intentionally or not—as these anti-immigration groups do. Taking these arguments seriously, contemporary U.S. anti-immigration groups play a supportive role in the increasing absolutization of power in the nation-state's wars on terror, drugs, and narco-terrorism as well as reflecting the predominance of material values—that is, the prevalence of neoliberal policies and values.[69] They also speak to the distinction between sovereignty/nationality and democracy that Honig analyzed.

On the other hand, the groups named above position themselves as *more* democratic than the average person or group, more efficient and responsive to citizens' needs than the government, and defending an invasion that others cannot quite see or appreciate.[70] In this way, they discursively place themselves outside the bounds of "bad" civil society. Moreover, they establish themselves as valid political actors in contradistinction to a group presumed to be inherently illegal; their patriotism is contrasted with Mexicans who carry the Mexican flag during mass protests. Their loyalty, often bolstered by military service, is opposed to Mexicans' alleged inability or unwillingness to serve in the military. And their groups are assumed to restore the rest of the nation to its former meaning and values, while Mexican American organizing, protests, and unionization is held to be evidence of separatism, ungratefulness, and even "invasion." In contrast, certain groups (e.g., LULAC, MALDEF, the National Movimiento Estudiantil Chicano de Aztlán, the National Council of La Raza, and other Mexican American political organizations) are portrayed as being separatist, disloyal, and a sign that certain types of immigrants are not assimilating. But this perspective tells us more about what U.S. expectations of assimilation are than about the immigrants themselves. Mainstream notions of assimilation are based on a wholesale rejection of one's former country, language, traditions, and behaviors in favor of what is considered American. It is conformity rather than difference (or *différance*);[71] homogeneity over plurality; and the demand for single, artificial loyalties over and above multiple ones. In this way, expectations of immigrants are closely in line with the intellectual conformity pervasive in American culture that Tocqueville saw in the early nineteenth century.

Further, Tocqueville recognizes the close linkage between the increasing centralization of governmental power and the greater predominance of intellectual and political conformity. On the one hand, this does not necessarily translate into political apathy on the part of the citizenry but rather intolerance to difference and dissent. On the other hand, I want to complicate the notion of "centralization" of the government and replace it with a similar notion: the increased use of prerogative power and continuous references to a "state of emergency." This substitution retains the spirit of Tocqueville's argument, which is to suggest that nondemocratic power dynamics and processes become increasingly prevalent as governmental power grows in and of itself. This includes the suspension of normal freedoms and civil liberties in favor of more restrictive policies that limit certain groups' movements, subject them to high levels of surveillance, and effectively curtail democratic freedoms.[72] Moreover, Tocqueville significantly remarked on how an economic ethos will make this linkage even deeper as people begin to love equality of conditions over democratic freedom, and thus turn to the government to maintain the former over the latter. Neoliberal policies are a contemporary analogue to this problem and tend to strengthen individual rights at the expense of the collective, business interests over individual freedoms, and substitute a material ethos for a more justice-oriented politics.

In this context, it can be argued that groups like American Patrol, the Minutemen, and Ranch Rescue are acting independently of the government (and often in opposition to it, in their opinion) but nonetheless uphold contemporary power dynamics—neoliberal policies, the increased deployment of absolute power, the greater pervasiveness of a state of emergency—in their local form. They exemplify how power is diffuse, local, and extralegal (as Foucault has analyzed) even as the wars on terror, drugs, and narco-terrorism are the paradigms within which they operate. For this reason, the meaning and operation of these groups are analogous to groups that lynched African Americans during the Jim Crow era. Organizations like the Ku Klux Klan were extra-governmental but were instrumental in upholding the apartheid system.

Oliver Cromwell Cox defines lynching as "an act of homicidal aggression committed by one people against another through mob action for the purpose of suppressing either some tendency in the latter to rise from accommodated position of subordination or for subjugating them further to some lower social status."[73] It is not directed against an individual but against a class of people, and the group that lynches feels that it is justified by its "right to punish."[74] In the same way, most of the anti-immigration groups discussed above argue that their actions—dressing in camouflage, patrolling the border, stopping individuals who appear to be of Mexican descent to check their identification, staging demonstrations in areas where there are day laborers—will send a message to all other Mexican would-be entrants. Significantly, lynching establishes "the socio-psychological matrix of the power relationship between the races."[75] Applied to today's current situation, the combination of anti-immigrant lobbying, border patrol groups, and paramilitary organizations serves to uphold the very power dynamic that the U.S. government wants to establish: a state of emergency undergirded by racial profiling, class bias, and gendered stereotypes. Moreover, these groups are merely responding to the narrow construction of the immigration "debate" that either posits immigrants as cheap, exploitable labor or as enemy-criminals to be punished and deported. Further, in times of anxiety—both in terms of national security and economic instability for the working classes—political action can relieve tension and function as a sort of negative bonding. It can displace problems endemic to the system onto a group of outsiders such that measures against this group appear as a political cure-all.

Conclusion: Democracy in America?

While it must be noted that Mexican immigrants and workers (here and on the border) exercise a considerable amount of agency at times—from acts of micro-resistance on the job, to unionizing, to staging mass protests, as in the spring of 2006 and recent protests in Arizona—these acts are not conventionally appreciated as strengthening U.S. democracy or civil society.[76] Rather, they have been portrayed as frightening acts of separatism, disloyalty, and even lawbreaking. It is, in fact, the figure of the illegal alien that determines these portrayals. On the other hand, anti-immigration groups with patriotic names pose themselves as the nation's most loyal actors. Their reception is more mixed, both being validated by mainstream sources (such as being featured on CNN without being identified as extremist groups) and criticized by others (most notably the Southern Poverty Law Center, the Anti-Defamation League, and the American Civil Liberties Union).

What is evident is that both sides are following time-honored traditions in American history—one of mass protest, self-help, and political mobilization from the grassroots level,[77] and the other of nativism and intolerance. Nevertheless, just because immigrants can resist exploitation and sometimes succeed is not proof that they are being treated democratically or according to any rule of law. Groups like the Minutemen, American Patrol, and Ranch Rescue—in conjunction with neoliberal policies and demands, U.S. wars fought on the domestic front, and the limited terms of the immigration debate—all undermine the democratic legitimacy of Mexican American efforts. Vigilante groups are examples of "negative" civil society in that they use the rule of law for undemocratic ends; they focus on national projects at the expense of democratic—that is, pluralist or inclusive—programs; their militarism can lead to more open and systematic acts of violence; their implications of racial hierarchies, both overt and tacit, go against democratic notions of equality; and they create an openly hostile, intimidating atmosphere on the border. Most important, these groups show that it is not just the state that can initiate and maintain a "state of emergency" or operate in a realm that is characterized by the suspension of law.[78]

As I have tried to show, broader social trends have already fashioned the "choices" these groups think they have. In the context of the war on terror, the war on drugs, and the war on narco-terrorism, combined with the Patriot Act and other legislation related to these "wars," immigrants' status is increasingly undecidable. Recent public debate only crystallizes these narrow choices, forcing American-born citizens to choose between treating Mexicans as exploitable labor or as potential terrorists. Finally, the ambivalent political and economic status of many Mexicans and Mexican Americans on the border and in the maquila program reinforce the antidemocratic power networks already operating, placing concerns of the nation and sovereignty above democratic processes and self-understanding. The groups or individuals that are the subject of controversy, new legislation, and vigilante acts are the most politically and economically vulnerable. That is, the ambivalent status of the Mexicans and Mexican Americans these vigilante groups are targeting makes them particularly vulnerable to attack with impunity.

The transnational subjectivities of Mexican American immigrants can both increase individual well-being through gains made in gray areas[79] at the same time that sovereign power is asserted, ensuring further political precariousness. Anti-immigrant discourse and policies, combined with "grassroots activism," reinforce binary modes of operation and allow for the contradictory situation in which these workers both sustain the low-tier workforce and yet are treated as potential threats to national security. Most important, we must question any "war" that punishes status more than criminal acts and that serves to exploit a denigrated subject. The combination of low-tier work conditions in a more global economy and the wars on drugs and terror lead only to more ambivalence and the strengthening of sovereignty over and above democratic activity.

In the next chapter, I explore two politico-economic spaces—the guest-worker program and the Border Industrial Program—that represent the crystallization of neoliberal policies. These ostensibly economic spaces suspend workers' political rights and paradoxically strengthen state sovereignty while also opening up borders to global forms of capital. In effect, they render workers stateless while participating in the program. Rather than viewing this statelessness as anomalous or a case of bad laws, I argue that these circumstances should be the starting point for invigorating democratic politics. If the United States begins to treat individuals who occupy politically ambivalent spaces as the norm, "we" may begin to envision a post-national citizenship and redirect the energy of political and civic organizations to cosmopolitan democracy rather than national projects. But the first step must be to recognize the very policies and actions that make immigrants stateless in the first place.

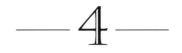

4

HOMO LABORANS, STATELESSNESS, AND TERROR

Economic Deregulation and the Strengthening of Sovereignty

In this chapter, I would like to suggest that two programs—the U.S. guest-worker program and the Border Industrial Program (or maquila program)—are spaces created in reaction to perceived political and economic emergencies. Both programs are legal and operate outside normal laws and practices, and both are viewed as temporary. But not only have they lasted far beyond the original "emergencies" that inspired their creation, but they also have a significant impact on low-tier informal work in the same industries. Although both are assumed to be free zones—meaning that they are supposed to be purely economic in nature—they serve two major political purposes. First, they seek to control entry (particularly illegal entry) into the United States and thus are instruments of immigration policy in general. Second, they contribute to the greater control and surveillance of low-tier immigrants, including the fortification of the border. In this way, these programs resolve the apparent split between those who are allegedly pro-immigration and anti-immigration by ensuring that immigrants are at once highly exploitable *and* politically rightless (and therefore easily tracked and deported).

Although both programs are portrayed as manifestations of American generosity to poorer countries, they are in reality instances of neoliberal policies that achieve at least three things: greater capital mobility, increased worker immobility, and, if possible, increased control over all low-tier immigrant workers (including an attempt to control illegal workers).[1] These two programs are significantly marked by the law (surveillance, a border fence, and other attempts to fortify the border) and lawlessness (whether through deregulation, toxic dumping, or lawbreaking with impunity). Importantly, they demonstrate how neoliberal policies undercut democratic equality and the rule of law, and yet strengthen state sovereignty through the suspension of law. Both are not only crystallizations of ideal neoliberal economic policies but also political policies—namely, how to deal with poorer immigrants, or would-be immigrants, of color. Gender roles, mixed with racial stereotypes, further complicate matters, explicitly highlighting femininity in the case of the maquila program and more tacitly oriented toward male workers in the guest-worker program.

I will first investigate the conditions of each program, focusing on how economic deregulation, coupled with the suspension of political rights, approaches what Giorgio Agamben calls a situation of "bare life." This is to pick up on underemphasized elements of Agamben's work, such as the use of prerogative power domestically and systematically, in a nonwar situation, and effecting a deterritorialized space through the suspension of not just political rights but also economic regulation and rights. I also briefly consider how the language of charitableness, economic reasonableness, and consent and contract all serve to obfuscate the highly dangerous conditions these workers occupy. As Carole Pateman has argued that legal reasoning about marital rape has been Hobbesian rather than democratic, I want to suggest that these employment contracts are similarly construed.[2] In effect, they are contracts that lead to the suspension of an individual's rights, and yet according to Hobbesian logic, they are legitimate. In contrast, Locke's ideal contract is not legitimate in conditions of coercion or if it effectively renders obsolete all other rights. Even in the mid-nineteenth century, Marx lambasted that "unconscionable freedom, Free Trade!,"[3] and similarly challenged the appearance of equality and freedom in the labor contract. More recently, Agamben has discussed how this veneer of consent simply shows that democracies can cynically use the notion of mutuality to mask unequal power relations.[4] My aim in this chapter is to highlight the political aspects of two related programs that have been discursively depoliticized, and to show the intimate relationship between the interests of global capital and the *strengthening* of sovereignty. For this reason, as I have argued in previous chapters, workers are not merely "invaders," welfare parasites, or job stealers, but also potential enemies or terrorists. Because the programs create free zones, they "deterritorialize national territory"[5] and make participants stateless; accordingly, any democratic solution to these issues must be trans-national rather than national.

Both create a sort of "free trade zone," affecting not only participants but also informal and formal labor relations outside these programs. Very broadly, free trade zones maximize corporate freedom based on govern-mental acquiescence and minimize workers' rights, deregulating safety, health, and environmental standards. They operate in denationalized space, realizing a suspension of the law and a challenge to territorial claims. The disciplinary effects of these programs are not only economic but also polit-ical, weakening democratic freedoms such as unionization and blocking the possibility of any formal political activity in the case of guest workers. Because these arrangements increasingly are viewed as the "responsible" or "humane" way to regulate illegal workers and poorer entrants, their conditions become normal.[6] This is important to note as the programs are regarded as temporary in key ways: guest workers are considered tempo-rary labor; guest-worker programs are supposed to ebb and flow with labor demand based on seasonal need and labor shortages; the structural adjust-ment policies that over time came to define the logic of the maquiladoras were a response to economic crisis;[7] and one of the main attractions of the maquiladoras is that companies rely on a flexible workforce and can hypo-thetically divest if needed.

In fact, this temporariness serves as the justification for harsh conditions, which include dangerous machinery, exposure to pesticides and other harm-ful chemicals, overcrowded and dilapidated housing, long hours, low pay, and the absence of any collective representation or political rights.[8] As the conditions have a normalizing effect, the programs themselves institute and establish major changes to labor expectations and relations. Significantly, they have an enormous impact on low-tier laborers' lives on the border and within the United States, weakening democratic agency and blocking political rights (whether human rights or citizenship rights).[9] Indeed, they create a group of people who are effectively stateless while they participate in the programs.

For these reasons, although most interpreters of Agamben's work focus on obvious manifestations of sovereignty and prerogative power, I believe that these free trade zones are excellent examples of how "bare life" is cre-ated through economic and political deregulation.[10] As Agamben argues, the disturbing trend in late modernity has been the increasing *permanence* of the state of emergency in democracies, which has been used in economic *and* political contexts.[11] The economic justification for using prerogative power demonstrates the degree to which the law is suspended not just during wartime but also in perceived economic crises; in fact, some of the most important examples of presidential decrees have involved economic intervention. Free trade zones operate according to a similar logic, relying on the suspension of the law, but rather than leading to the heavy economic intervention of the 1920s and 1930s, today's interventions diminish labor norms and deregulate working conditions. For this reason, they give the illusion of the absence of government. Economic deregulation is accompanied by the suspension of normal political rights and protections, and yet heavy police surveillance is required to enforce these conditions. This includes the strengthening of the Border Patrol, the construction of the border fence, the increased threat of detention and deportation, and rigid labor conditions that seek to control workers.[12] Finally, given that these conditions can last for years, they point to a situation in which this temporary, extralegal arrangement becomes the norm.

Nevertheless, the losses incurred by low-tier workers and their governments are effaced. Instead, both arrangements are viewed as charity from the developed to the developing world, and the irony of the label "Made in the U.S.A." is lost on most consumers.[13] Western countries have frequently used guest-worker programs and free zones in the postwar era to address labor shortages and stimulate the economy (whether in a developing country or a developed one). By presenting these arrangements as a "gift" from the developed world to the developing world and a logical solution to labor shortages,[14] these nations conceal the contribution the workers make as well as the debt and exploitation of resources a host country may incur.[15]

In the United States, the two programs are historically interrelated: the guest-worker program began in 1942 and ended in 1964, and the Border Industrial Program was created in part to give the same workers a job once the guest-worker program ended.[16] As I have discussed, today the guest-worker program is embraced by both Democrats and Republicans and is viewed as a humane solution to the immigration "problem." But to address concerns about border security after the events of September 11, 2001, and to quell conservative fears that Mexicans are invading the country, bringing disease, and engaging in criminal activity, Democrats' most recent proposals aim at expanding the guest-worker program while also requiring extensive background checks before participation is allowed and strict rules confining workers' freedom of movement.[17] Because the program is temporary and viewed as a sort of favor granted by the United States, the highly exploitative and politically unfree conditions of guest workers are seldom mentioned in the mainstream media and political debates.[18] In fact, those who support this program are viewed as being too "soft" on immigration (even including President George W. Bush, who supported expanding the program).[19] Like assimilation debates, conventional deliberations obscure quite a lot and the two sides are mutually reinforcing rather than truly different.

The dynamics of the Border Industrial Program, established as a model of an economic "free zone" and an effort to maintain U.S. competitiveness in the global economy, are ostensibly different than those of the guest-worker program. In contrast to the militarization of the border, this area has had a history of lax environmental protection, fewer taxes and duties, and, until recently, much fewer worker protections. Pictures of the maquila areas show shantytowns; piles of rubbish with warning signs; the maquilas themselves, some encircled by barbed wire; and white crosses, marking the rape-murders of hundreds of maquila workers.[20] This gives a different image of the border than that portrayed by supporters of ending Mexican immigration and building a border fence. Indeed, this free zone gives the impression of openness to investment and business, a source of labor made "cheap" by the suspension of regulations and laws (or lack of enforcement), and an area of extreme lawlessness and danger to women. Although one is seemingly marked by the abandonment of law and the other is apparently subject to bureaucratic rules and surveillance, both the maquila program and the U.S. guest-worker program share much in common, as I have indicated above. Further, while these programs have been around for decades, the war on terror and the construction of a border fence change their dynamics.

I am, in essence, making two broad sets of claims. The first concerns how the two programs have been set up in response to alleged crises and either suspended the law or created a second set of laws that effectively undermine workers' political agency and political status. They cannot be considered domestic programs, but rather sites of denationalized space. The many justifications for both programs, I believe, rest on unproved assertions indicative of broader crises today: the economic meltdown of 2008–9, the increasing needs of the global economy, and the wars on terror and drugs. In turn, the measures taken to address today's crises (my second set of claims) are justified through a rhetoric of self-evidence, thereby *enacting* what they purport to confirm. To put it differently, policies related to these crises, including the two programs in question, constitute sovereign decisions themselves rather than serving instrumental legitimizing functions ex post facto. I will first provide some background on these programs before further explicating my theoretical claims.

The U.S. Guest-Worker Program

Throughout U.S. history, farmers have relied on seasonal workers under often oppressive conditions, including slavery, indentured servitude, and sharecropping. Many of the circumstances from this history were very similar to those of guest workers today, except that recruited workers were not expected to leave the country.[21] The 1917 Immigration Act established the basis for the first official *temporary* labor market and permitted the secretary of labor to bypass ordinary immigration restrictions to allow these workers into the country.[22] Farmers became increasingly dependent on Mexican laborers (as opposed to workers from other countries), hiring them both legally and illegally. The U.S. guest-worker program (known as the Bracero Program) began in 1942, established by President Franklin Roosevelt via executive order to address predicted wartime labor shortages in the agricultural sector and to help build railroads.[23] Nevertheless, from this time up to the present, there is little evidence that labor shortages have really been significant enough to justify such a program.[24] Instead, farmers have fought to maintain subpar employment *conditions*, posing the problem as one of legality versus illegality. Thus they have fashioned a set of claims discursively to address an emergency that never materialized.[25]

Guest-worker programs have proved to be exceptional in several regards: they circumvent normal immigration law;[26] labor conditions deviate from normal labor regulations and safeguards; they actually preclude unionization;[27] and the labor contracts are highly unusual (in comparison to an ideal model of the Fordist work contract) in that they lead to the suspension of economic regulation and labor rights.[28] Interestingly, nearly every presidential administration since Lincoln's has recognized the exceedingly undemocratic and brutal aspects of these programs, not to mention how they suspend normal immigration laws, and yet even today guest-worker programs address only farmers' needs and not those of the workers. As Phillip Martin has pointed out, in a country that has celebrated books like

The Grapes of Wrath published in the 1930s and movements such as César Chávez's in the mid-1960s, it is perhaps surprising little has changed.[29] The preference for the rights of farmers over those of workers can perhaps be explained by a few factors: the ideal of the United States in the 1700s and 1800s as a country founded on material equality with an agricultural base;[30] the increasing power of the farm lobby in Congress; the fact that citizens' voices are viewed as legitimate and poorer foreigners' as illegitimate (intersecting with class, ethnicity, and race); and, most significant to my argument, the constant appeal to the idea of a crisis or emergency to justify guest-worker programs.

The Bracero Program was officially ended in 1964, although U.S. farmers continued to rely on guest workers and unauthorized migrant workers. While the guest-worker program did not quite end, it was relatively quiet until the 1980s when it was expanded through the Immigration Reform and Control Act.[31] Even though the 1986 expansion was not a response to war per se, it could also be viewed in terms of crisis, including concerns about sovereignty, borders, illegal entry, and illegal hiring. More broadly, worries about the United States' position as a political and economic superpower informed these debates.[32] In the post-9/11 era, calls to expand the guest-worker program reflect the same concerns as those of 1986: control illegal immigration, address alleged labor shortages, and track all poorer entrants. Today, these concerns are expressed in the context of the wars on terror and drugs combined with the experience of economic crisis. Throughout the history of this program, necessities of war, issues of national security, and, increasingly, concerns about the United States' position as a superpower have been intertwined with agricultural lobbying for cheaper workers and exceptions to labor regulation.[33] This combination of factors has led to allegedly temporary solutions, nearly always enacted as exceptions to regular immigration policy and labor standards, which continue to justify the contemporary guest-worker program. Indeed, Martin calls this "agricultural exceptionalism."[34]

Today's guest-worker programs can be split into two broad groups: so-called labor immigrants (certified H-2A), who continue to work predominantly in agriculture, and "human capital immigrants," who are allowed to work based on special talents.[35] This second group (certified H-1B) is capped at sixty-six thousand per year. As evidence of the perceived importance of guest workers in general, in 2006 there were at least six major proposals being considered in Congress, advocated by a bipartisan group.[36]

What is notable about the guest-worker programs is the degree to which they are both regulated by the law and yet allow for the legal suspension of the law. On paper these programs appear to be on par with jobs filled by American-born individuals, with the added bonus that employers are required to provide agricultural laborers housing, food, and transportation during the term of the contract. Participants must also be paid the same amount as U.S. workers for the same job, and employers must adhere to regular labor standards. Nevertheless, because temporary laborers are not given any sorts of legal protections or the right to recourse in the case of abuse, conditions are deplorable. This is particularly true of H-2A workers (who are my focus). Just as significantly, workers are tied to one employer, and they become illegal once the contract is terminated (for any reason).[37] For these reasons, the standards listed above have no enforcement mechanisms and the definitions are arbitrary. For example, housing is broadly defined, and although an inspector must approve the conditions, the results are often unsafe and unhygienic.[38] Men are packed into buses or abandoned train cars, given moldy mattresses, and often sleep side by side. They are given neither potable water nor refrigeration for their food. Employers define overtime work and hourly wages, and thus the workers are often shortchanged, despite loose provisions that allegedly ensure equal pay. They are also paid less when the number of hours worked are factored into pay, compared to American-born individuals. Because they are not allowed to change employers, they cannot complain—they are not allowed to unionize, have no right to follow a case in court, cannot bargain for wages, and must leave once their contract ends or is terminated.[39] As Vernon Briggs has argued, this setup remains controversial precisely because of the

> operational features of the program that are considered to be unfair and, if applied to citizens, would be illegal. They are unfair because employers do not have to pay social security taxes or unemployment compensation payroll taxes on H-2 workers that would be required if citizens were hired. The program also permits actions that would be illegal elsewhere in the economy because of the use of industry blacklists; the fact that workers are subject to arbitrary treatment and dismissals; and the use of a system whereby employers are permitted to request back by name the following year only 60 percent of those workers hired during the current year.[40]

Barry Yeoman, a reporter for *Mother Jones* magazine, similarly reports about the H-2A program:

> A six-month investigation of the program . . . reveals widespread complaints that growers have threatened workers at gunpoint, refused them water in the fields, housed them in crumbling, rat-infested buildings where sewage bubbles up through the drains, and denied them medical care after exposing them to pesticides. Farmers control their visitors, their mail, even their weekly shopping trips. A study by the U.S. General Accounting Office notes that H-2A workers, knowing they can be deported at any time, "are unlikely to complain about worker protection violations, fearing they will lose their jobs or will not be hired in the future."[41]

It is significant that the workers who are allegedly willing to work under any conditions regularly "escape."[42] In fact, Kitty Calavita calls guest workers "captive labor" and argues that escapes highlight workers' brutal conditions; for this reason, "the bracero's captive status had to be rigorously maintained."[43] Quite obviously, even by the standards of Friedrich Hayek, who is recognized as the father of neoliberalism, these conditions cannot be characterized as those of a free market.[44]

Workers are exposed to dangerous pesticides, men who work with tobacco often become sick and yet go untreated, many have lost fingers or limbs, and others have died from overexposure.[45] Finally, migrant children must be included in this group for they, too, are subject to a different set of laws than their American-born counterparts. Rather than protecting migrant children, the prevailing laws merely explain why they are allowed to work longer hours and in unsafe conditions.[46] I will argue below that these programs amount to a legal suspension of the law, a form of prerogative power that is not recognized as such.[47] As Agamben contends, the suspension of law does not always mean a legal void but rather a second set of laws, arbitrary actions and decrees that effectively remove any political rights or opportunities for redress.[48] To put it differently, they strip the individual of "personality" (i.e., nationality), reducing them to mere (or bare) life.[49] In this context, abuses can occur with virtual impunity.

Workers who participate in the H-1B program are considered more elite in comparison and yet face similar obstacles to workers in the H-2A program. While they are better off financially and hold higher-status jobs, this system still ensures that they are paid less than their American counterparts; that they often cannot get promoted because of laws requiring recertification or demands that they leave the country; that their employer determines their hours and overtime (since there are no mechanisms for challenging these accounts); and that various abuses (e.g., verbal or sexual) cannot be protested by these workers.[50]

What must be emphasized is that these employees are not considered citizens or even immigrants. Their legal status falls into a complex gray area. They are viewed as economic beings with no "right to rights";[51] nevertheless, they are subjected to economically deregulated conditions that in some sense undermine the idea that they are even economic beings, they are viewed as human beings with biological needs far below those of citizens, and so their status is economically over-determined (in important respects) and politically under-determined. Saskia Sassen discusses how these dynamics present new issues for nation-states and workers' rights: for example, workers who are hired through a regional trade agreement (like NAFTA) and whose contract is arranged by a private firm are monitored by contracting firms under NAFTA; thus their status is defined by a multinational trade pact (rather than by one nation-state) and monitored by a private contractor (rather than by a state's immigration services).[52] Abuses are possible because workers' status is defined economically but not politically.[53] This is not to idealize the nation-state or national citizenship as an alternative, but rather to show the democratic deficit that is created by these agreements and the limitations of the nation-state to deal with these issues.

Indeed, the crucial link between economic deregulation and the loss of human and political rights must be recognized. As Dani Rodrik has argued in "Feasible Globalizations," nation-states cannot achieve all at once economic deregulation, sovereignty, and democracy. Echoing Karl Polanyi, Rodrik contends that a "trilemma" arises when nation-states attempt to implement programs and policies aimed at all three objectives simultaneously. When states try to adopt predominantly neoliberal policies, they undermine democracy in at least three ways: (a) economic policy-making bodies like the IMF are not held accountable for democratic norms; (b) social safety nets are scaled back; and (c) social and cultural needs are trumped by economic austerity measures, such that investors' and corporations' demands are viewed as most important.[54] The result is that democratic agency and citizens' rights are undermined at the same time that their economic well-being is threatened. Thomas Friedman's notion of the "golden straitjacket" that every country must don in order to survive, leading to the growth of markets and the "shrinking of politics," is a similar admission that democratic politics are lost.[55] Ironically, Rodrik thinks part of the solution to current global inequality is a guest-worker system, with truly temporary labor and "forced savings."[56] Rodrik contends that if guest-workers have part of their paycheck forcibly withheld until they return to their home country, it will ensure that they are truly *temporary*. Nevertheless, Rodrik himself explains why his solution is precisely the problem.

His solution is no different than the current guest-worker program except that he believes policy makers should include forced savings to ensure that workers actually leave when their contracts expire.[57] Not recognizing the abusive nature of the program itself or how it is not an alternative to neoliberalism but rather its ideal manifestation, Rodrik advocates such a program because workers would benefit directly. To him, the dynamics of foreign direct investment and international financial institutions' intervention would be challenged, allowing workers to gain skills, education, and earnings directly rather than relying on trickle-down economics. But Rodrik ignores workers' conditions, their lack of political rights, and how policies instituting these deterritorialized spaces are precisely what he is warning about: the loss of national sovereignty, the loss of "embedded" economies,[58] the impossibility of a social safety net, and the loss of democratic agency. He also doesn't seem to recognize the irony of advocating "forced" savings in a program that is supposed to ameliorate inequality.

Similarly, a "pro-immigration" Heritage Foundation paper on the guest-worker program contends that "when three out of every 100 people in America are undocumented (or, rather, documented with forged and faked papers), there is a profound security problem. Even though they pose no direct security threat, the presence of millions of undocumented migrants distorts the law, distracts resources, and *effectively creates a cover for terrorists and criminals*."[59] The authors' answer is a "noncitizen" guest-worker program, which they deem "essential" in securing the border. They go on to argue that the program should not lead to citizenship, because "foreign migrants will be oversupplied."[60] Giving migrant workers the benefits of citizenship (e.g., welfare) will "distort the incentives to migrate to the U.S."[61] Instead, their legal status should be considered the same as a traveler. This no-nonsense paper is ostensibly pro-immigrant because it recognizes the great economic benefits of migrant work at all levels and proposes a solution that makes fewer entrants illegal. But it does not consider how working for three years in a confined area for one employer, being on-call for 24/7 (in the case of sheepherders, for example), or being subjected to physically unbearable conditions is a bit different than tourism.[62] Further, it easily links unauthorized immigration to terrorism. Because the terms of this debate have been narrowly construed—pro-immigration or anti-immigration; security threat or not; gift or no gift—labor conditions and relations are irrelevant. The added layer of the wars on terror and drugs serve to affirm binary thinking and efface the loss of democratic agency that workers experience.

In reality, the guest-worker program is the materialization of neoliberal demands for a free market, which lead to significantly unfree conditions. They are on U.S. territory and are recognized by the law, and yet once in place, these workplaces create a space of economic and political deregulation, suspending citizen and human rights for the term of the "contract." In effect, this labor contract renders participants stateless for the length of employment. All these conditions have been founded on and maintained by economic prerogative: the intertwining of economic measures and sovereign power. The Border Industrial Program operates in a similarly deterritorialized space.

The Border Industrial Program

As William Adler explains in his book *Mollie's Job,* the Border Industrial Program was established in part to help returning braceros find work. Additionally, Adler explains other, more compelling reasons to establish this program. In the 1960s, northern U.S. companies hired African Americans who were paid cheaper wages but who also most often joined unions. Southern states tried to attract these companies by offering tax breaks and right-to-work laws that would undermine unions and collective bargaining.[63] Many companies did move to the South, but as the maquila program developed, its proponents approached the same companies and promised an even weaker labor force in Mexico. In this account, the maquila program is the end of the line, as American employers tried to find an increasingly cheap workforce, weak labor standards, and tax breaks.[64] Although Mexican labor standards are technically higher than those in the United States, enforcement is much weaker, and in this particular program they were negligible in significant ways. Coupled with very lax environmental protections and even flimsier enforcement, this program offered greater potential profits than the opportunities in the southern states.

Maquiladoras are assembly plants that import parts from the United States, assemble them, and export them back to the United States and other countries. The only taxes that are paid are for the value added by the labor. Because U.S. companies needed to be convinced to move across the border, the Mexican government changed its laws regarding property rights and ownership to make the program more attractive. Its 1973 Law to Promote Mexican Investment and Regulate Foreign Investment allowed foreign ownership only up to 49 percent so that Mexican firms would not have to compete with foreign firms. This law changed in May 1989 to allow 100 percent foreign ownership in the maquila areas, which helped attract more foreign investment. Today, firms may have more than one owner or may be owned by a subsidiary, which is "a common practice among transnational corporations, designed to reduce liability in terms of laws, taxes, and regulations."[65]

The maquila program became especially profitable in the mid-1990s during the Mexican peso crisis.[66] As a result, already-cheap labor became incredibly cheap and thus, while businesses in the interior of Mexico were going bankrupt and poverty was skyrocketing,[67] the maquiladoras were generating considerable profits. Although the average citizen was not helped by this situation, the foreign currency created by the maquilas helped the Mexican government a great deal. In response to the peso crisis, the IMF and U.S. banks had offered Mexico the largest bailout loan of its kind, and it is now considered the second-highest bailout package ever (the U.S. provided $20 billion of the more than $50 billion rescue package).[68] As the government initiated structural adjustment policies and the populace suffered, transnational corporations greatly profited. The maquila program continued to develop and both the number of employees and factories hit a peak in 2000. But as workers' wages began to decrease with the peso devaluation, they staged walkouts, work stoppages, and union organizing drives. Today, it is argued that the number of maquilas is declining because workers are demanding too much, leading factory owners to threaten to move to China.[69] But up until recently, these factories have been very attractive to U.S. firms for three reasons: cheap labor, lack of enforcement of labor standards, and weak laws (particularly regarding environmental protection).

In a desperate situation due to the peso crisis, it has been argued that the Mexican government has a lot to gain by maintaining these conditions in order to retain these firms' interest. One of the most important elements in maintaining worker vulnerability is through the state-run unions, which are tied to the Partido Revolucionario Institucional (Institutional Revolutionary Party). Only one maquila has succeeded in establishing an independent union (Han Young), and this was after prolonged struggle by the workers.[70] The Mexican government has allegedly intervened in legal and illegal ways in order to combat any independent unions. For this reason, these corporations often view this area as being union-free. One example among many is the attitude of a manager who stated, "The absence of a union means that we have a virtual haven for productivity, free of bargaining fetters. This is so much easier than the U.S."[71]

Some of the conditions of the maquilas include not allowing bathroom breaks, not allowing employees to drink water, forced overtime, high levels of intensity and productivity, hiring and firing at will, and a long workweek. Depending on the plant, if employees complain, they can be dismissed or blacklisted.[72] Melissa Wright notes that these conditions are acknowledged to be less than tolerable and managers plan on keeping workers for a period of about two years, at which point their bodies begin to give out.[73] As many researchers have noted, the plants have also famously hired women and encouraged highly feminized work attire and cosmetic application—this despite the fact that the program was supposed to help returning braceros find work. Even though the gender disparity is far less severe than it was in the 1990s,[74] gender continues to serve as a reference for determining skill levels, pay, and what qualifies as management or engineering aptitude. More disturbing, sexual harassment, beauty contests (including one documented case of a forced beauty contest), and even rape-murder arguably *define* the maquila industry.[75]

Many authors have documented how young women have been required to wear revealing outfits, makeup, and high heels to their factory jobs.[76] Women workers deal with constant harassment by management and are often approached to act as prostitutes. Although a highly feminine appearance gets one hired, it does not necessarily lead to respect or advancement on the job. Very simply, the same characteristics that aid a woman's appearance in getting hired also make her appear vulnerable, incompetent, and "too ethnic" for administrative and managerial positions. As Wright has found through her case study of two Mexican women who did make it into the ranks of management at their maquiladoras, a worker's appearance is divided along national, gendered, and class lines.[77]

Dressing as a Mexican woman—high heels, bright colors, glittery acces-
sories, and bows in the hair—is seen as being unprofessional, prostitute-like,
traditional, and backward. Indeed, jobs typed as "female" *and* "Mexican"
are also called unskilled and therefore are lower paid, despite overwhelming
evidence that productivity levels in the factories are among the highest in
the world and there is a high degree of technological complexity in much
of the work involved.[78] Although Wright notes that an individual worker
can assimilate to an American style in order to attempt entry into management, she also remarks how the denigration of women is involved in this
transition, not to mention that the candidate must adopt a hostile attitude
toward workers' efforts to unionize and demand rights. In this way, gender
activates hierarchies that require an antagonistic approach to other workers
and other women.

Hence women workers who want to work at the managerial level not
only face a number of obstacles and prejudices, but they are required to support the status quo, which happens to be classist, ethnically prejudiced, and
sexist. Wright found in her interviews that managerial discourse constantly
focused on restraining Mexican women's sexuality. The managers she interviewed frequently emphasized that they "cannot tell the difference between
a prostitute and a female maquiladora worker,"[79] placing maquiladora workers in the context of all global workers, "as the embodiment of that sexu-
ally chaotic third world woman so common, according to corporate gurus,
to other industrial worksites around the globe."[80] With the growth of the
maquila industry, the demand not simply for young female workers but
those attired in a highly feminine manner could be viewed as a disciplinary
mechanism to put women back in their place as they begin to earn money
and act independently.[81] The policing of Mexican sexuality is not merely
discursive; rather, Cooney has found that "it is routine for pregnancy tests to
be administered in maquiladoras, and if they are positive women are fired on
the spot. Even worse, in certain cases women have been given pills to force a
miscarriage and told that it was a vitamin."[82] These practices in turn can be
directly linked to fears of Mexican women crossing the border and having
"anchor babies," thereby usurping U.S. welfare and public provisions.[83] In
this way, the policing and restraining of Mexican women's sexuality is tied to
issues of national sovereignty and material security. The result is a contradictory tangle of messages to maquila workers.

To put it in Foucaultian terms, factory conditions do not merely discipline
workers, subjecting them to tight schedules, heavy production standards,

surveillance, and normative judgments;[84] they also control them along bio-political lines: in this case, women's bodies are made into the "hysterical" bodies Foucault discusses at the end of *The History of Sexuality,* as managers focus not just on reproduction but also on how this reproduction will violate American national sovereignty and security.[85] Like the broader category of "sexuality," the reproductive capabilities of the "hysterical woman" are tied to widespread societal processes and concerns. As Mexican women's attire and behavior are used to control them—their high heels, lipstick, short skirts, and constant subjection to harassment are conditions of employment on factory floors—they are symbols of chaos, out-of-control sexuality and reproduction, which threatens gender, ethnic, class, and national borders. That nearly all women have been forced to dress this way to get hired and keep their job, and that some have been forced to participate in even more objectifying "company" events like beauty contests, show the coercive nature of this exercise. Judith Butler's arguments about conventional femininity as a drag show are particularly apt.[86] As Butler notes, women are constantly reminded that they will be punished for not *performing* their gender roles; and, ironically, one could add that they are also punished *for* performing them.

The maquiladora murders in Ciudad Juárez and Chihuahua—notably cities where independent unions are weakest[87]—demonstrate that the stakes of gender dynamics are high. This area of Mexico in particular has historically experienced high levels of domestic abuse.[88] As increasing numbers of women arrive for work, their economic independence could pose a threat to the gendered order of these border areas. The maquila workers themselves admit that they are exploited and yet have experienced some gains in terms of social status, economic well-being, and ability to act autonomously in the family.[89] This could be particularly true given the demographic flux in these border areas; traditional gender roles could be anchors in an area that has experienced so much change. Indeed, both the guest-worker program and the maquila program have transformed the demographics of Mexican rural areas, arguably producing a population that is less rooted and more transnational.[90] The Bracero Program radically altered gender relations in certain areas of Mexico: one-sixth of the male population participated in this program at one time, leaving behind women, families, and small farms and businesses.[91] With the maquila program, the same dynamics of displacement and change are reinforced through women's employment. For these reasons, gender roles may be heightened in this area and domestic violence is a facet of daily existence.

They are also considered challengers of traditional roles for women. Their forced drag show of short skirts, high heels, and makeup stands in stark contrast to the idealized role of a chaste, sacrificing mother figure who tends first to her children and not her job.[92] According to Jessica Livingston, maquiladora workers are also viewed as traitors who, like prostitutes, selfishly and blindly serve American needs. As Livingston puts it, "In this association between maquiladora workers and corruption, the women bear the resentment for the United States once again infiltrating Mexico's borders."[93]

Founded in these gendered dynamics, the rape-murders of approximately 375 women have been called "maquila murders" because they are viewed as an extreme method of keeping women in line. They are also seen as a continuation of the history of domestic violence that continues unchecked today. The rape-murders are more public, serving as a reminder to maquila workers that, without any warning, they could be next.[94] This is to suggest that the combination of conditions that define maquila workers' status leads to a legally ambivalent geopolitical space in which they can be harmed with impunity. Authorities shift responsibility to the workers themselves, blaming them for what they wear and implying that if women worked in bars at night, they must expect unwanted attention.[95] Further, the Mexican government and local police have refused to fully investigate murders and have attributed them to a serial killer or the drug trade. Neither explanation recognizes the intersection of class, territorial location, and gender in these attacks, or the role of foreign capital. Notably absent in these accounts is any responsibility of foreign corporations for women's safety or any type of binational efforts to aid these workers. In the end, the women themselves have invited this fate. Wright connects the "disposability" of women workers to the disposability of their lives: "When women workers are determined to be worthless or when women's corpses are dumped like trash in the desert, these discourses [of disposability] explain how, given these women's 'intrinsic worthlessness,' such events are both natural and unavoidable."[96]

Indeed, the space created by the BIP is purposely denationalized in order to abdicate responsibility, whether for workers' physical safety or environmental issues (among other things). Like neoliberal policies that allow for subcontracting and the removal of any corporate responsibility for workers' conditions, free zones are a product of international collaboration that allows its parties to renounce blame when convenient. A political void is created, effectively suspending the law and demonstrating precisely what

Hannah Arendt discussed in relation to the stateless: maquila workers do not have the right to have rights. To put it differently, they are bare life, serving as a negative type against which full citizenship is measured, and thereafter murdered with impunity.[97]

Lax environmental enforcement, even despite claims that NAFTA was the first "green" free trade agreement, works with the murders and abductions to further position these workers as bare life. Up until 2000, the Border Industrial Program required that transnational corporations bring their waste to the United States to be disposed of. Since 2000, Mexico is now responsible for toxic waste disposal. Neither arrangement has really mattered, however. Since the program's inception, companies have dumped toxic waste in rivers, refused to tell workers what they are being exposed to or what the long-term effects are, and failed to dispose properly of waste if they close. Employees deal with toxic conditions on the job, and when they return home, the water they drink and bathe in is also contaminated. Rivers and puddles are also considered dangerous and pollutants fill the air at certain times. The result has been increased risk of leukemia, skin ailments of workers and their children (through contact after work), and significant birth defects, including a number of children born with swelled brains (encephalitis).[98] Although workers have united to fight environmental hazards, the Mexican government has denied the severity of conditions, the United States has denied any responsibility, and individual corporations have not been accountable for their toxic waste dumping.[99] This refusal to take any action may be surprising given a class action lawsuit of maquila workers against selected transnational corporations during the 1990s in which workers won several million dollars.[100] But it is arguably cheaper to work on a case-by-case basis than to take full responsibility for an area that is now dangerously and maybe lethally polluted.

Hence in both programs workers are in limbo. In the guest-worker program, the worker is not a citizen or normal immigrant but something in between that is unaccounted for in domestic law. Understanding the status of these workers must include accounting for international and regional trade agreements and actors. But at the level of the nation-state, these workers appear to be a temporary anomaly. In the maquila program, workers from other towns and states who come to the maquilas to work are not considered city residents. Indeed, the fact that their status is in limbo has created enormous infrastructural problems, from bad roads, to inadequate education for workers' children, to horrendous living conditions, illegal access to electricity, inadequate sewage, and so on.[101]

Further, the state of affairs of both the agricultural guest-worker program and the maquiladoras are clearly similar in the following ways: both sets of workers are treated neither as immigrants or citizens; both are subjected to harsh and exacting work conditions that go beyond normal labor standards;[102] and both are subjected to conditions that lower the standards of "humane" treatment.[103] Both sets of workers have been physically and verbally attacked by employers, not to mention exposed to toxic chemicals and dangerous machinery. And both sets of circumstances are not only legal but arranged by governments, treasury departments, and transnational corporations following structural adjustment policies recommended by the Bretton Woods institutions.[104] Although the two programs are not usually connected in political analyses, I believe they should be. They are both instances of free trade zones: one on the southern border, which could be called a paradigm of the free trade zone (allowing for labor exploitation coupled with political disempowerment in a foreign country, so as to abdicate U.S. responsibility for injustice), and one that has developed within U.S. borders.

Mexico's policies leading up to the peso crisis were already neoliberal to an extent, evidenced by the event itself, which was a result of overspeculation of the nation's currency.[105] The Border Industrial Program was also evidence of the government's increasing willingness to deregulate the labor market by suspending regular labor and environmental protections in order to attract foreign capital. The effects of NAFTA (which began in 1994) and the structural adjustment policies implemented in the wake of the IMF loan further established the prevalence and strength of neoliberal policies and actions. Like the rules governing maquilas, these provisions are viewed as temporary austerity measures to get the economy on track, and yet their institutionalization and permanence are clear.

These unequal relations are replicated in free trade agreements abroad, making developing countries "partners" in the spread of U.S. economic dominance; it is a non-territorial type of power guided by a set of economic beliefs that reflect and add to U.S. power.[106] This is true even when U.S. power appears to be declining. Because of the veneer of consent and contract, not to mention aid, it appears that the Mexican government acts as an equal to that of the United States. The appearance of democracy, contract, and consent are also important in affirming the mutuality of these work conditions while obfuscating workers' rightlessness.

Consent? The Hobbesian Employment Contract

It is in this sense that the paradox of sovereignty can take the form "There is nothing outside the law." The originary relation of law to life is not application but Abandonment.

— Giorgio Agamben, *Homo Sacer*

A tacit assumption about increasingly casual or flexible labor conditions for low-tier workers is that there is still some degree of mutuality in hiring and determining labor conditions. This can be assumed only because neoliberal policies and free trade discourse obscure the degree of state intervention in these arrangements. While the labor contract may be forged voluntarily, the use of the law to suspend regular laws and protections has nothing to do with individual voluntarism. Depending on the circumstances, the adversarial or absent role that "host" or sending governments play in ensuring that workers do not organize unions or fight systematic abuses is a key part of workers' conditions.[107] But rather than mere abandonment, governments' acquiescence in exploitative conditions can involve force or threats of force; police interference in organizing activities or refusal to investigate disappearances, rapes, or murders; and public denials that workers are being harmed. Alternatively, the work that it takes to forge free trade agreements, create new work zones, or militarize the border is downplayed as the freedom of the market is exaggerated. The host states play a crucial role in these dynamics both through their absence or abandonment of workers at certain times, but also through their enforcement of these conditions, often outside what is considered the legal norm.

Further, because the dominant view in privileged countries like the United States is that workers are so desperate for employment that they will put up with anything, the coercive circumstances of the labor contract itself are not questioned.[108] Instead, it is argued that conditions are relatively better than the minimum standards of the sending country. But this argument does not justify exploitation, unfree conditions, or systematically risking workers' lives, nor does it explain why workers constantly protest conditions in various ways. What is at issue is not necessarily how the agreement is made, but the fact that agreeing to these labor contracts leads to the suspension of democratic rights and normal labor standards. Hence the key question is, Are contracts that effectively suspend an individual's political and civil rights valid? This is the sort of agreement that John Locke and Thomas Hobbes discussed—the question of whether a contract is legitimate when one party agrees to sell him- or herself or cede all autonomy to another person. Carole Pateman frames the problem in this way: "A person ought never to consent to be a slave, because this totally negates the individual's freedom and equality and hence, in a self-contradiction, denies that the individual is capable of consent."[109] While both Hobbes and Locke argue that this sort of compact violates the natural right to self-preservation, Hobbes is far more ambivalent about when there is an actual violation of this right through a contract. For instance, Hobbes does not believe that agreeing to a contract under threat of lethal force nullifies the contract.[110] On the other hand, he claims that no one can contract his life away.[111] Nevertheless, the fact that he conceives of this contract as only occurring once in the formation of a polity challenges the very idea that it is a contract at all for future generations. Further, as is well-known, his one-time contract gives power to a leader who is outside the law and, therefore, whose every action could be arbitrary and abusive. As ambivalent as Hobbes appears to be about violating one's natural rights through a contract that suspends these rights, his political solution to the disorder of the state of nature is precisely such a contract.

Pateman examines the marriage contract and the historical acceptance of marital rape in terms of Hobbes's social contract. Legal tolerance of marital rape shows that this "contract" is forged only once, and henceforth any action perpetrated by a husband onto a wife is considered legitimate in the eyes of the law. For this reason, she argues that the courts' and popular opinion's views of the marriage contract are Hobbesian in a society that considers itself a liberal democracy and, thus to an extent, anti-Hobbesian.[112] In contrast to Locke, who conceives of a social contract with some sort of exit (rebellion),[113] Hobbes argues that not only can contracts be forged in an atmosphere of fear, but once they are agreed on, anything that happens—barring life-threatening actions—is legitimate. Although future liberal theorists criticized Hobbes's antidemocratic impulses, they still believed that a marriage contract tacitly legitimated any future actions in the marriage, thus following his lead more than they were willing to admit.[114] Clearly, this relationship is not forged between democratic equals or autonomous individuals: in essence, the wife becomes an extension of the husband through marriage. In the case of marital rape, Pateman shows that because women are already constructed as naturally subordinate to men, legal decisions have tended to interpret submission as consent. For these reasons, she argues, "Unless refusal of consent or withdrawal of consent are real possibilities, we can no longer speak of 'consent' in any genuine sense."[115] Although exit (divorce) is now possible, she finds that the remaining resistance to implementing marital rape laws (or the resistance to making them enforceable) is the last vestige of what is essentially a Hobbesian contract in a country that imagines itself to be democratic.

The maquila and guest-worker "contracts" are similarly Hobbesian in that they legitimate—that is, make legal—any of the conditions to which the worker is subjected.[116] Like a woman who agrees to marriage can legally be raped by her husband without ever agreeing to rape, the laborer who agrees to work at these jobs can then legally be subjected to myriad dangerous circumstances even while attempting to challenge them. The importance of this observation cannot be overstated: political agency and political rights are not unified as currently conceived. The mere fact that workers can exit their contracts should not justify the multiple ways in which their autonomy and bodily integrity are undermined. In fact, it is the resistance launched by workers—unionization, demands for improved conditions, and the formation of environmental groups—that is portrayed as ungrateful, exploitative, and irresponsible. As the state decided on behalf of the married woman what actions on her body were permissible, so the contracting nation-states that forge these agreements, along with the Bretton Woods institutions, decide what workers can or should tolerate. Further, built into this relationship is a relation of natural subordination of Mexico to the United States based, among other things, on a history of presumed ethnic superiority,[117] economic supremacy, and other hierarchical criteria legitimized by the IMF. What is more, in the employment contract, the law itself becomes the constant referent for its suspension:[118] for example, if foreign workers are exposed to pesticides that citizens are not, legal arguments are made to justify this treatment.[119] This is why these two cases are not merely instances of neglect or abuse: Decades of legislation, policies, and bureaucratic decisions have created these exceptional programs. Further, their long historical legacy and their entrenchment in local economies show that these undemocratic conditions are a legal and systematic suspension of the law. If a contract is supposed to indicate autonomy, legitimacy, and equality, none of these conditions are met under these circumstances.

Moreover, although the circumstances of the two programs differ, the exercise of democratic rights and individual autonomy de facto nullifies the contract. This is truest when workers try to unionize, an activity that has been portrayed as purely economical and wasteful in more neoliberal times. The inequality of the work contract, including the discouragement or outright prohibition of unionization, is particularly significant if work is not merely instrumental to citizenship but also a crucial element of its enactment. Unionization at its best should be viewed as one of the most significant political activities in an individual's life. It clearly makes a difference with regard to health, safety, well-being, family time, and collective representation, not to mention wages and work conditions. The denial of the right to unionize, whether de facto in Mexico or de jure in the U.S. guest-worker program, is the denial of a political voice and access to political rights, and ensures that the work contract is, in fact, a Hobbesian contract. As writers like John Stuart Mill and Carole Pateman have asked, if a significant sphere of citizens' lives is not only undemocratic but also marked by despotic power enforced by the law, are these individuals truly citizens and is the society in which they live truly a democracy?[120]

The Rhetoric of Necessity

I would like to suggest that neoliberal politics and the consolidation of American military, political, and economic power have allowed U.S. elites to turn to moralizing language based on ideas of necessity and crisis, effectively depoliticizing most of the significant developments in the past two decades or so.[121] This gradual transformation can be traced to the emergence of neoliberalism in the 1980s, which led to the increasing coalescence of sovereign matters and economics. This challenges the idea that with the globalization of the economy and a "free" market the state has receded. Other factors have included the end of the Cold War and the brief decline of American power, which made it more steadfastly committed to neoliberalism and its resurgence as *the* superpower in the 1990s. As the United States viewed itself as the sole legitimate superpower, it was possible for discourse to become increasingly moral and ascetic, rather than directly political. The absence of challenges to U.S. power allowed a more naturalized account of its actions, grounded in self-evidence and necessity. This is true not only in the war on terror but also in its increasing institution of free zones and its pressure on other countries, via the Bretton Woods institutions, to do the same.

The increasing proliferation of free trade zones, free trade agreements, and the pressure to adopt flexible work conditions are directly linked to the policies known as the Washington Consensus. Using terms linked to freedom—free market, flexibility, free trade zones, right-to-work states—this set of policies has increasingly led to state control of worker-participants. As a model that is being pushed throughout the world, it may not be the norm but it certainly is the goal. This outlook is considered the antidote to U.S. economic problems and developing countries' poverty, but it forces an entirely new set of labor practices into the field, thus relying on necessity rather than "an objective situation." As Agamben explains, "Far from occurring as an objective given, necessity clearly entails a subjective judgment, and . . . obviously the only circumstances that are necessary and objective are those that are declared to be so."[122] This move then entails "a *suspension* of the order that is in force in order to guarantee its existence." The realm of necessity thus opened, a crisis is created while the "law remains in place."[123]

The perception of emergency coupled with the recourse to necessity enacts the political such that programs like those analyzed above are not merely responses to crisis but constitute a sort of crisis in and of themselves. Accordingly, they rely on fresh political and economic emergencies and threats to continually renew their raison d'être. And they seek to remove politics by force—by uprooting a group of workers and suspending their rights, both subjecting them to sovereign power and yet abandoning them to conditions considered far below those fit for citizens. In effect, these neoliberal arrangements do not only suspend the economic law, leaving politics untouched, but also open up spaces of prerogative power broadly defined.

Agamben notes in *State of Exception* that there are no legal theories of prerogative power (the legal suspension of the law), and this is because it is impossible to discuss what is purely political but void of normal legal procedures. It could also be surmised that prerogative power is taken to be an anomaly, as something that happens only during emergencies. Thus it could be argued that no systematic understanding of its role in everyday politics is necessary. Alternatively, the suspension of law, which entails stripping individuals of their legal rights, could be considered the termination of politics, not its origin.[124] But to Agamben, this form of political power is not purely anomalous or apolitical, but rather what is most political and is established through "the relation that binds and, at the same time, abandons the living being to law."[125] What he means by the second remark is that when individuals are, or have become, stateless, they are not purely in orbit and freer than the rest. Instead, they move from a citizen/criminal binary on domestic terrain to a more undecidable friend/enemy or state/stateless binary in the international sphere.[126]

Like the state of exception, this sort of statelessness (the status of refugees) should not be viewed as purely exceptional and therefore defying any systematic analysis, but actually foundational to understanding modern Western political power and belonging. Inspired by Hannah Arendt's critique of the nation-state and her conclusions about the impotence of human rights, Agamben shows throughout his book that states of emergency have increasingly been used in constitutional democracies since the early twentieth century. These acts to suspend the law have notably been legal and used in times of perceived military and economic crises (often the two have overlapped). What he finds is that democracies not only depend on this allegedly exceptional tool quite often, but they do so most often domestically and regularly, so that the exception becomes the norm.

The U.S. guest-worker program and the Border Industrial Program are perfect examples of what he is warning about. They are both evidence of the regular use of sovereign measures on domestic terrain. Although each was created during times of economic and political crisis, each has remained in place for decades longer than their original emergences, often being renewed by fresh crises. Further, it is important to note that the workers involved are not merely abandoned—they do not just lose political status altogether—nor are they suddenly freer than others. Rather, the law essentially *authorizes* abuses, harassment, exposure to chemicals, violence, and murder. No less important, the laws ensure that conditions are deregulated and that a hierarchical power relationship is created.

In both programs, the idea of necessity is a key reference point. Economic necessity is taken for granted in several ways: the constant need for cheaper and cheaper labor; the increasingly predominant assumption that these workers will do jobs Americans won't, at the same time that jobs became more flexible and right-to-work laws more prevalent; the assumption that profit stimulates economies even as workers' conditions suffer; the related acceptance of a hierarchy between employers (the givers) and employees (the takers); and the key assumption that decoupling economic "rights" from political ones is a legitimate exercise in a democracy. Again, although these programs preceded the turn to neoliberal policies, their expansion and politico-economic validation were fostered by neoliberalism. Most significant, they have gone from the margins to the center: at first outside Keynesian or Fordist arrangements entirely, while today they are the neoliberal ideal.[127] This is exemplified in the spread of maquila conditions throughout Mexico since the ratification of NAFTA. This does not mean that maquilas are now the predominant factory type in Mexico—what it means is that this model of a free zone is the ideal against which factories are now measured in conventional (neoliberal) articles and scholarly work.[128] Similarly, the U.S. guest-worker program has waxed and waned, but it has experienced a resurgence during a time when neoliberal market reforms predominate, coupled with concerns about the border and national sovereignty—first in the 1980s and increasingly since the attacks of 9/11. While conditions in the Bracero Program were considered shocking in the 1950s and 1960s, today the use of immigrant labor that is low paid, denied geographical mobility, tied to one employer, refused collective bargaining, and unable to bargain for wages is the economic ideal.[129] Unauthorized workers enjoy more freedom, but under similar conditions and with the constant threat of deportation looming over them.

As I noted above, U.S. labor shortages have never actually justified either program. In fact, in studying the history of the development of the BIP, the story is more one of undercutting: first between U.S. regions (unionized states versus right-to-work states), and then adding the border to the mix. The guest-worker program has similarly been founded on unproved predictions of labor shortages because, again, there is far more concern about maintaining labor conditions than ameliorating the conditions of the working class. Nor has either program led to less unauthorized entry. In fact, according to most in-depth analyses of migration patterns—particularly Saskia Sassen's theories—these programs would only stimulate migration, legal and illegal.[130]

But one further assumption must be questioned—why it is taken for granted that there is an immigration "problem" in the first place? And why must the solutions in a democratic country be militarization of the border, including a border fence; legal exploitation of workers; the abandonment of workers to pollution, assault, and death; and political rightlessness? Essentially, Mexicans symbolize all the United States' concerns, which today are the loss of a social safety net, a crisis in health care, a faltering economy, and the fear of terrorism. But in the context of the war on terror (and related wars), Mexicans' presence is viewed as not merely as an economic threat but also a sovereign one. As a result, both the government and vigilante groups have increasingly militarized the border. Nevertheless, the desire to remain competitive on the international market ensures that Mexicans are never denied access to this country. Rather, the goal is to ensure economic exploitability through increased surveillance and control. Hence a rhetorical enemy has been created who also happens to be viewed as the solution to U.S. labor issues.[131]

It is also important to note that quite a lot of political intervention has been necessary to create these "purely economic" conditions, whether of the guest-worker program or the BIP.[132] The particular capacities of each institution (the U.S. Treasury Department, the Bretton Woods institutions, NAFTA) are located in the regional or international sphere and are non-democratic. They may purport to be representative of the common good and the fostering of positive economic conditions for the good of all, but the decision making, the deals brokered between governments or nongovernmental organizations, and the conditions themselves are out of the public view.[133] Although the media may report on these programs, their actual conditions are not held to warrant public scrutiny largely due to the undecidable nature of the relationships—they do not fit into the old binaries of domestic/international, economic/political, immigrant/citizen.

Moreover, given the dynamics of the war on drugs, the war on terror, the increasing militarization of the border, the increased numbers of arrests by ICE, and the construction of the border fence, the status of these workers demonstrates how extreme economic measures can be meshed with these new, undeclared, deterritorialized wars. The same workers who are given the "gift" of work are also seen as potential terrorists who steal jobs and welfare, violate our sovereignty, and even, according to some, are attempting to colonize the Southwest through reproduction.[134] The language of necessity obscures boundaries, including the division between an internal enemy and an external one. At the same time, it makes wartime measures commonplace. In this milieu, efforts to unionize or stage political protests are not viewed as exercising democratic agency, but as irresponsible at best and threatening and disloyal at worst. The irony of this is that deterritorialized political power can abdicate responsibility when convenient, collecting profits but evading political accountability and undermining democratic equality.

Conclusion

The U.S. guest-worker program and the maquila program are examples of the suspension of law domestically for economic reasons, though with significant political consequences, and they demonstrate how temporary measures have become the norm. The focus on individuals as units of production leads to a situation in which workers' conditions and quality of life are far below what is considered adequate for citizens of either country.

The absence of political rights and the undecidable status of workers deterritorializes the spaces in which they work, rendering them stateless. Nevertheless, the lack of rights does not lead to the absence of politics—instead, they are subjects of sovereign power. They are considered threats to sovereignty through their potential illegality, border incursions, and reproduction, and they are considered economic threats as well. These two programs aim at intense control of immigrants' movement, reproductive capabilities, and political agency, while also abandoning them to their employers, unsafe machinery, dangerous pesticides, and toxic living environments. This abandonment, however, should not be viewed as the absence or neglect of government, but rather the strengthening of prerogative power and the dispersion of sovereign decision making.[135]

The relative absence of debate about workers' conditions in either program allows for consensus and greater discursive power to establish as necessary what did not previously exist. Those who are proponents of the guest-worker program—notably Presidents George W. Bush and Barack Obama, and Senator Dianne Feinstein—are considered "soft" on immigration. They, in turn, argue that economic necessity, the immigration problem, and the wars on terror logically lead to a program that controls workers' conditions and reduces illegality. At these two levels of operation—the bare, biological need of Mexicans and the deterritorialized space in which the wars on terror and drugs are fought—democratic rights, citizenship, and political agency are thought to have no place. These two realms of necessity instead create their own logic, which is replicated throughout the world in countries adhering to IMF dictates, accepting World Bank loans, establishing free trade zones, and signing free trade agreements. The proliferation of these dynamics in turn obscures the degree to which there is heavy political intervention, the active suppression of rights (broadly conceived), and the strengthening of state sovereignty. But this last point must be qualified.

As I have indicated above, states like Mexico may be relatively strengthened through the prerogative used in economic interventions, but they also serve as "junior partners" to U.S. power through the implementation of neoliberal reform.[136] Even today, when the ideas of Keynesian economics are being revived in the press (notably in the *New York Times*), there is little divergence from past policies. Improved labor conditions and relations are viewed as "socialist" and obstacles to "responsible" economic practices. Unions are considered outdated and corrupt, and workers continue to be played against one another if they protest, attempt to unioniz , or "escape" in some way.

To recognize that these issues are not merely happenstance, nor merely economic, is to recognize that the United States continues to strengthen its sovereignty and exercise prerogative power unchecked. This is true not despite crisis, but because of it. As the language of necessity is constantly invoked, coupled with the deceptive language of freedom (free market, deregulation, flexibility, free trade, etc.), these two programs move from the margins to the center and from temporary measures to permanent ones, affecting formal and informal labor relations outside the programs. The political may not shrink, but democracy does. This is a warning not only for policy makers but also political theorists who believe that politics can be decoupled from economic matters. This includes theorists ranging from Habermasians to authors like T. H. Marshall,[137] who establish a hierarchy of needs, placing political agency and rights as a second set of needs, granted only after basic economic require- ments have been met. Agamben and Žižek, following Arendt, critique the same hierarchy in human rights norms: if human rights organizations address only bare necessity, they replicate the very dangers they attempt to eradicate. Similarly, as long as U.S. politics is guided by crisis and notions of necessity, it will continue along this undemocratic path.

These two programs demonstrate that transnational programs are not temporary and must be dealt with politically at the transnational or inter- national level. The centrality of the nation-state in defining political status clearly leads to the effective statelessness of these workers, and thereby opens a space in which abuse can occur. This space may also leave room for new types of rights, political statuses, and, more generally, innovation and cre- ativity, as Sassen, Held, and Soysal have demonstrated in their work. But the combination of factors ensures that resistance can be viewed as the work of outlaws and enemies—individuals outside the politico-economic norm of national citizenship. First, the increased use of prerogative power domesti- cally and regularly—exercised not just on those who are clearly threatening but also potentially so—limits the political agency of worker-activists in important respects. Second, the fact that neoliberal principles are increas- ingly dominant permits the greater latitude for international conglomerates and business interests at the expense of workers. At best, one could argue that there is a clear democratic deficit. To put it differently, if corporations are now treated as individuals and yet given greater freedom than individu- als (e.g., privileging corporate rights over protesters' rights),[158] then at the regional level they will be even more supreme. They can act with impunity and unilaterally. In this context, if immigration law is one of the last areas in which the state can exercise sovereignty, it will certainly exert this power,[139] perhaps in direct proportion to the degree that the state loses control in the economic sphere.[140] This is why the free zones are a dream both for advocates of control and surveillance *and* "free marketers."

Human rights organizations are the logical institutions to fill this void, and they do help workers to a limited extent, which I will discuss in the conclusion. But as authors like Pierre Hassner, David Held, Michael Hardt, Antonio Negri, and Giorgio Agamben have pointed out, the UN's two missions—as a membership organization protecting national sovereignty and a human rights organization protecting individual and group rights against the nation-state—are directly at odds with each other. The result is that human rights are interpreted via the nation-state, which undercuts the effectiveness not only of UN missions but also those of any international human rights body.[141] As long as human rights norms remain subordinate to nation-states in various ways, solutions based on these rights will often replicate the very issues causing the abuses in the first place. In these cases, the political cannot be divorced from the economic, and democracy should not be put aside for the future.

But perhaps because of the ambivalence of an increasingly transnational, politically undecidable space, workers who are essentially stripped of rights—whether temporarily or for a longer period—still resist. This is important to note for at least two reasons. First, in discussing late modern deployments of prerogative power, the impression is often that it is absolute to the point of precluding agency. Clearly, that is not the case. Second, examples of resistance challenge the notion that Mexican workers are subservient, apolitical, or "stagnant" in some other way. Nevertheless, although there are numerous cases of resistance—from acts of "micro-resistance" (Foucault's term)[142] to unionization to the mass demonstrations of spring 2006—this does not lead to a broad overturning of power asymmetries. Further, just because people can resist and sometimes succeed is not proof that they are being treated democratically or according to any rule of law.

The suspension of economic laws is an act of prerogative power that must be taken seriously in order to understand that conventional arguments about assimilation and the immigrant experience are seriously deficient. The suspension of economic laws, the barring of political rights, and the inequality of the labor contract itself all leave these low-tier workers stateless. These dynamics in turn affect the conditions of other immigrant low-tier workers, whether illegal or legal.

Given the ongoing wars on terror and drugs, public and political discourse reinforce both dynamics by positing Mexicans (and other working-class immigrants of color) as invading the United States, stealing jobs, colonizing the Southwest, and draining public resources. Academic theorists who view immigrants as enacting the social contract or challenging the pernicious effects of nation-state sovereignty also position them as acting individually and autonomously. What I would like to suggest is that the processes of globalization and what appears to be a sovereignty-free area operate symbiotically with the operations of the United States' undeclared wars to simultaneously police and exploit working-class immigrants of color. Consequently, these workers operate in a sphere founded on arbitrary power and violence, whether they actually experience that or not. What is important to note is that this is true not only because of what is ordinarily conceived of as political forces, but also because of economic regulations and labor relations and norms. To put it differently, predominantly neoliberal policies unite economic and sovereign concerns, making Mexican immigrants (among others) a group that can be exploited and policed, treated as crucial to the international economy and yet a threat to sovereignty.

My argument challenges conventional models of assimilation, citizenship, and economic integration. More broadly, it disputes the autonomy and range of powers that immigrants are purported to have, on the one hand, and challenges the primacy of the nation-state in understanding immigration. If these two trends continue—a war without borders and a global economy of "free zones"—political solutions will not be found in the nation-state, but rather in supra- or subnational understandings of political belonging.

Conclusion

The Right to Rights?

In this chapter, I will argue that cosmopolitan politics—a commitment to democratic practices and rights performed on multiple levels—is the necessary solution to the problems I have considered in this book. But I would first like to frame this solution in terms of the critiques I have offered thus far. In this book, I have explored how a controversial immigrant group is caught up in three important processes: the continued primacy of the nation-state in defining political belonging; the operations of global capital in national territory; and the deployment of the war on terror, which has shaped recent immigration policy and rhetoric. I have analyzed these processes in terms of policy making, popular views and stereotypes, economic trends, and the activity of civil society. Since the mid-1980s, but particularly beginning in the mid-1990s, U.S. policy has initiated greater efforts to tighten the border, increase deportations, boost arrests of "criminal aliens," and cut off incentives to migrate to the United States by restricting access to the social safety net.[1] These efforts have been supported in the media and by increased anti-immigration grassroots activity. At the same time, there are significant challenges to the wish for a self-contained, bordered country: immigration, both authorized and unauthorized, continues at very high rates; global capital "denationalizes national territory" in a variety of ways and affects labor standards and work conditions; and the new, undeclared wars on terror and drugs necessarily efface borders in the United States and abroad. These challenges in turn reinforce the anxious desire to seal the border; to protect from foreign invasion; and to preserve national integrity, including the nation's "core values."[2] The backlash since 2006 is evidence of these anxieties.

Specifically, the immigration proposals of 2006–7 posited immigrants as exploitable labor (from the "pro"-immigrant camp) or security threats (the anti-immigration camp). As I argued in the introduction and the previous chapter, these two positions have been inextricably bound to each other and reveal far more about American political concerns than they do about the immigrant groups targeted in these proposals. Further, although the two positions reflect historical trends of marginalizing "labor immigrants," they are also relatively new and unique given the greater predominance of neo-liberal politics and the wars on terror and drugs. There are two significant consequences to these views of controversial immigrants.

In the first place, they portray immigrants as individuals who are simply leaving their home countries due to poverty and overcrowding.[3] This picture of individual rationality is divorced from migrant pathways that have historically been established, economic demands for "cheap" and "docile" labor, and linkages to these groups and areas that the United States has actively developed. It allows conventional interpretations of immigration to emphasize economic factors apart from all other elements that inspire an individual or family to leave their country. It also serves as a justification for neoliberal policies aimed at making workers' status purely economic at the expense of political protections, rights, and action. In turn, the economic viewpoint is indicative of a hierarchy of needs in which work under any conditions is primary and democratic agency and action is not only second-ary, but seen as threatening and disruptive.

Second, the key categories of liberal politics reinforce the portrayal of immigrants in individual, economic terms. Liberal notions such as the social contract, the individual as the unit of analysis, equality, and free will para-doxically depoliticize understandings of immigrants' situation. Among other things, these analytical categories obscure the effects of alarmist and nativist discourse, media portrayals of hyper-reproduction and disease,[4] and policies that treat controversial immigrants as threats to national security. That is, they emphasize the notion of individual choice without considering context of reception, how policies shape actions, and the importance of family ties or community. Hence, the liberal perspective of individual rights, individual volition, rationality, and the mutuality of contracts functions with the eco-nomic perspective to privilege the economic at the expense of the political.

Not surprisingly, the United States' stance toward human rights and development has operated according to the same logic by fostering eco-nomic development to the detriment of democracy, broadly conceived. This is important to note for three reasons: (a) these policies are allegedly designed to aid development in poorer countries and stop the flow of immigration into the United States, but in fact they often initiate or reinforce significant immigration flows; (b) they mask the increased use of sovereign measures not only abroad but domestically through a rhetoric of goodwill and economic beneficence; and (c) they thereby limit and constrain the very institutions that should serve the needs of an increasingly transient population.

Authors such as Saskia Sassen, Alejandro Portes, and Rubén Rumbaut have demonstrated in their work that foreign direct investment, regional trade agreements, military interventions, and economic aid actually stimulate migration rather than deter it.[5] Second, free trade agreements and foreign direct investment actually make borders more (conceptually) porous rather than less—they are a hybrid of U.S. and foreign effort that "deterritorialize national territory" in the areas where they operate. Third, when displaced workers begin to migrate to the United States, immigration law in general and guest-worker policies in particular treat workers as purely economic units and do not account for the breakup of families or communities that occurred because of these patterns. These separations lead to attempts at reunification, whether officially sanctioned or not. Therefore, as Sassen argues, "because immigration is thought to result from unfavorable socioeconomic conditions in other countries, it is assumed to be unrelated to U.S. economic needs or broader international economic conditions. In this context, the decision becomes a humanitarian matter; we admit immigrants by choice and out of generosity, not because we have any economic motive or political responsibility to do so."[6]

Although there are complex reasons for migration, what is important in these observations is that each of these efforts neutralize or undermine democratic politics in favor of "development" or "humanitarian intervention," ironically producing or exacerbating the effects they are alleged to ameliorate. Very often, the uprootedness caused by each of these types of interventions leads to migration. Immigration policy, however, does not recognize these dynamics and instead criminalizes the groups affected.[7] As U.S. policy is increasingly oriented toward the figure of the "illegal alien" and the terrorist,[8] broadly conceived, it is aimed at the border and enforcement mechanisms, including the increased use of detention centers, the greater militarization of the southern border, the symbolic commitment to building a border fence,[9] expedited hearings and rapid deportations, and the promotion of the guest-worker program as a "humane" response to unauthorized entry. These policies are blunt instruments that preclude democratic agency, mutual interaction, and the exercise of rights; rather, they deal with controversial immigrants along a legal/illegal binary that ignores the complexity of immigration law and processes. Further, these policies affect entry and shape immigrants' political status and agency once within the country.

Immigration policy is not only ineffective in stopping the flow of migration from certain geographical areas, it is significantly undemocratic in its principles and implementation. Recognizing that borders and the nation-state are political arrangements rather than natural givens, policy must cease the split in which it treats its own citizens democratically (ideally, anyway) and certain foreigners as enemies. Further, democratic principles should not only guide immigration policy but also be directly aligned with local, domestic, regional, and international economic policies. In fact, the hierarchy of economic reasoning and profit above democratic rights and agency should be reversed.[10]

Moreover, the free market and neoliberal policies are supported not by democratic institutions and law but acts of sovereignty characterized by war and crisis. For these reasons, there is a clear democratic deficit in areas or statuses outside the bounds of the nation-state. What this means is that not only do victims of genocide and war need some sort of political status and rights at the regional or international level, but so do individuals who have become stateless in less explicit, seemingly banal ways; that is, through the statelessness produced in U.S. guest-worker sites, sweatshops, and detention centers. Because these issues are endemic to the nation-state as it has developed and the partnership between global capital and the sovereign state, I argue with Saskia Sassen that workers made invisible at the nation-state level may have the greatest hope of political action at the regional and international levels.[11] But as I have just noted, U.S. stances on economic development and human rights have tended to privilege the economic at the expense of the democratic. I will explore the issue of human rights below and argue that the term "post-national citizenship" better captures the needs of individuals and groups whose political status is undecidable and who occupy deterritorialized spaces.

Human Rights

The very phrase "human rights" became for all concerned—victims, persecutors, and onlookers alike—the evidence of hopeless idealism or fumbling feeble-minded hypocrisy.

—Hannah Arendt, *The Origins of Totalitarianism*

In the system of the nation-state, the so-called sacred and inalienable rights of man show themselves to lack every protection and reality at the moment in which they can no longer take the form of rights belonging to citizens of a state.

— Giorgio Agamben, *Homo Sacer*

Given the issues I have raised in this book, there is a clear democratic deficit in many of the relationships in which controversial immigrants are involved, and I believe cosmopolitan politics could provide the basis for political agency that national citizenship alone cannot.[12] But human rights and cosmopolitanism would not serve immigrants as a transcendent status but rather a hybrid one, reflecting the amalgam of memberships and loyalties of these individuals as well as the ambivalent space in which many of them reside. I will suggest below that post-national citizenship is one way to conceive of this hybridity, and that it is something immigrants often perform today de facto, if not de jure. Hybridity indicates that individuals have rights based on political performance within the confines of the United States, but it also connotes a broader notion of political status in their transnational movements and actions.[13] Nevertheless, human rights as they have been implemented at elite levels have often been fraught with contradictions.

Hannah Arendt famously commented that the group who needed human rights the most, the stateless, was precisely the group who had no rights.[14] In fact, she notes that because individuals have the right to refugee status but no state is obligated to offer asylum, the sovereign right of deportation is often the tool of choice in dealing with individuals whose status is undecidable. In this context, Arendt argues that the stateless by definition are "outlaws"[15] and have "no right to rights,"[16] a phrase I have repeated throughout this book. When human rights aid has been administered, it has most often been in the form of the means to sustain biological life—food, water, medicine, makeshift shelters—and has operated at the level of bare life rather than addressing the political origins of abuse and rightlessness. In this way, international organizations often maintain the separation between economic subsistence (mere life) and political status. For example, placing stateless individuals in refugee camps simply reproduces the individual's political displacement, addressing only the need for food and shelter.[17] Bretton Woods institutions reinforce this separation through their conditional aid and development programs that continue to silence the majority of the people, further impoverishing them and funneling money to local elites.[18] There are two ways to view this issue and Arendt has formulated both: only citizens are truly viewed as human, but contradictorily, only when all other markers of a group or individual are stripped does this person appear to be human and nothing more.[19] Both formulations amount to arguing that individuals stripped of their political status cannot rely on human rights as currently implemented.

Since noting this difficulty, various authors have continued to remark on the limitations of human rights as rights. These criticisms have been formulated most radically by authors like Agamben, Slavoj Žižek, and Hardt and Negri, not to mention complementary appraisals of development by authors such as Gayatri Spivak and Arundhati Roy.[20] Although each analysis must be taken on its own terms, they can be summarized as stating that human rights and development organizations most often end up replicating the very problems they seek to eradicate. Agamben would argue that all the issues these authors discuss hinge on the primacy of bare life in configuring national sovereignty and the reproduction of this model of rights at the international level by various agencies. The development of human rights in this direction has arisen for several reasons.

First, there is the claim that economic well-being will lead to democracy, that one presupposes the other.[21] This claim has become increasingly significant since neoliberal politics have become predominant at the state level (notably in the United States and the United Kingdom) and in the transformation of the Bretton Woods institutions in the 1980s. In turn, neoliberal politics and rhetoric tend to naturalize poverty, effacing the historical and political roots of famine and starvation.[22] This mind-set affects views of immigrants arriving to the United States from poorer countries, as well as views of the sending countries themselves.

Human rights organizations often reproduce this dynamic, whether intentionally or not. This is perhaps because they have no choice but to use the language and legal mandates already set at the international level, which in turn reflect the Cold War struggle in defining human rights. Based on Cold War divisions, the United States has historically recognized political oppression, legitimizing the claims of political abuse in communist countries but not allegations they label as economic or social. Today, rather than broadening the basis of claims for political asylum, the United States has categorized increasing numbers of refugees as "economic" who would have previously been considered political.[23] This split, of course, merely reinforces the reduction of the stateless individual to bare life.[24] When it is argued that individuals should be granted rights, they are based on notions of humanity and human dignity rather than political identification or inclusion. This transfers the role of bare life from state sovereignty and citizenship to international sovereignty and human rights. As Nirmal Trivedi remarks, "Because humanitarian law is replete with advocacy efforts for life on behalf of those abandoned by the law . . . it is vital for us to see how the way the debate and the struggle is couched cooperates with biopolitics and thereby does not oppose the state of exception that the law can make possible."[25] That is, human rights organizations end up arguing that certain groups are worthy of life[26] and therefore political status, rather than attempting to shatter the bond between sovereignty and bare life. For this reason, the conception of human rights as a status conferred by birth or existence simply replicates citizenship based on blood or birth. Law then continues to define life worth living and life not worth living.

A second set of critiques similarly argues that human rights rhetoric seeks to depoliticize crises by calling them "humanitarian interventions" and by emphasizing the victimization of groups but effacing the political and historical roots of these problems.[27] Mapped onto this is the rhetoric of good and evil, pure and tainted, innocent and guilty, which further obscures complex political and economic realities. In these rhetorical efforts, human rights are administered and defended "beyond power."[28] As Wendy Brown states, this amounts to human rights conceiving of "itself as something of an antipolitics—a pure defence of the innocent and the powerless against power, a pure defence of the individual against immense and potentially cruel or despotic machineries of culture, state, war, ethnic conflict, tribalism, patriarchy, and other mobilizations of instantiations of collective power against individuals."[29] For these reasons, humanitarian interventions are viewed as operating in the realm of morals rather than power, politics, and violence.[30] Žižek similarly argues that the appeal to moral superiority obscures political motives and the use of violence. This is evident in "humanitarian" interventions in which the United States sees itself as a neutral, benevolent party rather than a key global actor with clear economic and political interests.[31] Thus fighting on behalf of human rights, or on the morally righteous side of a good/evil axis of power, obscures American political motives and the use of force and violence. Žižek contends that this mind-set is like George Orwell's phrase "war is peace" in that American leaders interpret their violence to be morally virtuous and divorced from other motives. Hence the United States justifies bombing a country to establish democracy, invading another country to "secure food transportation and distribution,"[32] and reviving torture methods to fight "just wars." American usurpation is then conveniently hidden under an ethical veil. These radical critiques are indicative of significant problems in human rights implementation—many that the United Nations High Commissioner for Refugees freely admits[33]—and relevant to the more general U.S. policy orientation toward controversial immigrants.

A third, related critique is offered by Bronwyn Leebaw, who observes that human rights actors, in their desire to appear impartial, have been forced to distance themselves from the political underpinnings of crises.[34] This has not happened in a monolithic way, as actors can be split into two groups: the humanitarian movement (e.g., the Red Cross) that administers aid amid crisis and must very often prove that it has no political agenda just to be admitted into a country; and the human rights movement (e.g., Amnesty International), which has sought to address political injustice and expose human rights abuses. Nevertheless, in its desire to be viewed as impartial, even the latter group has "responded to political dilemmas by simultaneously accommodating and denigrating political compromise. This threatens to undermine their critical role in exposing abuses of power as well as their ability to inspire political mobilization in support of the values they espouse."[35] Further, as the two strands of human rights actors have increasingly worked together, their aims have become narrower politically. The purported goal of limiting their political scope is to be taken seriously by all sides in complex conflicts. But "although these elements of humanitarian logic were incorporated as a way to alleviate political conflict, they might better be understood as strategies of avoidance."[36] As actors struggle to act impartially, they seek to distance themselves from "politics," even as they must be familiar with—and even rooted in—a situation's politics in order to help. The result is the minimizing of politics and, thus, a sort of fatalism, according to Wendy Brown.[37] As Leebaw points out, however, the very ability to interact in "human rights" contexts belies more political awareness and commitment than humanitarian rhetoric would suggest. The question is, What is the political in this context?

From an Agambenian perspective, the limbo of the stateless and refugees is precisely the most political sphere. It is not a legal void or politically meaningless, as some of Agamben's critics charge, but rather the sphere in which sovereignty can manifest itself to its fullest potential.[38] Whether refugees are treated badly is then pure luck. When individuals become stateless, Arendt has argued that "the prolongation of their lives is due to charity and not to right, for no law exists which could force the nations to feed them; their freedom of movement, if they have it at all, gives them no right to residence, which even the jailed criminal enjoys as a matter of course; and their freedom of opinion is a fool's freedom, for nothing they think matters anyhow."[39] Agamben sees the link between bare life and sovereignty in an even starker fashion: because bare life is the precondition of all citizenship, any individual or group could fall into this rightless state.[40]

Although I believe both diagnoses are correct, one could ask if this "secret tie" uniting sovereignty and bare life were not also always accompanied by forms of the political that Agamben does not recognize as political: acts of spontaneity and passion,[41] such as the immigrant protests of spring 2006 in major U.S. cities;[42] unauthorized workers leading union movements despite their political status, as has happened in Los Angeles;[43] and acts of micro-resistance in maquiladoras and guest-worker escapes. To put it differently, the power mechanisms that Agamben has analyzed so well cannot be absolute or totalitarian in democracies, particularly when sovereign agents and power mechanisms are dispersed.[44]

Another notion of the political has continuously appeared throughout contemporary history and has not always been complicit with institutional, sovereign power. From this perspective, James Ingram has suggestively interpreted Arendt's famous phrase "the right to have rights" as "the right to politics."[45] Rather than viewing rights as commodities or the protection of one's private property, rights are broadly conceived as political performance on the part of the actors concerned. This is not "power" acting on behalf of "victims," but the enactment of democratic practices by the groups whose interests are at stake. Bonnie Honig has called this "taking," which involves the enactment of rights or the performance of citizenship when one has not been granted these rights or statuses. "Taking" leads to multiple affiliations, thus challenging the centralization of power, and denationalizes democracy, "not because they [democratic cosmopolitans] do not value affective ties and membership but precisely because they do."[46] This view of the possibilities for political action entails a utopian vision[47] when considering democratic political action: one that includes not only what has succeeded but also what has failed; not only what has relied on official truths but also what has operated on the margins; not only what has been recorded and codified but also what has been passed down orally; and not only what has been included in territorial belonging but also what is deterritorialized. The starting point analytically would then be one Agamben has suggested:

rather than give a deterritorialized group statehood or national citizenship (his example is the Palestinians), create a relationship of deterritorialization between the areas or groups in question.[48]

The result would perhaps be the revival of Hedley Bull's neo-medievalism, as Andrew Linklater has suggested.[49] This does not eradicate the nation-state, but instead provides for a "complex network of overlapping authorities."[50] While overlapping economic authority certainly already exists at the regional and international level, Linklater and other cosmopolitan writers argue for the greater presence of actors, groups, and regions that are not motivated by profit but by democratic politics. This could only happen, I believe, if these groups do not act *only* in a "fugitive" manner,[51] however laudable this is, but *also* have institutional recognition in international government organizations.[52] A second proviso is that the policies and influence of the Bretton Woods institutions must be held to democratic standards. The current perception that these organizations are (and should be) acting in a completely different realm than—or even in opposition to—the United Nations, the International Court of Justice, and humanitarian nongovernmental organizations undermines their original missions.[53] As Joseph Stiglitz has argued, these institutions are public and dedicated to aiding development and the world economy.[54] Unless their actions are held to democratic standards, including transparency, accountability, and permitting the active participation in decision making of all nation-states under their auspices, they will continue to counteract any democratic efforts at the international level.[55] As they are currently run, they continue to act as partners to wealthier nations, fostering inequality and exploitation.

A third proviso is the reform of the United Nations itself. Since its inception, the UN has been an institution that has unquestionably helped countless individuals and given legitimacy to former colonies attempting to ameliorate inequality at the international level.[56] Nevertheless, there is the contradictory mandate of the United Nations: it is both a membership institution, protecting the sovereignty of each nation-state, and more recently a human rights institution, protecting individuals from the abuses of nation-states.[57] This contradiction makes any action at the human rights level limited at best. In the end, the UN has historically protected the rights of nation-states over and above individuals, even if its agencies would like the focus to shift exclusively to the protection of human rights.[58] The two solutions to this are to change its mission to one exclusive focus and to make this body a supranational rather than international one.[59] An additional problem is that its parliamentary form is highly undemocratic in significant respects. The veto power of five major states, the membership of states that are not democratic, the lack of checks and balances within the organization, and the absence of judicial review are some of the most glaring issues.[60]

Today, migrant groups are already working in a variety of ways to create democratic spaces that meet their new conditions; they do not need to be guided by these elite institutions but rather included, as legitimate actors outside any particular nation-state. The presence of environmental groups, ethnic groups like the Roma, and workers' organizations in both the United Nations (with the creation of a second assembly of representatives of these deterritorialized groups)[61] and Bretton Woods institutions (as overseers of the political effects of economic policies) would not necessarily mean their co-option (i.e., their participation in the further inscription of bare life at the heart of sovereignty). In challenging the very foundations of the nation-state, political participation cannot merely replicate the bare life–sovereign tie. Rather, their presence could alter the meaning of rights, participation, and citizenship, not to mention work and work conditions. As is the case with national governments, the United Nations should be only one of several institutions in which political activity can be legislated and adjudicated between nation-states. But an analytical change of focus is also required: the citizen should not be the paradigm for a more democratic political status; instead, the stateless and deterritorialized spaces should be the starting points.

Agamben argues that the figure of the refugee or stateless individual is "perhaps the only thinkable figure for the people of our time and the only category in which one may see . . . the forms and limits of a coming political community."[62] This is because the refugee has been the necessary product of an increasingly inclusive *and* exclusive logic of the nation-state since the early twentieth century.[63] As Arendt showed in her work, the emergence of mass statelessness, disenfranchised minorities, the drawing and redrawing of borders, and forced population exchanges in the early to mid-twentieth century were testimony to the fact that these stateless groups were not anomalous but rather "the most symptomatic" of contemporary politics.[64] Accordingly, the stateless were not merely cast aside but held as the negative figure against which citizenship was positively valued.

They are living proof of the undemocratic practices and institutions that secure and maintain the state, not to mention the capitalist enterprises that entrench their undecidable status. Today, the figure of the purely economic immigrant and that of the illegal alien are new representatives of these older processes. As borders became even tighter in the 1990s in the United States and across Europe while global capital became more mobile, terrorists and illegal aliens have been increasingly viewed as the two faces of the enemy: the cultural-political enemy and the economic enemy. And these two have increasingly been intertwined.

As I stated above, human rights aid has most often addressed individuals at the level of bare life, but this does not have to be the case. In truth, there is quite a lot about human rights efforts that have been politically creative and spontaneous, even if these efforts are (certainly) not the norm. Some key examples are self-help groups established by women immigrants, addressing issues such as language acquisition, unionization, and domestic violence.[65] Indeed, Sassen notes that "the practices and claims enacted by nonstate actors in [international civil society] may well contribute to creating international law, as is most clearly. the case with both the international human rights regime and the demands for rights made by firms and markets with global operations."[66] Note Sassen's reversal: the institutions do not define the scope of individuals' political actions, but rather "nonstate actors" help establish international law.[67] Yasemin Soysal likewise sees human rights norms transforming notions of citizenship, work relations, and state sovereignty, particularly in Europe. Soysal's work preceded the events of September 11, but it presents an important alternative view. European countries have provided for immigrants' political agency in a variety of ways, including giving them local voting rights, funding organizations representative of each group, giving immigrant groups consultative status at municipal levels, and allowing them to unionize. None of these efforts have been seamless and many of the provisions have since been eliminated, but Soysal shows how they do not merely add on to the nation-state but help create "postnational citizenship."

Post-national Citizenship

In this spirit, human rights should not be conceived as rights that are granted (somehow, by someone) in the context of the failure of a nation-state to enforce the rule of law. This would mean that they are merely the rights of the dispossessed, based on victimization. Thus, as Jacques Ranciére argues, "ultimately, those rights appear actually empty. They seem to be of no use. And when they are of no use, you do the same as charitable persons do with their old clothes. You give them to the poor. Those rights that appear to be useless in their place are sent abroad, along with medicine and clothes, to people deprived of medicine, clothes, and rights."[68] First, "human rights" may be better termed "post-national citizenship" because this phrasing emphasizes the political and performative nature of rights, rather than those founded on mere existence or humanity. Post-national citizenship also enlarges the area of political action from the mere possession of rights to different political possibilities.[69] Significantly, this citizenship should not lead to the individualization of rights that has characterized human rights norms in the past few decades; this process has led only to depoliticization of the political and economic conditions that caused displacement in the first place.[70] And practically speaking, policies that address the individual have resulted in splitting up families and communities. Rather, post-national citizenship should allow for the practice of rights in a political sense, which necessarily entails accounting for community and recognizing that many communities may overlap or even challenge one another. The term also suggests that the nation-state does not perfectly "house" individuals; it recognizes that there are post-national spaces, relationships, and political arrangements that reflect the significance, including the relative permanence, of deterritorialized spaces.[71] Post-national citizenship is constituted precisely because these spaces and times exist within and between nation-states.

Second, they therefore do not have to be exercised "above" citizenship rights; in fact, unauthorized immigrants often exercise political agency "below" citizenship. But subscribing to a vertical notion of power, or power as "concentric circles" (as Nicholas Xenos characterized Martha Nussbaum's cosmopolitanism[72]), does not provide an adequate view of the matter. If power is in fact a network or web (as Foucault argues),[73] cosmopolitan politics is power that is or could be generated locally and specifically at times (e.g., unionization movements of nonresidents, environmental groups, or women's rights groups), regionally at others (e.g., the formation of an independent service workers' union that monitors and protects labor conditions under NAFTA), and globally at meetings such as those held by women workers in Beijing (in 1995, under UN auspices) and in Huairou, China (as part of the Nongovernmental Organization Forum, organized by women workers from around the world).[74] In this respect, Michael Peter Smith explicitly challenges the popular slogan "think globally, act locally" and the implication that all truly democratic politics must be local.[75]

However, third, individuals and groups must be able to operate as legitimate actors at all these levels and this requires two things. In the past two decades, there has been an increasing restriction on the occupation of public space and mass protest.[76] For example, recently various global cities have required parade and demonstration permits, often favoring economic or purely cultural activities but denying political activism that is considered out of the mainstream or on the Left.[77] Combined with the increasing tendency of the George W. Bush administration to use free speech zones and exclusion zones, as well as legal efforts to protect corporate interests in public space, mass political activity at the grassroots level has increasingly been viewed as criminal rather than democratic. Laws that criminalize immigrant activity, including the threat of deportation, surveillance, and curtailment of economic activity, are one element of this broader trend that privileges corporate power and has tended to privatize public space. In this context, the mass protests of 2006 were viewed by some as an outrage because of the significant (presumed) participation of unauthorized immigrants, while unionization efforts by unauthorized immigrants can be interpreted as an offense on multiple levels: economic, political, and legal. Similarly, protests in support of the DREAM Act in 2010 have been portrayed as the criminal usurpation of public space and a method of flaunting protesters' illegality. A significant reversal of these policies and attitudes is needed if all individuals are to act as democratic agents.

Another issue is harder to capture empirically: assimilation norms that posit some groups as being traditional and backward also ignore their political activities or devalue them as criminal.[78] Analysts view elite institutions as shaping immigrants' activities in an enlightening and rational way that the immigrants themselves are not capable of. This is exemplified in Seyla Benhabib's analysis of the French government's attempt to ban the wearing of the veil in public schools. Although she rightly discusses the French arguments for separation of church and state (laïcisme), she does not see that these justifications may *also* be neocolonial, gendered, and racialized, even if also democratic.[79] Alternatively, she wonders if these "traditional" girls will ever stand up for themselves:[80]

> Traditional Muslim girls and women are not supposed to appear in the public sphere at all; ironically, precisely the realities of Western democracies with their more liberal and tolerant visions of women's role permits these girls and women to be educated in public schools,

[and] to enter the labor force. . . . My prediction is that it is a matter of time before these women, who are learning to talk back to the state, also will engage and contest the very meaning of the Islamic traditions that they are now fighting to uphold. Eventually, these public battles will initiate private gender struggle about the status of women's rights within the Muslim tradition.[81]

The problem is that there is quite a lot of evidence that they already do, but this is apparent only if one pays attention to informal democratic activity on many levels. Yasemin Soysal has already recorded the establishment of a wide array of grassroots groups across Europe in her study of Turkish migrants; and Trica Keaton has explored how girls of Maghrebi descent identify themselves in hybrid terms, and how girls who consider themselves Senegalese and French call themselves SENEF (Senegalese-French).[82] Among other examples, some of the girls Keaton worked with participated in a group called Ni Putes Ni Soumises (Neither Whores Nor Submissives), which challenged forced marriages and honor killings.[83] More informally, many acknowledged the struggle in identifying with a home country where they did not feel welcome and being in a new culture that constantly told them they were not "truly" French. In their political actions, the girls employed a range of references from their countries of descent, human rights norms, and French democratic principles in asserting their identities and political pathways. For this reason, one cannot argue that these disenfranchised individuals simply claimed the French democratic rights denied to them, which would indicate that the French principles (for example) are better than their current enactment. Instead, if the laws were not only democratic but also gendered and racist, the girls' assertion of a hybrid identity does not serve as a bridge between two poles, but rather produces something new, enlarging the meaning of these identities and political practices even as they remain marginalized.[84]

Similarly, when controversial or marginalized groups are examined in the U.S. media and by mainstream academics, it is constantly asked why "they" (e.g., the homeless, poor single mothers, poorer minorities, immigrants) do not fight back. They are painted as apathetic, passive, and victims of themselves. When they work at low-paying jobs in bad conditions, their initial agreement is also taken as a sign of this submissiveness. But attention must be paid to how individuals and groups define their democratic agency *given* the unequal treatment and policies that denigrate, make invisible, or criminalize their activities.

Benhabib's attention to elite and formal democratic processes over and above evidence of informal democratic practices marks a more widespread tendency in political theory and media analyses to ignore the following: the pairing of democratic *and* sovereign (including prerogative) decisions and policies; gendered, class-biased, and racist norms built into seemingly neutral processes; and laws and policies that silence the possibility of "rational discourse."[85] A change of focus, from the formal and elite to those whose political status is undecidable, brings attention to the exclusionary logic of the nation-state as well as the bio-political dynamics of sovereignty. In this context, the multitude of efforts—from unionizing, to community organizing, to women's groups, to legal self-help activities—can be seen as the response to various concerns by the individuals involved in these processes. What is needed is not rousing individuals from apathy or extricating them from tradition, but greater legitimacy for noncorporate and nonprofit actors, greater political support for controversial groups, and the acknowledgment of the various ways to perform rights.

Moving what has been viewed as marginal to the center of a democratic politics would require strengthening various elements of civil society at all these levels, so that nongovernmental organizations would no longer be organized around emergencies and the worst abuses of power.[86] Instead, these groups would become vehicles of exercising positive political rights and serve as more permanent checks on sovereign, national power as well as operating as gadflies to international organizations. Nongovernmental organizations would then be in a position to fight the criminalization of democratic activities, from protests to unionization to alternative self-help groups. But as long as groups helping immigrants and refugees operate only on an emergency basis—stepping in to prevent the worst political or economic abuses—they will never perform as institutions for the emergence of positive political activity and rights, helping to legitimate nonelites, the poor, and those whose status defies the nation-state. In sum, it must be recognized that building a civil society involves multiple and competing institutions for democratic purposes and should not merely reflect a "state of emergency."

Further, beginning with the figure of the refugee to think about a new politics will ideally challenge extant notions of inclusion and foster dialogue, debate, and action based on working relationships (activism, community work, employment) rather than static identities. As Arendt noted, it was when Jews were stripped of their nationality that they were no longer identified as neighbors, teachers, artists, mothers, fathers, or doctors; they became "unidentifiable beggars, without nationality, without money, and without passports."[87] In the past, extraordinary individuals could find asylum, their unique stories evoking the sympathy of one government or another. But encountering thousands of "faceless" and "nameless" refugees evoked the opposite response. Today, laws and norms that portray immigrants as economic and illegal similarly efface the multiple affiliations and talents of individuals, reducing them to mere need and want. Analytically, beginning with the figure of the refugee to identify not only the key problem but also to point the way to a more democratic approach means that statelessness is not viewed as anomalous but rather descriptive of various statuses, spaces, and relationships that go beyond, below, and in between the nation-state and are a regular feature of a more global world. Rather than making all individuals "human" and thus stripping all their particularity, an analysis based on statelessness would allow for a multiplicity of political identities and sites that would then preclude the possibility of "refugees in orbit."

Soysal's research on guest-worker policies in "corporatist" and "centralized" countries pre–September 11, 2001, suggests that these forms of post-national citizenship have existed in various instances, thus giving us glimpses of how to create a new democratic politics. Importantly, this form of citizenship has happened not because workers waited for governments to grant them rights, but through the unique interaction among (a) human rights norms and governments; she argues that human rights norms have forced governments to protect migrant workers, ensure their rights in the workplace, and give them a voice in local and federal politics;[88] (b) the needs of industry for labor and yet government reluctance to nationalize these guest workers (Germany is a crucial example);[89] governments allowed workers limited political rights, mobility, and protections such that their exclusionary logic *inadvertently* created a new form of political inclusion;[90] and (c) the growing strength of international organizations, including the International Court of Justice, UN agencies, the International Labour Organization, and migrants' organizations. Evidence of these dynamics is the use of human rights discourse and democratic notions to assert migrant identity, the demand for dual citizenship, and, more broadly, claims that enlarge the meaning of citizenship.[91] Her research is a complex example of political participation based on individual and group action (rather than allowing a nation-state to define workers' status), and it demonstrates how governments must inevitably respond to nongovernmental groups' demands.

In particular, she has highlighted how countries that provide voting rights, funding for language retention and cultural expression, workers' groups, and consultative organs based on immigrant self-definition ideally foster a dynamic interaction that permits "incorporation" rather than assimilation. Soysal utilizes the term "incorporation" rather than "assimilation" because she argues that the latter entails giving up "traditional" or "backward" values for modern (superior) ones, while the word "incorporation" recognizes how immigrants already work, live, and act in a host country, enacting multiple identities and affiliations, as well as accounting for the context of reception created by host countries.[92] Viewing integration as incorporation challenges conventional notions of assimilation by challenging the monolithic and coercive elements of straight-line assimilation. To Soysal, the formation of types of post-national citizenship was not purely accidental, but rooted in a greater European commitment to human rights after World War II. This dedication may have been largely formal, inadequate, or even cynical, but the result has been a deeper commitment to human rights rhetoric, a belief that integration must happen through respecting immigrant culture, and the very preliminary evidence of what Soysal thought was complete: post-national citizenship. Unfortunately, when she was writing there were significant problems with anti-immigrant racism and, shortly after the publication of her book, a significant tightening of borders in Europe and the United States in the 1990s. After September 11, many of the programs she studied lost their funding or are now considered obsolete, given the threat of terrorism.[93]

Thus Soysal's optimism must be tempered. Saskia Sassen's work focuses on many of the same power mechanisms that provide for immigrant agency, but she importantly recognizes key obstacles: workplace inequality and worker exploitation; a democratic deficit for guest workers and service workers in North America (and other areas); the gendered division of labor that increasingly makes women more invisible, even as they sustain key parts of the global economy; racism and the criminalization of poverty; and the greater polarization of wealth since key economic processes and institutions have proceeded according to neoliberal demands. Additionally, although Sassen might not put it this way, the United States in fact has drawn its borders tighter than Europe, and its leadership in the international arena can be characterized as having imperial pretensions, seeking the breakdown of *other* polities' borders but not its own. And significantly, the U.S. guest-worker program has never allowed for the political freedoms that were eventually afforded such workers in Europe by the 1970s and 1980s.[94] Finally, although the Obama administration has begun to dismantle key provisions from the war on terror (e.g., certain torture methods or the continued use of the Guantánamo detention center), the war on drugs and the economic crisis will continue the symbiotic relationship between prerogative power and other forms of sovereign power and global capital.[95] Current refugee policy and practices reflect the worst of these realities.

In sum, Soysal provides crucial examples of how human rights norms are necessarily being implemented to provide political status for groups that are increasingly transnational, but Sassen reminds us of the very real obstacles that block political action, from worker exploitation to the privileging of corporate interests to service agreements that effectively make participants stateless. On the one hand, Soysal, along with others like David Held, David Beetham, and Pierre Hassner, reminds us that cosmopolitan practices, institutions, and political activity have increased in the past few decades. Thus cosmopolitanism is not a future project that needs to be artificially imposed on an extant system.[96] On the other hand, Sassen's work illustrates the complexity of achieving democratic aims, even if the need for democratic political activity is urgent.

Hybridity?

As I suggested above, one way to envision this sort of politics is to look at hybrid forms of political identification, speech, and relationships. The notion of hybridity does not directly confront stereotypes about immigrants, but the practice of hybridity challenges the monolithic treatment of immigrant groups and serves as an example of agonistic democracy that can undermine the predominance of the deployment of state sovereignty domestically. The concept of hybridity has been mocked by authors from Zygmunt Bauman[97] to Hardt and Negri[98] as a construct imagined by elite academics and having no bearing on "reality." In fact, their mockery echoes Samuel Huntington's and Francis Fukuyama's critiques of multiculturalism as the promotion of unrealistic, unassimilable values by elites who are out of touch with the true nature of everyday life.[99] Nevertheless, to draw on an older example, the historical development and usage of the word "Chicana/o" shows a different trajectory, as Gloria Anzaldúa has argued.[100]

Chicana/o importantly demonstrates the mixture of American and Mexican identity into a new political and cultural reality: one that combines languages, for example, but also creates new words and new forms of self-expression. To Anzaldúa, the expression of Chicana/o identity is a language of rebellion against homogenizing terms like "Hispanic" and the assertion of a self-created status.[101] Operating on the level of language is not an elite exercise, but rather reflects the painful realities of being forced to speak English in schools and in work settings, of having Tex-Mex versions of Spanish denigrated both by some Mexicans and many Americans. Nevertheless, the word also has political and geographical connotations. First, as Anzaldúa argues, this is a politics that remains on the border and is inhabited by individuals who refuse to conform to various norms imposed by either their traditional cultures or their "host" country.[102] Attention to the border brings the focus on territory that was originally inhabited by "Chicanos' ancient Indian ancestors."[103] In this way, to claim a border culture and call oneself Chicana/o is to affirm a historical legacy. Mexicans cannot be "invaders" or simply be viewed as coming to the United States due to individual volition; rather, the history of bordering states and Mexican American relations demonstrates a more complex power dynamic that cannot be reduced to individual, rational choice. Indeed, it is precisely the memory of what Mexicans once had here (or the idea that the United States gradually encroached on Mexican territory) that threatens authors like Samuel Huntington so much, as he argues that this legacy makes Mexican immigrants exceptional in comparison to all other immigrants *and* potentially threatening to core U.S. values. Simultaneously recognizing that Mexican culture and American culture have informed one another, he splits (in the Freudian sense) the Mexican from the American, positing the Mexican as all that is bad and the American as all that is good.

But the act of asserting a hybrid identity does not allow for this either/or binary. As Anzaldúa contends, the reality of Mexican immigrants' lives in the United States is the creation of new identities that defy and challenge any cultural, political, or economic hierarchies. Authors, policy makers, and vigilante groups formulate the border as a "war zone" but don't recognize that "the convergence has created a shock culture, a border culture, a third country."[104] Anzaldúa is not relying on the experiences of an elite academic to make these arguments, but rather her experience of the reality of crossing the border, attending public schools in the Southwest, and watching the INS detain a family member.[105] Inverting the dominant paradigm of unauthorized immigrants as being inherently criminal and stealing "our" jobs, she calls them "refugees in a homeland that does not want them."[106]

As I have argued with Agamben, the stateless and refugees must become the model for a new citizenship that works in between and around borders, and which challenges the logic of bio-power.[107] By invoking and acting out a politics that contests dominant paradigms *and* which undermines sovereign power (including illegal crossings),[108] the assertion of Chicano/a politics points the way toward post-national citizenship. It suggests a political identity and movement based on multiple loyalties and the beginning of political action by the agents who need it most.

Although the current political climate is changing, immigration will remain a heated subject until the broader processes I have traced are challenged. In addition to arguing for cosmopolitan politics, I have made the case throughout this book why national immigration policy must also change. Matters of immigration straddle many borders—including academic disciplines, policy, and territory—and thus occupy an undecidable conceptual space. Nevertheless, it is clearly unjust to subject a considerable proportion of a population to undemocratic practices and expectations. Matters of immigration cannot be divorced from the status of democracy—they are inextricably tied to how individuals and groups act politically. Klaus Bade has argued that immigration policy does not just serve the purpose of shaping who enters a country or how, but also regulates the relationship between a state and resident foreigners.[109] It is this relationship that should be held to the same democratic standards as all others. It is easy enough to state that the border fence must be ripped down, the guest-worker program dismantled immediately, detention centers shut down, and mass deportation ended, and to argue that no individuals should ever be barred from political action, even if by "consent." In this book I have provided reasons why these arrangements should change and why these changes are urgent. The crucial but necessary challenge is to work together to tackle these problems on every level, placing democratic agency and processes above economic profit and law-and-order policies. It is time to act.

Notes

Introduction

1. Despite this attention, there was a noticeable silence on the immigration issue after the candidates for president were nominated in 2008. I believe this is because Senators Obama and McCain had sponsored the Secure America and Orderly Immigration Act of 2006 and therefore were too similar on this issue to give fodder to an increasingly divisive campaign.

2. As one fact sheet on immigration states, "It is obvious there is no more defining issue in our Nation today than stopping illegal immigration. The most basic obligation of any government is to secure the Nation's borders." "Dianne Feinstein on Immigration," *On the Issues*, July 8, 2008, accessed October 6, 2008, http://www.ontheissues.org/International/Dianne_Feinstein_Immigration.htm. See also Editorial, "The Nativists Are Restless," *New York Times*, February 1, 2009.

3. See Mae M. Ngai, "No Human Being Is Illegal," *Women's Studies Quarterly* 34, nos. 3/4 (Fall/Winter 2006): 291–95.

4. Associated Press, "Feds Deny Protests Affected Immigration Arrests," MSNBC.com, June 23, 2007, http://www.msnbc.msn.com/id/19389988/print/1/displaymode/1098: "During the height of the 2006 immigration debate, from April through June, the number of arrests jumped to 4,516. That was more than double the 2,234 arrests for the same period of 2005."

5. Associated Press, "Border Patrol Swells to More Than 18,000," National Border Patrol Council, December 4, 2008, http://www.nbpc.net/index.php?option=com_content&task=view&id=181&Itemid=57; Kevin R. Johnson, "The Forgotten 'Repatriation' of Persons of Mexican Ancestry and Lessons for the 'War on Terror,'" *Pace Law Review* 26, no. 1 (Fall 2005): 17.

6. Jim Salter, "Amendment Would Require English," *Belleville News-Democrat*, October 3, 2008.

7. See Karen Lee Ziner, "Governor's Advisory Panel to Report on Concerns of Immigrants," *Providence Journal*, October 5, 2008; Mark Hemingway, "SAVE-ing Immigration Reform," *National Review*, March 14, 2008; Gregg Krupa, "Metro Detroit Area Deportations Climb 45 Percent in One Year," *Detroit News*, December 4, 2008. President Obama has expanded the deportation program.

8. See Alejandro Portes and Rubén G. Rumbaut, *Immigrant America: A Portrait*, 3rd ed. (Berkeley: University of California Press, 2006), esp. 34–36, 371–72. I discuss this backlash in the next chapter.

9. This is true even as the language of war is receding under the Obama administration.

10. See Cheryl Shanks's intellectual history of debates preceding the 1965 Immigration Act and those leading up to the 1986 Immigration Reform and Control Act (IRCA):

Immigration and Politics of American Sovereignty, 1890–1990 (Ann Arbor: University of Michigan Press, 2001).

11. On the use of the terms "illegal" and "unauthorized," please see Mae M. Ngai, *Impossible Subjects: Illegal Aliens and the Making of Modern America* (Princeton: Princeton University Press, 2004), xix, xx. Both are highly inaccurate (not to mention derogatory in the first case), and I use them only for the sake of convenience.

12. This was known as the Sensenbrenner Bill (H.R. 4437) or, more formally, the Border Protection, Antiterrorism, and Illegal Immigration Control Act of 2005.

13. See Richard Vogel on the various proposals for a guest-worker scheme proposed in 2006: "Transient Servitude: The U.S. Guest Worker Program for Exploiting Mexican and Central American Workers," *Monthly Review*, January 2007.

14. Subsequently a proposal in May 2007 combined the worst of these proposals, making political and economic conditions harder for poorer immigrants and easier for elite foreigners. Similar measures have since been proposed, but nothing has been passed.

15. Statement of Dr. Erik Camayd-Freixas, U.S. District Court for the Northern District of Iowa, regarding a hearing on "the Arrest, Prosecution, and Conviction of 297 Undocumented Workers in Postville, Iowa, from May 12 to 22, 2008," Subcommittee on Immigration, Citizenship, Refugees, Border Security, and International Law, July 24, 2008, accessed January 11, 2009, http://judiciary.house.gov/hearings/pdf/Camayd-Freixas080724.pdf. It is important to note that Camayd-Freixas believes that Mexicans are a proxy for real terrorists, and thus he charges that the arrests have been executed cynically. In other parts of this book, I cite public figures who honestly appear to believe that Mexicans themselves are security threats. Like during the Cold War, the construction of a prototypical enemy is most likely a mix of both approaches.

16. This is not to argue that there is only one sort of foreigner that should be the focus of analyzing anti-immigration efforts. First, other groups are also the targets of these efforts. Second, in time, Mexicans will no longer be a controversial group; another group with similar characteristics will be.

17. On the treatment of the Irish, see relevant passages in James M. McPherson, *Battle Cry of Freedom: The Civil War Era*, Oxford History of the United States (New York: Oxford University Press, 2003).

18. See Johnson, "Forgotten 'Repatriation,'" 21–23; Daniel Kanstroom, *Deportation Nation: Outsiders in American History* (Cambridge: Harvard University Press, 2007).

19. Nevertheless, the dynamics of the period now called the first Red Scare (during the interwar period) and the second Red Scare did lead to shocking numbers of deportations and highly exclusive political practices. But the border itself was not necessarily an instrument of control then in the way it is today. Second, despite important similarities, I believe the wars on terror and drugs, combined with neoliberalism, do lead to a different contemporary context. With regard to these historical eras, see "Statement by Emma Goldman at the Federal Hearing in re Deportation, October 27, 1919, Emma Goldman Papers, Berkeley Digital Library, accessed December 2, 2010, http://sunsite.berkeley.edu/Goldman/Exhibition/plea.html; Gardner Jackson, "Doak the Deportation Chief," *The Nation*, March 18, 1931; Reuben Oppenheimer, "The Deportation Terror," *New Republic*, January 13, 1932.

20. See Peter Andreas, *Border Games: Policing the U.S.-Mexico Divide* (Ithaca: Cornell University Press, 2000).

21. From this time period, see Saskia Sassen, *Globalization and Its Discontents: Essays on the New Mobility of People and Money* (New York: New Press, 1998); Yasemin Soysal, *Limits of Citizenship: Migrants and Postnational Membership in Europe* (Chicago: University of Chicago Press, 1994); Peter Skerry, *Mexican Americans: The Ambivalent Minority* (Cambridge: Harvard University Press, 1993); Dowell Myers, "The Changing Immigrants of Southern California"

(Research Report LCRI-95-04R, University of Southern California School of Urban and Regional Planning, Los Angeles, October 25, 1995); Alejandro Portes and Rubén G. Rumbaut, *Immigrant America: A Portrait*, 2nd ed. (Berkeley: University of California Press, 1996); Peter Brimelow, *Alien Nation: Common Sense About America's Immigration Disaster* (New York: Random House, 1995); Nicolaus Mills, ed., *Arguing Immigration: The Debate over the Changing Face of America* (New York: Simon and Schuster, 1994).

22. See Linda Bosniak, "The Citizenship of Aliens," *Social Text* 56 (Autumn 1998): 29–35.

23. See Samuel Huntington's "The Hispanic Challenge," *Foreign Policy*, March/April 2004; and *Who Are We? The Challenge to America's National Identity* (New York: Simon and Schuster, 2004).

24. Like treatments of homelessness and the homeless, political scientific analyses of immigration often tend to focus on individual immigrants, ignoring the context of reception, the effects of the market as they interact with increasingly strict immigration laws, and the political dynamics of discourses that depoliticize immigrants' current situation.

25. Susan Eckstein, "Cuban Émigrés and the American Dream," *Perspectives on Politics* 4, no. 2 (July 2006): 298.

26. See Jack Citrin, Amy Lerman, Michael Murukami, and Kathryn Pearson, "Testing Huntington: Is Hispanic Immigration a Threat to American Identity?," *Perspectives on Politics* 5, no. 1 (March 2007): 31–48. Although some notable scholars in the fields of sociology and geography have more complex accounts of these notions, it is significant that the field of political science has more conventional, simplistic notions of the immigration process.

27. Bonnie Honig, *Democracy and the Foreigner* (Princeton: Princeton University Press, 2001); Sassen, *Globalization and Its Discontents*; Soysal, *Limits of Citizenship*.

28. This is not to say that individual analyses are worthless; in fact, quite the opposite. Ethnographic work and sociological investigations of "subjectivity," for example, provide important insights into the immigrant experience. Without these, most theories would have no ties to reality. See Rhacel Salazar Parreñas's discussion of these approaches in *Servants of Globalization: Women, Migration, and Domestic Work* (Stanford: Stanford University Press, 2001).

29. I explore this connection in *America's New Working Class: Race, Gender, and Ethnicity in a Biopolitical Age* (University Park: Penn State Press, 2008).

30. In the next chapter, I discuss the conservative work of authors like George Borjas, but also mainstream accounts of authors like Rogers Brubaker, Richard Alba, and Victor Nee to examine how they often perpetuate these categories even as they seek to challenge their substance.

31. See, for example, Thomas Friedman's arguments in *The Lexus and the Olive Tree: Understanding Globalization* (New York: Anchor Books, 2000) or, from the other side of the political spectrum, Zygmunt Bauman, *Globalization: The Human Consequences* (New York: Columbia University Press, 1998).

32. This language of the loss of control is evident in Patrick Buchanan, *State of Emergency: The Third World Invasion and Conquest of America* (New York: St. Martin's Press, 2006). Peter Andreas aptly challenges this rhetoric (and its symbolism) in *Border Games*. For dramatic examples of the degree to which the deportation and detention systems (a) affect a significant number of immigrants and (b) operate outside not only the boundaries of citizenship but also even the most minimal human rights norms, see Mark Dow, *American Gulag: Inside U.S. Immigration Prisons* (Berkeley: University of California Press, 2004); Kanstroom, *Deportation Nation*; Johnson, "Forgotten 'Repatriation.'"

33. I discuss this term at length in chapter 2 of *America's New Working Class* and also in an earlier version of the chapter, published as "Domestic War: Locke's Concept of Prerogative and Implications for U.S. 'Wars' Today," *Polity* 39, no. 1 (January 2007): 1–28.

34. And, of course, the state itself is a site of contestation, as the political theorist Jacqueline Stevens has recently reminded me in private correspondence.

35. See Buchanan, *State of Emergency*, for a not particularly subtle argument that Mexicans and other "Third World" immigrants are invading the United States and that immigration must be stopped.

36. On these processes, see Michael Peter Smith's recent work, such as "The Two Faces of Transnational Citizenship," *Ethnic and Racial Studies* 30, no. 6 (November 2007): 1096–1116; see also Kevin R. Johnson, "'Melting Pot' or 'Ring of Fire'? Assimilation and the Mexican-American Experience," *California Law Review* 85, no. 5 (October 1997): 1259–1313.

37. See Saskia Sassen, "Bits of a New Immigration Reality: A Bad Fit with Current Policy," *Border Battles: The U.S. Immigration Debates*, July 28, 2006, accessed August 1, 2009, http://borderbattles.ssrc.org/Sassen/.

38. Parreñas, *Servants of Globalization*, 80.

39. Ibid., 108. Saskia Sassen discusses how immigration law targets the individual immigrant at the border, ignoring community, family, and migrant networks that build linkages to host countries. See *Globalization and Its Discontents*. Others have also criticized U.S. policy for its individualistic implementation of immigration policies that ends up dividing families.

40. William Adler, *Mollie's Job: A Story of Life and Work on the Global Assembly Line* (New York: Scribner, 2000), 215.

41. See Gloria Anzaldúa, *Borderlands: The New Mestiza/La Frontera* (San Francisco: Aunt Lute Books, 1999).

42. See, for example, Michael Peter Smith, "Can You Imagine? Transnational Migration and the Globalization of Grassroots Politics," *Social Text* 39 (Summer 1994): 15–33.

43. See Joseph Nevins, *Operation Gatekeeper: The Rise of the "Illegal Alien" and the Making of the U.S.-Mexico Boundary* (New York: Routledge, 2002) on the recent historical roots of this relationship.

44. Contrary to other political thinkers, I hold that Foucault's notion of disciplinary power is compatible with Giorgio Agamben's concept of bare life. On the relationship between these two concepts, see Giorgio Agamben, *Homo Sacer: Sovereign Power and Bare Life*, trans. Daniel Heller-Roazen (Stanford: Stanford University Press, 1998), 3, 119, 120; and see Foucault's discussion of disciplinary power and bio-power in *The History of Sexuality*, vol. 1, *An Introduction*, trans. Robert Hurley (New York: Vintage, 1980), 139. According to Foucault, these two forms of power are "not antithetical" but are "two poles of development."

45. *History of Sexuality*, vol. 1, is the main text in which Foucault explicates his notion of bio-power. Significantly, these two theories illuminate the connection between super-exploitation and the treatment of the new working class bio-politically and as bare life.

46. *Discipline and Punish* is the main text in which Foucault introduces the concept of disciplinary power. *Discipline and Punish*, trans. Alan Sheridan (New York: Vintage, 1979).

47. Foucault, *History of Sexuality*, 1:139.

48. Ibid.

49. See Bauman, *Globalization*.

50. See also Roxanne Doty, *Anti-immigrantism in Western Democracies: Statecraft, Desire, and the Politics of Exclusion* (New York: Routledge, 2003).

51. On anchor babies, see Buchanan, *State of Emergency*, 258–60.

52. Agamben, *Homo Sacer*.

53. See Hannah Arendt, *The Origins of Totalitarianism* (New York: Harcourt Brace Jovanovich, 1979).

54. I am referring to the repatriation drive of 1930 in which the U.S. government forcibly removed approximately one million people of Mexican descent, about 60 percent of whom were U.S. citizens, and to Operation Wetback in the 1950s. See Johnson, "Forgotten 'Repatriation.'"

55. I want to thank one of my anonymous reviewers who subsequently identified himself—James Martel of San Francisco State University—for pushing me to define the term "bare life" further and suggesting instead "undecidable life."

56. For criticisms, see Jacqueline Stevens's blog *States Without Nations*, http://stateswithoutnations.blogspot.com/; Anna Marie Smith, *Welfare Reform and Sexual Regulation* (New York: Cambridge University Press, 2007); and, to a lesser extent, Andrew Norris, "The Exemplary Exception: Philosophical and Political Decisions in Giorgio Agamben's *Homo Sacer*," *Radical Philosophy*, May/June 2003. For an excellent critique of these criticisms, see James Martel, "Can We Do Away with Sacrifice?," *Political Theory* 34, no. 6 (December 2006): 814–20.

57. To put it differently, Agamben wants to show that Nazism was not outside the Western tradition but a dangerous manifestation of the unity of bio-power and sovereignty in a Western democracy.

58. As I discuss in chapter 4, the use of prerogative power does not therefore mean an absence of law, but rather the institution—by decree, for example—of regulations, procedures, or laws that make their subjects politically inferior in important respects (such as the right to sustain one's life). The legal situation of the prisoners at Guantánamo Bay during George W. Bush's administration is an example of this. In making this argument, I am disagreeing with Nasser Hussain, "Beyond Norm and Exception: Guantánamo," *Critical Inquiry* 33, no. 4 (Summer 2007): 734–53; see Jacques Rancière, "Who Is the Subject of the Rights of Man?," *South Atlantic Quarterly* 103, no. 2/3 (Spring/Summer 2004): 297–312.

59. As Saskia Sassen has put it. See *Globalization and Its Discontents*.

60. See Linda Bosniak, *The Citizen and the Alien* (Princeton: Princeton University Press, 2006), 100; on the detention-deportation system, see Dow, *American Gulag*; Mark Dow, "A Response to David Mikhail's *Sleepwalker*," *Boston Review*, March 16, 2009; Associated Press, "Report to Blast Conditions at Georgia Detention Center," WTVM.com, April 10, 2009, accessed April 10, 2009, http://www.wtvm.com/Global/story.asp?S=10162792; Arthur H. Rotstein, "Study: Female Immigrant Detainees Get Poor Care," *Arizona Republic*, January 14, 2009; Editorial, "The Shame of Postville, Iowa," *New York Times*, July 13, 2008; Nina Bernstein, "Punishment over a Detainee's Death," *New York Times*, January 10, 2009; Statement of Dr. Erik Camayd-Freixas (see introd., n. 15).

61. Agamben, *Homo Sacer*, 110.

62. Ngai, "No Human Being Is Illegal," 293; see Bosniak's discussion of plenary power in "Citizenship of Aliens," and also Bosniak *The Citizen and the Alien*, 50–51, 53.

63. On the other hand, I do *not* argue that this term can be used loosely: the fact that individuals subject to prerogative power had an undecidable political status is one necessary component in defining this power dynamic. Thus I do not believe that there are a "thousand sovereigns," nor do I argue that, for example, the police exercise prerogative power per se. The political powers of those wielding power must also be considered.

64. Doty similarly argues that "this phenomenon [anti-immigrant vigilantism] shifts our attention from 'the state' and sovereignty narrowly conceived to more nebulous realms where the sensibilities, ideologies, desires, and numerous other forces that constitute 'statecraft from below' are played out." "States of Exception on the Mexico-U.S. Border: Security, 'Decisions,' and Civilian Border Patrols," *International Political Sociology* 1, no. 1 (June 2007): 118.

65. I discuss prerogative power and my particular uses of Agamben and Foucault in much more detail in *America's New Working Class*.

66. The use of the term *différance* refers to the work of Jean-François Lyotard and Jacques Derrida, who argued that difference (or otherness or alterity) should not simply be interpreted as the opposite of mainstream or normal, but as something entirely new and undecidable.

67. As I discuss in the next chapter, Alba and Nee also fall into a sort of trap by revising the canonical model but still reinscribing its basic categories. See Richard Alba and Victor

Nee, "Rethinking Assimilation Theory for a New Era of Immigration," *International Migration Review* 31, no. 4 (Winter 1997): 826–74.

68. See Huntington, "Hispanic Challenge."

69. On the predominance of the economic viewpoint, see Sassen, *Globalization and Its Discontents*, 31. Ironically, Patrick Buchanan makes a similar argument, claiming that the majority of pro-immigrant advocates (like George W. Bush) are part of a "cult of economism." See Buchanan, *State of Emergency*, 74.

70. See Soysal's discussion *Limits of Citizenship*, introd. and chap. 3, esp. pp. 29–31; Sassen, *Globalization and Its Discontents*, introd., chaps. 2 and 6; Parreñas, "Introduction: Migrant Filipina Domestic Workers in Rome and Los Angeles," in *Servants of Globalization*, 1–22.

71. See Jacqueline Stevens's discussion of the paucity of theoretical analyses on the role of the nation-state in *Reproducing the State* (Princeton: Princeton University Press, 1999).

72. Bosniak, *The Citizen and the Alien*, 6.

73. For example, see Parreñas's discussion of integration in the introduction to *Servants of Globalization* or Soysal's notion of integration (versus assimilation) in *Limits of Citizenship*.

74. See Perry Bacon Jr., "Are the Immigration Protests Creating a Backlash?," *Time*, March 29, 2006; "Thousands March for Immigrant Rights," CNN.com, May 1, 2006, http://articles.cnn.com/2006-05-01/us/immigrant.day_1_thousands-march-largest-protests-immigration-laws?_s=PM:US; Doug Hagin, "The Ugly Truth About Illegal Immigration Protests," *RenewAmerica*, April 3, 2006, http://www.renewamerica.us/columns/hagin/060403; "Illegal-Alien Advocates Play Down Mexican Flag," *World Net Daily*, April 10, 2006, http://www.wnd.com/?pageId=35649. More recently, protesters have advocated for the DREAM Act (which was defeated on December 18, 2010) and challenged the constitutionality of harsh immigration measures in Arizona.

75. See Hagin, "Ugly Truth," among others.

76. *POV: Farmingville*, directed by Carlos Sandoval and Catherine Tambini (New York: New Video Group, 2004), DVD; Leo R. Chavez, "A Glass Half Empty: Latina Reproduction and Public Discourse," *Human Organization* 63, no. 2 (Summer 2004): 173–88.

77. This is true because their views can be linked directly to the debates of 2006–8. Thus, even though their numbers may be fairly low, their views and physical presence in key areas throughout the country serve an important symbolic function.

78. See Adler, *Mollie's Job*; Amnesty International, "Mexico: Intolerable Killings: Ten Years of Abductions and Murders in Ciudad Juárez and Chihuahua" (AMR 41/026/2003, Amnesty International, London, August 9, 2003); Paul Cooney, "The Mexican Crisis and the Maquiladora Boom: A Paradox of Development or the Logic of Neoliberalism?," *Latin American Perspectives* 28, no. 3 (May 2001): 55–83; Leslie Salzinger, "From High Heels to Swathed Bodies: Gendered Meanings under Production in Mexico's Export-Processing Industry," *Feminist Studies* 23, no. 3 (Autumn 1997): 549–74; Vogel, "Transient Servitude"; Melissa Wright, "*Maquiladora* Mestizas and a Feminist Border Politics: Revisiting Anzaldúa," *Hypatia* 13, no. 3 (Summer 1998): 114–31; Barry Yeoman, "Silence in the Fields," *Mother Jones*, January/February 2001; Joy Zarempka, "Modern Slavery: Abuse of Domestic Workers," *Off Our Backs* 30, no. 7 (July 2000): 12; Verónica Zebadúa-Yañez, "Killing as Performance: Violence and the Shaping of Community," *e-misférica* 2, no. 2 (Fall 2005), http://hemi.nyu.edu/journal/2_2/pdf/zebadua.pdf.

79. For example, see Lornet Turnbull, "New State Import: Thai Farmworkers," *Seattle Times*, February 20, 2005.

80. See Sassen, *Globalization and Its Discontents*, 156.

81. This is true even if unauthorized immigrants are freer in many respects. Unlike guest workers, they must constantly face the threat of deportation and this ensures similar work conditions, even if the unauthorized immigrant is technically free to change employers. See Abel Valenzuela, "Working on the Margins: Immigrant Day Labor Characteristics

and Prospects for Employment" (Working Paper 22, Center for Comparative Immigration Studies, University of California, San Diego, May 2000); Parreñas, *Servants of Globalization*; Pierrette Hondagneu-Sotelo, *Doméstica: Immigrant Workers Cleaning and Caring in the Shadow of Affluence* (Berkeley: University of California Press, 2001).

82. See William P. Simmons, "Remedies for the Women of Ciudad Juárez Through the Inter-American Court of Human Rights," *Northwestern University Journal of International Human Rights* 4, no. 3 (2006): 492–517. The suit has now been dropped.

83. Giorgio Agamben, "We Refugees," trans. Michael Rocke, *Symposium* 49, no. 2 (1995): 114–19.

84. Regarding the term "articulation," see Chantal Mouffe, "Feminism, Citizenship, and Radical Democratic Politics," in *Feminist Social Thought: A Reader*, ed. Diana Tietjens Meyers (New York: Routledge, 1997), 532–46.

Chapter 1

1. See Portes and Rumbaut, *Immigrant America*, 2nd ed., 6–7, 269–300, for a discussion of conventional views of assimilation; in the third edition, see pp. 34–36, 346–51.

2. See Soysal, *Limits of Citizenship*, and Sassen, *Globalization and Its Discontents*. See also Parreñas, *Servants of Globalization*, introd. There are several other notable authors (many whom I cite in this book) who see the limits of the nation-state in determining assimilation norms and who truly challenge the canonical model, but my point is that these voices are not supported by *conventional* norms of assimilation in the broader public and thus remain well-known only among academics.

3. Soysal argues that rather than looking at formal notions of citizenship or assimilation, the informal incorporation in Europe of immigrants into educational systems, welfare institutions, unions, and politics is evidence of a new, post-national form of citizenship. See *Limits of Citizenship*, chap. 1. Sassen also complicates the presuppositions of assimilation and would mostly likely concur with Soysal's concept of integration, though perhaps not her conclusions. See Sassen, *Globalization and Its Discontents*.

4. Sassen recognizes this more than Soysal. See Sassen, *Globalization and Its Discontents*, and Soysal, *Limits of Citizenship*.

5. Rogers Brubaker, "The Return of Assimilation," *Ethnic and Racial Studies* 24, no. 4 (July 2001): 531–48; see Russell A. Kazal, "Revisiting Assimilation: The Rise, Fall, and Reappraisal of a Concept in American Ethnic History," *American Historical Review* 100, no. 2 (April 1995): 437–71, for a different timeline but similar argument, ending with the proclamation that the canonical (Chicago School) notion of assimilation was dead.

6. Alba and Victor, "Rethinking Assimilation Theory," 827.

7. I am obviously assuming that these authors' ideas can be taken to represent the mainstream literature on immigration and assimilation. Together with Mary Waters, George Borjas, Alejandro Portes, and Rubén Rumbaut, they are the dominant scholars in conventional literature. As stated above, authors like Saskia Sassen and Yasemin Soysal are prominent (in the sense that they receive high academic praise), but because their arguments are farther to the left politically and are less "assimilable" to public opinion, they must be considered alternative.

8. Portes and Rumbaut aptly refer to this as "forced assimilation." See *Immigrant America*, 3rd ed., conclusion.

9. Or they merely use the term superficially—for example, admitting that the United States is racist but continuing to expect immigrants to overcome this obstacle (rather than

focusing on changing the host society). This failure is the basis of Soysal's radical challenge to conventional notions of immigration. See *Limits of Citizenship*.

10. See Soysal's critique of this tendency in *Limits of Citizenship*, 4–6, 29–31, 110–18.

11. On the canonical model of assimilation, see Alba and Nee, "Rethinking Assimilation Theory." A more popularized version of many of the same conceptual categories can be found in Samuel Huntington's "Hispanic Challenge."

12. See Bonnie Honig's discussion of immigrants performing the social contract in *Democracy and the Foreigner*.

13. See, for example, Buchanan, *State of Emergency*, 5. This distinction between old and new is also found in the literature on homelessness (only with the values reversed) and serves the rhetorical function of discrediting one group and overly valuing the other, not to mention obfuscating the various contexts in which any group operates as well as the "context of reception."

14. See George J. Borjas, "Assimilation, Changes in Cohort Quality, and the Earnings of Immigrants," *Journal of Labor Economics* 3, no. 4 (1985): 463–89.

15. On human capital immigrants, see Alba and Nee, "Rethinking Assimilation Theory"; see also Borjas, "Assimilation, Changes in Cohort Quality, and the Earnings of Immigrants"; Portes and Rumbaut, *Immigrant America*, 3rd ed., 67–76. With regard to broader criticisms of "labor" immigrants and calls to stop their entry, see Huntington, "Hispanic Challenge," and the last round of immigration proposals in 2006/7 that called for a point system rewarding education and skills, much like the one in the United Kingdom.

16. See Brubaker, "Return of Assimilation," 541.

17. See Sassen, *Globalization and Its Discontents*, chap. 3.

18. For example, see Portes and Rumbaut, *Immigrant America*, 3rd ed., chap. 2; see also Pierrette Hondagneu-Sotelo, "Feminism and Migration," *Annals of the American Academy of Political and Social Science* 571, no. 1 (September 2000): 107–20, who claims that the primary type of migration in the twentieth century has been "labor migration"; and Honig's critique of this in *Democracy and the Foreigner*, chap. 4.

19. As Cheryl Shanks notes, this is truer today than in the past; with the end of the Cold War and the growing predominance of neoliberal values and policies, immigrants have been increasingly considered in economic terms—as factors of production—and in turn, economic logic has increasingly informed sovereign decision making. See *Immigration and Politics of American Sovereignty*.

20. Wealthier Arab Americans are obviously anomalies in this historical trend.

21. Arendt, *Origins of Totalitarianism*, chap. 9. Although her arguments about the Israeli-Palestinian issue challenge the idea of nation-states solving the problem of homelessness/ statelessness, she implies that the democratic territorial state (minus the nation) could ameliorate the conditions of statelessness. See James D. Ingram, "What Is a 'Right to Have Rights'? Three Images of the Politics of Human Rights," *American Political Science Review* 102, no. 4 (November 2008): 401–16, for an excellent contemporary discussion of interpretations of Arendt's politics and solutions to human rights issues.

22. See Alba and Nee, "Rethinking Assimilation Theory."

23. See ibid.; Brubaker, "Return of Assimilation"; and Alba in E. J. Graff, "Crossing Borders," *Radcliffe Quarterly*, Summer 2004; many of Alba's statements in Graff's article are unsubstantiated—including the idea that the French are more religious than Americans, that France has not been a country of immigration, and that the United States has never had a core identity.

24. Alba and Nee, "Rethinking Assimilation Theory," 835.

25. Brubaker, "Return of Assimilation," 543.

26. Borjas, "Assimilation, Changes in Cohort Quality, and the Earnings of Immigrants."

27. See, for example, Robert Kuttner, "Illegal Immigration: Would a National ID Card Help?," in Mills, *Arguing Immigration*, 82–84.

28. I explore these issues in *America's New Working Class*.

29. See Brubaker, "Return of Assimilation," 543; Alba and Nee, "Rethinking Assimilation Theory," 835–36.

30. Portes and Rumbaut, *Immigrant America*, 2nd and 3rd eds.

31. The assessment of skill levels must be viewed not as a fixed economic matter but rather as a political one—the charge of a group being low skilled often reflects matters of degrees rather than absolute differences, and it has been used to justify lower wages and less seniority for women, African Americans, and controversial immigrant groups. I discuss this in *America's New Working Class*, chaps. 4, 5; see also, among others, Jacqueline Jones, *American Work: Four Centuries of Black and White Labor* (New York: Norton, 1998); William Julius Wilson, *When Work Disappears: The World of the New Urban Poor* (New York: Vintage, 1997); Kathleen Paul, *Whitewashing Britain: Race and Citizenship in the Postwar Era* (Ithaca: Cornell University Press, 1997); Edna Bonacich, "A Theory of Ethnic Antagonism: The Split Labor Market," *American Sociological Review* 37, no. 5 (October 1972): 552.

32. I argue this point in *America's New Working Class*.

33. Further, because citizenship law and global dynamics have been analyzed in male terms, Sassen has remarked that women immigrants will never emerge as a "labor aristocracy" or be fully included as citizens. Recognizing that neoliberal policies and nation-state citizenship are at odds, she hopes that women immigrants will instead act as political agents in the international arena. See *Globalization and Its Discontents*, chap. 5.

34. See, for example, Patricia Williams, *Alchemy of Race and Rights: Diary of a Law Professor* (Cambridge: Harvard University Press, 1992); Wendy Brown, *States of Injury: Power and Freedom in Late Modernity* (Princeton: Princeton University Press, 1995).

35. Something authors like Brubaker, Alba, and Nee think is unjust and no longer prevalent.

36. See Adler, *Mollie's Job*.

37. This argument is at the heart of Sassen's work; see *Globalization and Its Discontents*, chap. 3.

38. As Kimberlé Crenshaw and, more recently, Ange Marie Hancock might argue. See Crenshaw, "Mapping the Margins: Intersectionality, Identity, Politics, and Violence Against Women of Color," *Stanford Law Review* 43, no. 6 (1991): 1242–65; Hancock, "When Multiplication Doesn't Equal Quick Addition: Examining Intersectionality as a Research Paradigm," *Perspectives on Politics* 5, no. 1 (March 2007): 63–79.

39. See Linda Bosniak, "'Nativism' the Concept, Some Reflections," in *Immigrants Out! The New Nativism and the Anti-immigrant Impulse in the United States*, ed. Juan F. Perea (New York: New York University Press, 1997), 288: "What I wish to emphasize about the debate over costs is its unspoken normative backdrop: it presumes that determining who is right in empirical terms on the cost question is dispositive of the immigration policy issue. It presumes, in other words, that if immigrants could somehow be definitively determined to cost more than they contribute, then restrictionists' efforts to curtail immigration would be basically unassailable on normative grounds."

40. For a critique of the T. H. Marshall–type of argument that welfare is the "teleological completion of the liberal state," see Sheldon Wolin, "Democracy and the Welfare State: The Political and Theoretical Connections between *Staatsräson* and *Wohlfahrsstaatsräson*," in *The Presence of the Past: Essays on the State and the Constitution* (Baltimore: Johns Hopkins University Press, 1989), 151–79.

41. See Borjas, "Assimilation, Changes in Cohort Quality, and the Earnings of Immigrants"; Alba and Nee, "Rethinking Assimilation Theory."

42. See Citrin et al., "Testing Huntington"; Bacon, "Are the Immigration Protests Creating a Backlash?"; Hagin, "Ugly Truth"; "Illegal-Alien Advocates Play Down Mexican Flag" (see introd., n. 74).

43. See Sandoval and Tambini, *POV: Farmingville.*

44. See Cindy Rodriguez, "Vocal Opposition: Migrants Say Eatery Forbade Them to Use Spanish," *Boston Globe,* November 12, 2000.

45. See Huntington's suggestion in "Hispanic Challenge" that groups like LULAC (League of United Latin American Citizens) are evidence that individuals of Mexican descent are not assimilating.

46. See Doty, "States of Exception."

47. See Julia Preston, "As Immigration Plan Folded, Grass Roots Roared," *New York Times,* June 10, 2007.

48. Prime examples are Bill O'Reilly and Lou Dobbs. See Portes and Rumbaut's excellent analysis of nativism in the conclusion to *Immigrant America,* 3rd ed.

49. See Wolin, "Democracy and the Welfare State"; Carole Pateman, *Disorder of Women: Democracy, Feminism, and Political Theory* (Stanford: Stanford University Press, 1992); Arnold, *America's New Working Class.*

50. Note that this frames the issue in male terms. See Leonard Feldman on the idea of Mexicans as "substitute" soldiers (Mexicans who enter the U.S. military in exchange for citizenship papers after they have served): "The Citizen-Soldier as a Substitute Soldier: Militarism at the Intersection of Neoliberalism and Neoconservatism," in *Security Disarmed: Critical Perspectives on Gender, Race, and Militarization,* ed. Barbara Sutton, Sandra Morgen, and Julie Novkov (New Brunswick: Rutgers University Press, 2008), 198–212. See also David McLemore, "Immigrant Soldiers Serve the U.S.," *Dallas Morning News,* November 28, 2006.

51. This is most evident in the recent popularity of claims that Mexicans want to recolonize their lost territory (the movement for Aztlán), discussed by Huntington in "Hispanic Challenge," and by politicians like Tom Tancredo. On Tancredo, see Carl F. Horowitz, "Tom Tancredo's Job—Book Review: In Mortal Danger," *Social Contract Press* 17, no. 1 (Fall 2006), http://www.thesocialcontract.com/artman2/publish/tsc_17_01/tsc_17_1_horowitz_review.shtml.

52. See Anzaldúa, *Borderlands.*

53. Nicholas Xenos, "A Patria to Die For" (paper presented at the annual meeting of the International Studies Association, Toronto, April 1997), http://www.polisci.umn.edu/centers/theory/pdf/Xenos_APatriatoDieFor.pdf. Xenos is discussing debates between Richard Rorty and Martha Nussbaum, among others, but see also Michael Walzer, "The Obligation to Die for the State," in *Obligations: Essays on Disobedience, War, and Citizenship* (Cambridge: Harvard University Press, 1970), 77–98; Feldman, "The Citizen-Soldier as a Substitute Soldier."

54. Xenos, "A Patria to Die For," 2.

55. Quoted in ibid., 8.

56. Ibid., 9.

57. Ibid., 13.

58. This is not to idealize the past but to denaturalize what is now taken as fact, namely, fixed and natural borders as well as monolithic, inevitable, and natural conceptions of patriotism, democracy, and citizenship.

59. See, for example, Bonnie Honig's critique of Michael Walzer in *Democracy and the Foreigner,* 85.

60. Xenos, "A Patria to Die For," 20.

61. Ibid., 20–21.

62. Ibid., 21–23. Steven Johnston expresses a similar reservation about Seyla Benhabib's *Another Cosmopolitanism,* ed. Robert Post (New York: Oxford University Press, 2006):

see Johnston, "Benhabib's Cosmopolitan Imperative," *Theory and Event* 10, no. 3 (2007), doi:10.1353/tae.2007.0077.

63. Xenos, "A Patria to Die For," 18.

64. See Ali Behdad's *A Forgetful Nation* (Durham: Duke University Press, 2005), especially chapters 2 and 4, on the importance of national memory in the process of nation-building.

65. For example, see Rodriguez, "Vocal Opposition."

66. See Huntington's discussions of language, which conflate bilingualism with a refusal to speak English, as well as Francis Fukuyama's arguments about this subject: Huntington, "Hispanic Challenge"; Fukuyama, "Immigrants and Family Values," in Mills, *Arguing Immigration*, 156, 161, 163; Fukuyama, "Identity Crisis: Why We Shouldn't Worry About Mexican Immigration," *Slate*, June 4, 2004, http://slate.msn.com/id/2101756/.

67. For example, see Salter, "Amendment Would Require English." As of October 2008, approximately thirty states passed English-only laws that require that only English be used in government proceedings, which includes not only meetings ranging from the local to state level, but also during conference calls, Internet exchanges, and message boards.

68. Fukuyama, "Immigrants and Family Values," 167.

69. As Huntington implies in "Hispanic Challenge."

70. Robert King, "Should English Be the Law?," *Atlantic Monthly*, April 1997, 11. See also the results from the 2000 census, which states that about 92 percent of the population speak English very well: Hyon B. Shin and Rosalind Bruno, "Language Use and English-Speaking Ability" (Census 2000 Brief C2KBR-29, U.S. Census Bureau, Washington, D.C., October 2003). And see Portes and Rumbaut, *Immigrant America*, 3rd ed., chap. 2.

71. See Alba and Nee, "Rethinking Assimilation Theory," on the normal trajectory of language acquisition, which should be viewed in generational terms rather than looking at immigrants who have been here only a short period of time. Class must also be taken into account as well, as there is no federal program universally available to immigrants to learn English. Finally, age must be taken into account—younger people learn foreign languages more quickly and easily than do older people.

72. Honig, *Democracy and the Foreigner.*

73. King, "Should English Be the Law?," 12.

74. For example, as Arendt does in *Origins of Totalitarianism*, chap. 9.

75. Honig, *Democracy and the Foreigner*, chap. 3.

76. See Mary Kaldor, "Reconceptualizing Organized Violence," in *Re-imagining Political Community: Studies in Cosmopolitan Democracy*, ed. Daniele Archibugi, David Held, and Martin Köhler (Stanford: Stanford University Press, 1998), 91–110.

77. See David Held, "Democracy and Globalization," in Archibugi, Held, and Köhler, *Re-imagining Political Community*, 11–27.

78. Even if the process can be peaceful for any individual immigrant. The point is that there are significant costs if an immigrant appears to be refusing to learn English.

79. Crenshaw, "Mapping the Margins." See also Gloria Anzaldúa, "How to Tame a Wild Tongue," in *Out There: Marginalization and Contemporary Cultures*, ed. Russell Ferguson, Martha Gever, Trinh T. Minh-Ha, and Cornel West (Cambridge and New York: MIT Press and the New Museum of Contemporary Art, 1990), 203–12.

80. Authors like Pierre Hassner have explored this charge in today's context. See "Refugees: A Special Case for Cosmopolitan Citizenship?," in Archibugi, Held, and Köhler, *Re-imagining Political Community*, 273–86.

81. Portes and Rumbaut also discuss this notion and, interestingly, conceive of the additional category: context of exit. This is particularly significant in the lives of refugees fleeing violent situations. See *Immigrant America*, 3rd ed., 175–88. See also Parreñas, *Servants of Globalization*.

82. See Soysal, *Limits of Citizenship*, chap. 3, esp. pp. 29–31.

83. See ibid.; Paul, *Whitewashing Britain*.

84. For example, see Nathan Glazer, "The Closing Door," in Mills, *Arguing Immigration*, 38–41.

85. Alba and Nee, "Rethinking Assimilation Theory," 864.

86. See Kazal, "Revisiting Assimilation," on this historical trajectory.

87. I consider the consequences of September 11, 2001, and legislative action based on these events, in much more detail in *America's New Working Class*.

88. Brubaker ignores Brimelow, Glazer, and D'Souza, among others, by accounting for their critiques of ethnic identity and differentialism but not their claims that immigrants are not assimilating. See Brubaker, "Return of Assimilation."

89. On this backlash, see Portes and Rumbaut, *Immigrant America*, 2nd and 3rd eds.; Mills, "Introduction: The Era of the *Golden Venture*," in Mills, *Arguing Immigration*, 11–27; see also Hondagneu-Sotelo, "Feminism and Migration," 110–11.

90. On this hostility toward the poor, see, for example, Wolin, "Democracy and the Welfare State"; David Garland, *The Culture of Control: Crime and Social Order in Contemporary Society* (Chicago: University of Chicago Press, 2001).

91. Although, technically speaking, both "wars" began in the 1970s—but I do not think they were recognized as such, nor did they have the same impact, until the 1990s. On the increased concern about poor immigrants, questions of legality, and the quest to fortify the southern border in the 1980s and early 1990s, see Nevins, *Operation Gatekeeper*.

92. See Portes and Rumbaut, *Immigrant America*, 3rd ed., 20–22, 346–47.

93. For example, see Sassen, *Globalization and Its Discontents*, 37–49.

94. See Nevins, *Operation Gatekeeper*, on this time period.

95. Portes and Rumbaut, *Immigrant America*, 2nd ed., 278.

96. See Shanks, *Immigration and Politics of American Sovereignty*; Sassen, *Globalization and Its Discontents*.

97. Portes and Rumbaut, *Immigrant America*, 2nd ed., 279. See Robert Kuttner, "Illegal Immigration," for an argument regarding immigrants' parasitism on the United States, as well as the charge that many use false documents.

98. See Portes and Rumbaut, *Immigrant America*, 3rd ed., 280.

99. Mike Davis, *City of Quartz: Excavating the Future in Los Angeles* (New York: Vintage, 1992), 354.

100. For example, see Borjas, "Assimilation, Changes in Cohort Quality, and the Earnings of Immigrants."

101. On the backlash of the 1990s, see Hondagneu-Sotelo, "Feminism and Migration"; Hondagneu-Sotelo, *Doméstica*; Perea, *Immigrants Out!*

102. Nevins, *Operation Gatekeeper*, 2.

103. On the Arizona legislation, see Randal C. Archibald, "Arizona Enacts Stringent Law on Immigration," *New York Times*, April 23, 2010.

104. See Edward Said, "The Essential Terrorist," in *Blaming the Victims: Spurious Scholarship and the Palestinian Question*, ed. Edward Said and Christopher Hitchens (New York: Verso, 1988), 149–58, who argues that the United States had been attempting to launch some sort of war on terror since the 1970s.

105. Nancy Gertner and Daniel Kanstroom, "The Recent Spotlight on the INS Failed to Reveal Its Dark Side," *Boston Globe*, May 21, 2000.

106. See ibid.; Patrick J. McDonnell, "Judges Rule Against Indefinite INS Jailings," *Boston Globe*, July 12, 1999; Editorial, "Secret Trials in America," *Boston Globe*, December 4, 1999.

107. Dow, *American Gulag*, 9.

108. See Mills, "Introduction: The Era of the *Golden Venture*," 24; Charles A. Radin, "Fears of Deportation Bias," *Boston Globe*, June 26, 2000; Mark Babineck, "Agents Indicted in

Death of Mexican Immigrant" *Boston Globe*, September 26, 2002; Teresa Mears, "Immigrants Are Told to Pay Back Aid," *Boston Globe*, October 19, 1997; Knight-Ridder, "Case Spotlights Use of Codes to Label U.S. Visa Applicants," *Boston Globe*, June 8, 1997; David Bacon, "INS Declares War on Labor," *The Nation*, October 25, 1999; Richard Chacon, "Imprisoned by Policy, Convicts Deported by U.S. Languish in Haitian Jails," *Boston Globe*, October 19, 2000; Agnes Blum, "Helping Those Who Get One-Way Tickets to Haiti," *Boston Globe*, June 9, 2002; "Haitians Decry Unequal Treatment," *Boston Globe*, January 13, 2000.

109. For more recent examples, see Statement of Dr. Erik Camayd-Freixas (see introd., n. 15).

110. See Ngai, "No Human Being Is Illegal."

111. See Carol Swain's repeated references to illegal immigration as if it were absolutely self-evident that there is a "problem" or even a crisis. Carol Swain, introd. to *Debating Immigration*, ed. Carol Swain (New York: Cambridge University Press, 2007), 1, 3, 10, 11.

112. See, for example, Rogers Smith and Peter Schuck, *Citizenship Without Consent: Illegal Aliens in the American Policy* (New Haven: Yale University Press, 1985).

113. As Peter Francese argues, the unauthorized entrant "breeds disrespect for a law that cannot be enforced." "Aging America Needs Foreign Blood," in Mills, *Arguing Immigration*, 88.

114. Although Carol Swain appears to have some sympathy for the protesters of 2006, she also argues that the "the protesters have led to a backlash." Introd. to Swain, *Debating Immigration*, 7.

115. See Sassen, *Globalization and Its Discontents*.

116. See Doty, "States of Exception," as well as the website for the Southern Poverty Law Center, http://www.splcenter.org/.

117. For example, conservative politicians like Tom Tancredo, Jim Sensenbrenner, and Steve King.

118. Alba and Nee, "Rethinking Assimilation Theory," 836, 837.

119. See Wilson, *When Work Disappears*.

120. See Sassen, *Globalization and Its Discontents*, chaps. 7, 8.

121. See, for example, Linda Chavez, "Immigration Politics," in Mills, *Arguing Immigration*, 34.

122. Peter Schuck's arguments bridge the two, as he attributes single motherhood to Mexicans. See "Alien Rumination," *Yale Journal of Law* 105, no. 7 (May 1996): 1963–2012.

123. See Brown, *States of Injury*; Smith, *Welfare Reform and Sexual Regulation*.

124. See Smith, *Welfare Reform and Sexual Regulation*; Chavez, "Glass Half Empty." See also Pierrette Hondagneu-Sotelo's discussion of the importance of accounting for gender, reproductive practices, and challenges to gender roles in studying migration in "Feminism and Migration."

125. See, among many others, Glazer, "Closing the Door," in Mills, *Arguing Immigration*, esp. 43.

126. Laurence Auster and Nathan Glazer often invoke this idealized view of the past. See Auster, "The Forbidden Topic," in Mills, *Arguing Immigration*; Glazer, "Concluding Observations," in Swain, *Debating Immigration*. In fact, the early twentieth century up through the 1930s was a period of eugenic thinking (including racial distinctions, fears about disease, and inferences based on economic class); linguistic intolerance; anti-Semitism and anti-Catholicism; and what is now called the first Red Scare. See primary documents from this period in Kathleen R. Arnold, ed., *Anti-Immigration in the United States: A Historical Encyclopedia* (Santa Barbara, Calif.: ABC-CLIO, 2011).

127. Frank D. Bean and Gillian Stevens, "Assimilation Redux," *Contemporary Sociology* 33, no. 4 (July 2004): 406; see also Alba and Nee, "Rethinking Assimilation Theory," 846,

860; Jane Junn and Natalie Masuoka, "Asian American Identity: Shared Racial Status and Political Context," *Perspectives on Politics* 6, no. 8 (December 2008): 729–40.

128. Alba and Nee, "Rethinking Assimilation Theory," 838.

129. Peter Schuck seems to take this approach—premised on the idea that racism is largely over in the United States—in his review of Peter Brimelow's racially oriented *Alien Nation*, but Schuck himself raises the issue of race numerous times in this review, arguing that it is an important category but not explaining why. See Schuck, "Alien Rumination."

130. In another context (but relevant to this discussion), see Melissa Wright's discussion of national, gender, and class divides in "*Maquiladora* Mestizas and a Feminist Border Politics." Briefly, to succeed in a maquiladora involves repudiating all that is not only Mexican but also *mejicana* (i.e., Mexican womanhood) through dressing differently, speaking only English, and being willing to combat unionization.

131. Peter Skerry, *Mexican Americans: The Ambivalent Minority* (Cambridge: Harvard University Press, 1995).

132. Mary Waters, *Black Identities: West Indian Immigrant Dreams and American Realities* (Cambridge: Harvard University Press, 1999). See her discussion in the introduction about American versus West Indian perceptions of race and racism.

133. See Johnson, "'Melting Pot' or 'Ring of Fire'?," on passing.

134. See Sandoval and Tambini, *POV: Farmingville*, a documentary about a town that is "invaded" by Mexican and Central American immigrants; the immigrants are charged with being Peeping Toms and menaces to girls and women, among other things.

135. I discuss this at length in chapter 5 of *America's New Working Class*.

136. Portes and Rumbaut, *Immigrant America*, 3rd ed., conclusion.

137. See Deborah Solomon's interview with Huntington, "Three Cheers for Assimilation," *New York Times Magazine*, May 2, 2004, 21.

138. A problematic enough term in itself; see Portes and Rumbaut, *Immigrant America*, 2nd ed., conclusion.

139. Eckstein, "Cuban Émigrés and the American Dream," 298. Luis Fraga and Gary Segura in the same issue of *Perspectives on Politics* are the most radical of this group of authors: "Culture Clash? Contesting Notions of American Identity and the Effects of Latin American Immigration," *Perspectives on Politics* 4, no. 2 (June 2006): 279–87.

140. See Richard Alba, "Mexican Americans and the American Dream," *PS: Political Science and Politics* 4, no. 2 (June 2006): 289–96.

141. See Waters, *Black Identities*, chap. 6.

142. Bean and Stevens, "Assimilation Redux," 406.

143. Brubaker, "Return of Assimilation," 540.

144. See Alba and Nee on the straight-line account, "Rethinking Assimilation Theory," 832.

145. Simone Weil, *The Simone Weil Reader*, ed. George A. Panichas (Mt. Kisco, N.Y.: Moyer Bell, 1985).

146. Honig, *Democracy and the Foreigner*, 8; see esp. chaps. 1 and 4.

147. Ibid., 74.

148. Ibid., 70.

149. As Sassen would say in *Globalization and Its Discontents*; regarding the increasing synthesis of sovereign matters with economic ones, see Garland, *Culture of Control*; Shanks, *Immigration and Politics of American Sovereignty*; Arnold, *America's New Working Class*.

150. As Andrew Linklater puts it in "Citizenship and Sovereignty in the Post-Westphalian State," in Archibugi, Held, and Köhler, *Re-imagining Political Community*, 116.

Chapter 2

1. The internment of the Japanese occurred in a similar context and obviously had harsher repercussions. Nevertheless, there are parallels: the racialization of an ethnic group; the precariousness of naturalization; and the profiling of specific groups as outsiders while others, like Germans and German Americans, were not interned in such great numbers. See Fred Lee, "The Japanese Internment and the Racial State of Exception," *Theory and Event* 10, no. 1 (2007), doi:10.1353/tae.2007.0043.

2. Regarding policies in the 1990s that served to construct an increasingly threatening figure of the "illegal alien," see Nevins, *Operation Gatekeeper*; on today's increasing linkage between what were once ordinary matters of immigration and national security, see Johnson, "Forgotten 'Repatriation,'" 21–23.

3. See, for example, John O'Sullivan, "Tearing Up the Country," *National Review*, February 9, 2004.

4. And yet, obviously, not more restrictive in numbers. The Johnson-Reed Act of 1924 led to the lowest numbers of immigrants in U.S. history.

5. Regarding this change to "post-Clausewitzean" forms of warfare, see Kaldor, "Reconceptualizing Organized Violence."

6. Proponents of such a view include Samuel Huntington, Lawrence Auster, and the Federation for American Immigration Reform.

7. See Buchanan, *State of Emergency*, 258–60; Wright, "*Maquiladora* Mestizas and a Feminist Border Politics," 118; Robin Jacobson, "Characterizing Consent: Race, Citizenship, and the New Restrictionists," *Political Research Quarterly* 59, no. 4 (December 2006): 645–54; Associated Press, "Georgia Lawmaker Wants to End 'Birthright Citizenship,'" *Atlanta Journal Constitution*, May 25, 2009; see also popular websites' discussions of this term, including: *Wikipedia*, s.v. "Anchor Baby," accessed October 9, 2008, en.wikipedia.org/wiki/Anchor_ baby; "Anchor Babies," The American Resistance, accessed October 9, 2008, http://www.the americanresistance.com/; "Anchor Babies: Part of the Immigration-Related American Lexicon," Federation for American Immigration Reform, accessed October 9, 2008, http://www .fairus.org/; "Anchor Babies: Is Citizenship an Entitled Birthright," American Patrol, http:// www.americanpatrol.com/REFERENCE/anchorbaby_FAIR.html.

8. See Jacobson, "Characterizing Consent."

9. See Wright, "*Maquiladora* Mestizas and a Feminist Border Politics," 118.

10. This program was established in 1964, creating a free zone on the Mexican border that allowed "foreign manufacturers to assemble goods without having to abide by existing import-export duties and regulations." Adler, *Mollie's Job*, 215. Significantly, employment and factory regulations are lax in this area.

11. See Dow, *American Gulag*, 13.

12. Arendt, *Origins of Totalitarianism*, 296.

13. In the conclusion of *America's New Working Class*, I discuss and problematize this distinction.

14. See, for example, John Derbyshire, "In Defense of Racial Profiling," *National Review*, February 19, 2001.

15. See Wolin, "Democracy and the Welfare State," and my own work on prerogative power in *America's New Working Class*.

16. For example, Pierrette Hondagneu-Sotelo examines domestic workers' conditions, which are both "free" of state control (and thus workers have a measure of autonomy) and yet not regulated or protected in any way, combined with legal measures such as California Proposition 187, which would have constrained the actions and choices of these workers and their families to a great extent. See Hondagneu-Sotelo, *Doméstica*.

17. Associated Press, "Report to Blast Conditions at Georgia Detention Center"; Rotstein, "Study: Female Immigrant Detainees Get Poor Care"; Editorial, "Shame of Postville, Iowa" (see introd., n. 60); Bernstein, "Punishment over a Detainee's Death"; Statement of Dr. Erik Camayd-Freixas (see introd., n. 15); Dow, *American Gulag*; Dow, "Response to David Mikhail's *Sleepwalker*."

18. Mark Dow argues that detention of foreign entrants and the use of anti-terror charges have been firmly in place since the 1980s. See Dow's "Response to David Mikhail's *Sleepwalker*" and *American Gulag*; see also Nevins, *Operation Gatekeeper*, 142.

19. Arnold, *America's New Working Class*, conclusion; see also Johnson, "Forgotten 'Repatriation,'" 22: "Recent years have seen record levels of deportations, with 80–90 percent of those deported from Mexico and Central America, for immigration violations wholly unrelated to terrorism."

20. Statement of Dr. Erik Camayd-Freixas, 16 (see introd., n. 15).

21. Dow, *American Gulag*, 13. He argues that "this 'failure' was the result of calculated political rhetoric, and the verbal and physical abuse of detainees must be viewed as the predictable enactment of such rhetoric by those charged with the day-to-day custody of the prisoners."

22. Although it is beyond the scope of this book, one could surmise that Mexican immigrants are a sort of proxy for Arab Americans and others targeted in the war on terror. Because the latter population is relatively small, it may be far more satisfying for lawmakers and the public to go after the most numerous group as well. Camayd-Freixas implies this in his statement (see introd., n. 15).

23. For a compelling argument about immigrants' capacity to resist bio-political and disciplinary power dynamics that subordinate (and worse) these individuals, see Paul Apostolidis, *Breaks in the Chain: What Immigrant Workers Can Teach America About Democracy* (Minneapolis: University of Minnesota Press, 2010).

24. William Branigin and Gabriel Escobar, "INS Deportations Rising," *Boston Globe*, April 25, 1999; John Budris, "Jailed Immigrant a Man Without a Country," *Boston Globe*, May 9, 1999; Gertner and Kanstroom, "Recent Spotlight on the INS"; David L. Marcus, "Three Times and Out," *Boston Globe*, October 14, 1998; McDonnell, "Judges Rule Against Indefinite INS Jailings"; Teresa Mears, "As INS Jails Fill, a Release Plan Surfaces," *Boston Globe*, February 14, 1999; Teresa Mears, "The Woes of Immigrants Forced to Emigrate," *Boston Globe*, March 26, 2000; "Secret Trials in America" (see chap. 1, n. 102); Associated Press, "U.S. Deportations at Record Level," *Boston Globe*, May 14, 1997.

25. See Kanstroom, *Deportation Nation*.

26. See Associated Press, "U.S. Deportations at Record Level"; Gertner and Kanstroom, "Recent Spotlight on the INS"; Mears, "Woes of Immigrants Forced to Emigrate."

27. A term used to describe crimes that are not felonies if committed by citizens; see Kanstroom *Deportation Nation*, 3, 10–12.

28. Dow, *American Gulag*, 179, 180.

29. See ibid.

30. Ibid., 51.

31. Dow made this comparison in private correspondence with the author (September 2009). I asked him what the difference was between these two cases, and his response was that there are no pictures. That is, there are pictures from Abu Ghraib but there have been no pictures of the multitude of systematic abuses characterizing the domestic detention program.

32. Regarding the convoluted rules about habeas corpus and detainees, see Dow, *American Gulag*, 189.

33. U.S. Commission on International Religious Freedom, "Report on Asylum Seekers in Expedited Removal" (USCIRF, Washington, D.C., February 2005); Dow, *American Gulag*.

34. The facilities end up treating these people in even harsher ways—if that is possible—because they do not want to educate or give work to "lifers" when they have no chance of ever using the skills outside the prison system. Mariel Cubans are an example of a group held indefinitely, although some have managed to be released. See Dow, *American Gulag.*

35. Kanstroom *Deportation Nation,* 5.

36. See Dow, *American Gulag,* on immigrant detention.

37. See Associated Press, "Feds Deny Protests Affected Immigration Arrests"; Krupa, "Metro Detroit Area Deportations Climb 45 Percent."

38. See, for example, Justin Akers, "Vigilantes at the Border: The New War on Immigrants," *International Socialist Review,* September/October 2005, http://www.isreview.org/issues/43/minutemen.shtml.

39. Associated Press, "U.S.-Mexico Border Fence Almost Complete," MSNBC.com, January 27, 2009, http://www.msnbc.msn.com/id/28878934/ns/us_news-security/.

40. Quoted in Tamar Jacoby, "Debating Immigration," *National Review,* October 10, 2005. More generally (and critically), see Timothy Dunn and Joseph Nevins, "Barricading the Border," *NACLA Report on the Americas* 41, no. 6 (November/December 2008): 21–25.

41. See, for example, Jason Beaubien, "Juarez Sees Huge Spike in Drug-Related Murders," *All Things Considered,* December 11, 2008, http://www.npr.org/templates/story/story.php?storyId=98135986; Jason Beaubien, "Drug Deaths, Violence Plague Border in Tijuana," *Morning Edition,* December 1, 2008, http://www.npr.org/templates/story/story.php?storyId=97457815; Jason Beaubien, "Economy, Drug Wars Hurt Cross-Border Business," *Morning Edition,* December 4, 2008, http://www.npr.org/templates/story/story.php?storyId=97752572; Som Lisaius, "Border Patrol Unveils Military-Style Off Road Vehicle," KOLD.com, March 9, 2009, http://www.kold.com/global/story.asp?s=9975398&ClientType=Printable.

42. See, for example, U.S. Customs and Border Protection, "Fact Sheet: U.S. Customs and Border Protection: Protecting Our Southern Border Against the Terrorist Threat" (U.S. Department of Homeland Security, Washington, D.C., August 20, 2004), http://www.america.gov/st/washfile-english/2004/August/20040823170937GLnesnoM0.2022669.html. The creation of the Office of Counternarcotics Enforcement in 2004 under Homeland Security is one example of the connection between these two wars.

43. See Amnesty International, "Mexico: Intolerable Killings"; Simmons, "Remedies for the Women of Ciudad Juárez"; Zebadúa-Yañez, "Killing as Performance."

44. See, for example, "Migrant Domestic Workers Face Abuse in the U.S.," Human Rights Watch, June 14, 2001, http://www.hrw.org/en/news/2001/06/13/migrant-domestic-workers-face-abuse-us; Basav Sen, "Legalizing Human Trafficking," in *Real World Globalization: A Reader in Business, Economics, and Politics,* 9th ed., ed. Betsy Rakocy, Alejandro Reuss, and Chris Sturr (Boston: Dollars and Sense, 2007), 154–64. For background on domestic workers' conditions, see Hondagneu-Sotelo, *Doméstica;* Parreñas, *Servants of Globalization.*

45. See, for example, Associated Press, "Day Laborers, Orange County Sheriff's Department Reach Tentative Settlement," *Los Angeles Times,* August 20, 2008; John Garcia, "PRLDEF Welcomes Settlement in Mamaroneck That Protects Day Laborers from Further Harassment" (press release, Promoting Justice for Latinos, New York, June 11, 2007); Akito Yoshikane, "Day Laborers Sue Chicago," *In These Times,* January 31, 2008; see also the anti–day laborer website "Day Laborers," http://www.daylaborers.org/.

46. See Editorial, "Mr. Obama and the Rule of Law," *New York Times,* March 22, 2009; Charles Savage, "Obama's Embrace of Bush Tactic Criticized by Lawmakers from Both Parties," *New York Times,* August 9, 2009.

47. On Operation Gatekeeper, see Nevins, *Operation Gatekeeper.*

48. Foucault, *History of Sexuality,* 1:104.

49. Ibid., 137.

50. This second type of power is similar to Max Weber's analysis of the Protestant ethic, which he characterizes as saving, self-denial, and working beyond a level that is comfortable. But Foucault argues that disciplinary power operates more broadly. See Weber, *The Protestant Ethic and the Spirit of Capitalism*, trans. Talcott Parsons (New York: Routledge, 2001).

51. Foucault, *History of Sexuality*, 1:139.

52. Ibid., 140, 141.

53. Ibid., 139.

54. This is justified in the Fourteenth Amendment and further affirmed by the Supreme Court decision granting the children of unauthorized immigrants the right to public education (*Plyler v. Doe*, 1982).

55. *Wikipedia*, s.v. "Anchor Baby," accessed December 16, 2008, en.wikipedia.org/wiki/Anchor_baby. According to the site, "In a September 3, 2008, debate in Danville, Virginia, Republican Congressman Virgil Goode declared that the greatest threat to America's national security was 'anchor babies.'"

56. On these stereotypes, see Grace Chang, *Disposable Domestics: Immigrant Women Workers in the Global Economy* (Boston: South End Press, 2000), 4: "Men as job stealers are no longer seen as the major 'immigrant problem.' Instead, the new menace is immigrant women who are portrayed as idle, welfare-dependent mothers and inordinate breeders of dependents."

57. Similar to "welfare mothers." Foucault, *History of Sexuality*, 1:153. See also 104, 146–47.

58. Ibid., 104.

59. In chapter 4 I will discuss this in further detail. Maquila workers are technically still Mexican citizens, but most are not residents of the cities in which they work. Therefore municipal governments do not always provide electricity, sewage, or safe roads for these workers; nor are their children automatically eligible to attend school. Further, the work areas themselves are effectively free zones—not American or Mexican, but essentially deterritorialized space.

60. As Agamben has argued in *Homo Sacer*.

61. See, for example, Fukuyama, "Immigrants and Family Values."

62. Jacoby, "Debating Immigration," 26–27.

63. Honig, *Democracy and the Foreigner*, 74.

64. Fukuyama, "Immigrants and Family Values."

65. Though I am not arguing that her work as a whole is xenophilic.

66. See Schuck, "Alien Rumination," for a discussion of each of these categories.

67. See Fraga and Segura, "Culture Clash?"

68. See Huntington, "Hispanic Challenge."

69. See Jones, *American Work*, 370.

70. See Wilson, *When Work Disappears*; Jones, *American Work*; Salzinger, "From High Heels to Swathed Bodies."

71. See Alejandro Lugo, "Cultural Production and Reproduction in Ciudad Juárez, Mexico: Tropes at Play Among Maquiladora Workers," *Cultural Anthropology* 5, no. 2 (May 1990): 180–82.

72. See Kristen Hill Maher, "Identity Projects at Home and Labor from Abroad: The Market for Foreign Domestic Workers in Southern California and Santiago, Chile" (Working Paper 75, Center for Comparative Immigration Studies, University of California, San Diego, May 2003).

73. Salzinger, "From High Heels to Swathed Bodies," 549.

74. See Sassen, *Globalization and Its Discontents*; Grace Chang, "The Global Trade in Filipina Workers," in *Dragon Ladies: Asian American Feminists Breathe Fire*, ed. Sonia Shah (Boston: South End Press, 1997), 135–43.

75. Patricia Fernández-Kelly, "Reading the Signs: The Economics of Gender Twenty-Five Years Later," *Signs* 25, no. 4 (Summer, 2000): 1110. On the feminization of labor, see Hondagneu-Sotelo, *Doméstica*, introd., esp. 22–25.

76. Wilson, *When Work Disappears.*

77. Paul Apostolidis, "Hegemony and Hamburger: Migration Narratives and Democratic Unionism Among Mexican Meatpackers in the U.S. West," *Political Research Quarterly* 58, no. 4 (December 2005): 647–58.

78. Sassen, *Globalization and Its Discontents,* chaps. 5, 6.

79. See Valenzuela, "Working on the Margins"; see also the anti–day laborer website "Day Laborers," http://www.daylaborers.org/.

80. See Fukuyama, "Immigrants and Family Values," 153.

81. Huntington, "Hispanic Challenge," 3–4.

82. See Nick Ervin, "Immigration and the Environment" in Mills, *Arguing Immigration*; Donald Mann, "The President's Letter: A Message from NPG President Donald Mann," *Population and Resource Outlook,* Winter 2005/6; Chavez, "Glass Half Empty."

83. See Jacobson, "Characterizing Consent."

84. See Honig, *Democracy and the Foreigner,* 64–66.

85. Chavez, "Glass Half Empty," 2.

86. See Antonio McDaniel, "Fertility and Racial Stratification," in "Fertility in the United States: New Patterns, New Theories," supplement, *Population and Development Review* 22, no. 1 (1996): 134–50. See also Schuck, "Alien Rumination," regarding the view that immigrant (Mexican) reproduction is a serious issue.

87. Wright, "*Maquiladora* Mestizas and a Feminist Border Politics," 117.

88. Honig, *Democracy and the Foreigner,* 65; see also Trica Keaton, "Arrogant Assimilationism: National Identity Politics and African-Origin Muslim Girls in the Other France," *Anthropology and Education Quarterly* 36, no. 4 (December 2005): 405–23.

89. Chavez, "Glass Half Empty," 1.

90. See Susan Bordo's discussion of minority men in *Unbearable Weight: Feminism, Western Culture, and the Body* (Berkeley: University of California Press, 1993), 9, 11, 283, 287.

91. See Richard J. Herrnstein and Charles Murray, *The Bell Curve: Intelligence and Class Structure in American Life* (New York: Free Press, 1994).

92. See Frosty Wooldridge, "Spiral of Immigrant Corruption in America," *American Daily,* February 14, 2006.

93. See Gayatri Chakravorty Spivak, "Cultural Talks in the Hot Peace: Revisiting the 'Global Village,'" in *Cosmopolitics: Thinking and Feeling beyond the Nation,* ed. Pheng Cheah and Bruce Robbins (Minneapolis: University of Minnesota Press, 1998), 329–48.

94. See Salzinger, "From High Heels to Swathed Bodies," 1997; Associated Press, "Day Laborers, Orange County Sheriff's Department Reach Tentative Settlement"; John Garcia, "PRLDEF Welcomes Settlement in Mamaroneck"; Yoshikane, "Day Laborers Sue Chicago."

95. Sandoval and Tambini, *POV: Farmingville*; see also Johnson, "Forgotten 'Repatriation,'" 24.

96. As James Martel has suggested to me.

97. See Robert Miles and Malcolm Brown, *Racism,* 2nd ed. (London: Routledge, 2003), 65–66; Antonio McDaniel, "Fertility and Racial Stratification"; Chavez, "Glass Half Empty."

98. See my discussion in *America's New Working Class,* chap. 4, of the reemergence of pseudoscientific racism.

99. See Jacobson, "Characterizing Consent"; Miles and Brown, *Racism*; Skerry, *Mexican Americans*; Dan Seligman, "Facing Race," *National Review,* April 19, 2004.

100. Huntington, "Hispanic Challenge"; see also Samuel Huntington, "The Special Case of Mexican Immigration: Why Mexico Is a Problem," *American Enterprise* 11, no. 8 (December 2000): 20–22."

101. Huntington, "Hispanic Challenge," 12.

102. See also Miles and Brown, *Racism*, 99.

103. Preston, "As Immigration Plan Folded, Grass Roots Roared."

104. Crenshaw, "Mapping the Margins"; see also Hancock, "When Multiplication Doesn't Equal Quick Addition."

105. See Miles and Brown, *Racism*, 88.

106. See Colette Guillaumin, *Racism, Sexism, Power, and Ideology* (New York: Routledge, 1995).

107. Miles and Brown, *Racism*, 9, 19, 87–99; José Antonio Padín, "The Normative Mulattoes: The Press, Latinos, and the Racial Climate on the Moving Immigration Frontier," *Sociological Perspectives* 48, no. 1 (Winter 2005): 54. Asian Americans also have an ambivalent racial status; see Junn and Masuoka, "Asian American Identity."

108. See Gavin Miles McInnes, "Calling Immigration Reformers Racists Is Stupid and Hypocritical and I'm Fed Up with It," VDare.com, n.d., accessed February 7, 2006, http://www.vdare.com/mcinnes/060207_reformers.htm. See also Roxanne Doty's discussion of whether vigilante groups are racist. As she notes, the two Minuteman projects have tried to dissociate themselves with racist and extremist groups. Nevertheless, much of their discourse and presuppositions are unconsciously racialized. See "States of Exception," esp. 122, 123.

109. Huntington, "Hispanic Challenge," 11; emphasis added.

110. See Mario Vargas Llosa, "Sleeping with the Enemy?," *Salmagundi*, Fall 2005/2006, among others.

111. Miles and Brown, *Racism*, 99.

112. Such parties include the Council of Conservative Citizens (Joe McCutchen), European-American Unity and Rights Organization, Pioneer Fund, American Nationalist Union, National Socialist Movement, American Front, KKK, Olaf Childress, Council of Conservative Citizens (S.C.), and the Aryan Nation.

113. Jim Naureckas, "Racism Resurgent: How Media Let *The Bell Curve*'s Pseudo-Science Define the Agenda on Race," *Extra!*, January/February 1995.

114. Ibid., 7–8; see also Adam Miller, "Professors of Hate," *Rolling Stone*, October 20, 1994; Charles Lane, "The Tainted Sources of 'The Bell Curve,'" *New York Review of Books*, December 1, 1994.

115. Although, as I discuss in the previous chapter, I do not mean to idealize the state.

116. See Agamben, "We Refugees."

Chapter 3

1. See Susy Buchanan and Tom Kim, "The Nativists," *Southern Poverty Law Center Intelligence Report*, Winter 2005; Susy Buchanan and David Holthouse, "Playing Rough," *Southern Poverty Law Center Intelligence Report*, Fall 2005; Susy Buchanan and David Holthouse, "'The Little Prince': Minuteman Leader Has Troubled Past," *Southern Poverty Law Center Intelligence Report*, Winter 2005; Bill Berkowitz, "Lou Dobbs' Dubious Guest List," CommonDreams.org, July 1, 2006, http://www.commondreams.org/headlines06/0701-08.htm; Bud Kennedy, "Few Minutes with Minutemen Is Plenty of Time for GOP Group," *Fort Worth Star-Telegram*, June 29, 2006; Ali Winston, "Ground Zero for Immigration," *The Nation*, August 28, 2006;

"The Puppeteer," *Southern Poverty Law Center Intelligence Report*, Summer 2002; see also the websites for individual groups.

2. Agamben, *Homo Sacer*, 122.

3. See Wolin, "Democracy and the Welfare State."

4. Foucault, *History of Sexuality*, 1:80–91. In investigating the same groups, Roxanne Doty arrives at a similar conclusion, although she approaches this issue by referring to the ideas of Carl Schmitt and securitization theory. See Doty, "States of Exception."

5. See Chantal Mouffe, "Feminism, Citizenship, and Radical Democratic Politics," in *Feminist Social Thought: A Reader*, ed. Diana Tietjens Meyers (New York: Routledge, 1997), 536.

6. See Weber, *Protestant Ethic*.

7. This is why they are important symbols of anti-immigration sentiment today on both the Left and the Right. These groups may not be numerous, but they are interesting in their connection to popular and governmental views of immigrants. For an opposing view, see Alexander Cockburn, "King of the Hate Business," *The Nation*, April 29, 2009.

8. For contemporary discussions on civil society, see Thomas Carothers and William Barndt, "Civil Society," *Foreign Policy*, Winter 1999/2000; Simone Chambers and Jeffrey Kopstein, "Bad Civil Society," *Political Theory* 29, no. 6 (December 2001): 837–65; Sheldon Wolin, *Tocqueville Between Two Worlds: The Making of a Political and Theoretical Life* (Princeton: Princeton University Press, 2001), 309–10.

9. See, for example, "ADL Says Armed Anti-immigration Groups in Arizona Share Ties to White Supremacists," Anti-Defamation League, May 6, 2003 (updated April 2005), http://www.adl.org/PresRele/Extremism_72/4255_72.asp.

10. See Doty, "States of Exception." Members of Ranch Rescue, American Border Patrol, and the Minuteman Civil Defense Corps have been arrested, and some were then expelled from their groups for their illegal acts. Recently, the founder of Minutemen American Defense and two others were arrested for murdering a man and his nine-year-old daughter in a home invasion. See Toby Herschler and Teresa Jun, "Border Militia Activist One of Three Charged in Arivaca Double Murder," KOLD.com, June 12, 2009 (updated June 29, 2009), http://www.kold.com/Global/story.asp?S=10526682&nav=14RSJ9PS. Timothy Dunn brought this incident to my attention (private correspondence, July 2009).

11. On the damage that negative images and representations do for minorities, see Kimberlé Crenshaw, "Beyond Racism and Misogyny: Black Feminism and 2 Live Crew," in Meyers, *Feminist Social Thought*, 246–63.

12. "ACLU Immigrants' Rights Project Staff Travels to Arizona to Support Monitoring Efforts by ACLU Arizona," American Civil Liberties Union, April 16, 2005, http://www.aclu.org/immigrants/gen/11733prs20050416.html; see also Johnson, "Forgotten 'Repatriation,'" 24–25.

13. Minuteman Project welcome statement, accessed January 30, 2006, http://www.minutemanhq.com/project/AboutMMP.html.

14. See, for example, Mark Krikorian, "American Dhimmitude," *National Review Online*, March 30, 2006, http://www.nationalreview.com/articles/217196/american-dhimmitude/mark-krikorian. Similar alarmist views appear in the *National Review* over the past ten years as well as in *U.S. News and World Report*. Peter Brimelow's arguments in the *National Review* as well as in his book *Alien Nation* are clear examples of this. See also Chavez, "Glass Half Empty," which gives empirical information about the number of articles in each journal regarding negative stereotypes about Mexicans and Mexican Americans.

15. See Buchanan, *State of Emergency*, 105, 119–37; see also the documentary *POV: Farmingville*, directed by Carlos Sandoval and Catherine Tambini; the websites of anti-immigration groups such as the Minutemen, the California Coalition for Immigration Reform, and American Patrol; and VDare.com, the *Barnes Review*, and MichelleMalkin.com. It should be noted,

however, that Chris Simcox has stated that he does not subscribe to the Reconquista theory: see Doty, "States of Exception," 122.

16. Buchanan and Kim, "The Nativists."

17. Not to mention AM radio stations, such as KRLA 870 in Los Angeles. See also Huntington, "Hispanic Challenge"; Valerie Richardson, "Mexican Aliens Seek to Retake 'Stolen' Land," *Washington Times*, April 16, 2006; Berkowitz, "Lou Dobbs' Dubious Guest List."

18. See Jacoby, "Debating Immigration." President George W. Bush signed the proposal into law on October 26, 2006; see also Ted Robbins, "Bush Signs Border Fence Act; Funds Not Found," *All Things Considered*, October 26, 2006, http://www.npr.org/templates/story/story.php?storyId=6388548. And see "Narco-terrorism," July 2003, accessed December 9, 2010, http://www.au.af.mil/au/aul/bibs/narco/narco.htm, for information on the war on "narco-terrorism."

19. Sassen, *Globalization and Its Discontents*, 7.

20. See ibid., chap. 3.

21. Ibid., 7.

22. Ibid., chap. 3.

23. Although space constraints here do not permit a full explanation, it can be shown that immigration policy since 1965 has still been racially oriented. For example, "Operation Vanguard" specifically targeted Mexican immigrants, and racial profiling since the Patriot Act has penalized only certain groups. I argue this point more fully in chapter 4 of *America's New Working Class*.

24. See Deborah A. Boehm, "Gender(ed) Migrations: Shifting Gender Subjectivities in a Transnational Mexican Community" (Working Paper 100, Center for Comparative Immigration Studies, University of California, San Diego, April 2004).

25. See Simmons, "Remedies for the Women of Ciudad Juárez"; UCLA online announcement for the conference "The Maquiladora Murders; or, Who Is Killing the Women of Juárez?," n.d., accessed December 9, 2010, http://www.sscnet.ucla.edu/chavez/maqui_murders/index.htm; Lydia Alpízar, "Impunity and Women's Rights in Ciudad Juárez," *Human Rights Dialogue* 2, no. 10 (Fall 2003), http://www.carnegiecouncil.org/resources/publications/dialogue/2_10/articles/1056.html.

26. See Nevins, *Operation Gatekeeper*.

27. On the construction of the "illegal alien" in public rhetoric, see ibid.; on the 1986 IRCA, see Shanks, *Immigration and Politics of American Sovereignty*.

28. Jones, *American Work*, 376; see also Nevins, *Operation Gatekeeper*, 78.

29. Nevins, *Operation Gatekeeper*, 78.

30. Granted, many were fleeing wars in Central America and should never have been deemed illegal, but rather should have been classified as refugees. See my discussion of this history in chapter 4 of *America's New Working Class*; see also Shanks, *Immigration and Politics of American Sovereignty*.

31. Doty, "States of Exception," 118.

32. "Proposition 187 Approved in California," *Migration News* 1, no. 11 (December 1994), http://migration.ucdavis.edu/mn/more.php?id=492_0_2_0.

33. As of August 2010, SB1070, a law that allowed what is effectively racial profiling, prohibited sanctuary cities and further criminalized the employment of unauthorized day laborers. See "Legal Battle Looms over Arizona Immigration Law," CNN.com, July 28, 2010, http://www.cnn.com/2010/US/07/28/arizona.immigration.law/index.html. Since its passage, it has been challenged in the courts (at different levels, including a challenge by the Department of Justice) and spurred numerous protests, but it has also garnered widespread national support.

34. Doty, "States of Exception," 122.

35. Ibid., 123.

36. Ibid., 118. Spencer has actively supported Arizona's SB 1070, giving numerous interviews and staging a protest on his property. See Curtis Prendergast, "Pro-1070 Rally Held at Border Fence," *Sonoran Chronicle*, August 18, 2010, http://sonoranchronicle. com/2010/08/18/pro-sb-1070-rally-held-at-border-fence/.

37. See Akers, "Vigilantes at the Border"; Doty, "States of Exception."

38. "Border Emergency Declared in New Mexico," CNN.com, August 13, 2005, http:// articles.cnn.com/2005-08-12/us/newmexico_1_ravages-and-terror-mexican-border-las-chepas?_s=PM:US.

39. See Buchanan, *State of Emergency*.

40. For this view, see Huntington, "Hispanic Challenge"; Lawrence Auster, "The Second Mexican War," *FrontPage Magazine*, February 17, 2006. Simcox has denied that he subscribes to the Reconquista theory (despite quotes that may suggest otherwise).

41. See, for example, Wooldridge, "Spiral of Immigrant Corruption in America."

42. For example, neo-Nazi groups and white supremacists: see "Vigilante Watch," *Southern Poverty Law Center Intelligence Report*, Spring 2003, accessed February 27, 2006, http://www.splcenter.org/intel/intelreport/article.isp?sid=10; Dan Baum, "Patriots on the Borderline," *Los Angeles Times Magazine*, March 16, 2003; Mike Gonzalez, "Illegal Immigration Forebodes Grim Future for America," *Pasadena Independent*, n.d., accessed February 18, 2006, http://www.americanpatrol.com/_WEB2006/060217.html.

43. In the past few years, it has been charged that Mexican immigrants bring tuberculosis and leprosy into the country. More recently, the swine flu scare has served as an excuse for attempts to quarantine the southern border areas and closely watch recent entrants. See, for example, Buchanan, *State of Emergency*, 29–31; Oscar Avila and Margaret Ramirez, "Health Departments Fight Tuberculosis on Both Sides of the U.S. Border with Mexico," *Chicago Tribune*, February 16, 2009. Most recently, fears about the swine flu provoked some to call for sealing the southern border.

44. See, for example, "Extremists Declare 'Open Season' on Immigrants: Hispanics Target of Incitement and Violence," Anti-Defamation League, May 23, 2006, http://www .adl.org/main_Extremism/immigration_extremists.htm.

45. See Baum, "Patriots on the Borderline."

46. See Akers, "Vigilantes at the Border."

47. Oliver Cromwell Cox, *Race: A Study in Social Dynamics* (New York: Monthly Review Press, 2000).

48. Arendt, *Origins of Totalitarianism*.

49. Sheldon Wolin, "What Revolutionary Action Means Today," in *Dimensions of Radical Democracy: Pluralism, Citizenship, Community*, ed. Chantal Mouffe (New York: Verso, 1992), 242.

50. For a different but complementary analysis of Tocqueville's and his contemporaries' views of foreigners and foreignness in American nation-building, see Behdad, *A Forgetful Nation*.

51. See Honig, *Democracy and the Foreigner*, chap. 1.

52. See ibid., chap. 4.

53. Ibid., 91; emphasis added.

54. Ibid., 99.

55. Ibid., 74.

56. Wolin, "What Revolutionary Action Means Today," 242.

57. Ibid., 242–44, 249.

58. See Huntington, "Hispanic Challenge"; Hagin, "Ugly Truth"; "Illegal-Alien Advocates Play Down Mexican Flag" (see introd., n. 74).

59. See, for example, Hagin, "Ugly Truth"; Pastor Ralph Ovadal, "Romanizing America Through Illegal Immigration," Educate-Yourself.org, April 6, 2006, http://www.educate-yourself.org/cn/romanizingmaericathroughillegalimmigration06apr06.shtml.

60. Alexis de Tocqueville, *Democracy in America*, ed. J. P. Mayer, trans. George Lawrence (New York: Harper Perennial, 2000), 435.

61. Ibid., 515, 516.

62. Ibid., 312–15.

63. Ibid., 525–28.

64. Ibid., 628–89.

65. See ibid., bk. 2, chaps. 4–7, and pp. 509–24.

66. John Stewart Mill, *Principles of Political Economy* (New York: Oxford University Press, 1994), 136–38 (and bk. 4 more generally); see also Tocqueville, *Democracy in America*, 522.

67. See Tocqueville, *Democracy in America*, bk. 2, chap. 7, and pp. 521–24.

68. Two examples of critiques of civil society arguments are Carothers and Barndt, "Civil Society," and Chambers and Kopstein, "Bad Civil Society."

69. I use the term "absolutization" in a qualified sense to indicate the increased suspension of the law.

70. See, for example, "Extremists Declare 'Open Season' on Immigrants" (see n. 41, above); "Illegal-Alien Advocates Play Down Mexican Flag" (see introd., n. 74). Many of the statements by right-wing groups are not only against immigrants but also the president (whether that be George W. Bush, Barack Obama, or anyone else).

71. See Joan Scott's accessible and insightful discussion of this Derridean term in "Deconstructing Equality-versus-Difference: Or, the Uses of Poststructuralist Theory for Feminism," in Meyers, *Feminist Social Thought*, 757–70.

72. As with Patriot Act measures, the recent experiment in eight major cities to put electronic ankle bracelets on refugee applicants, guest-worker provisions, and broader discouragement of unionization nationwide. These measures do not lead to a legal void, but rather policies that make some individuals or groups the subject of political power in such a way that they become subordinate members of society. Regarding the ankle bracelets, see Daniel Zwerdling, "Electronic Anklets Track Asylum Seekers in U.S.," *Morning Edition*, March 2, 2005, http://www.npr.org/templates/story/story.php?storyId=4519090.

73. Cox, *Race: A Study in Social Dynamics*, 250.

74. Ibid.

75. Ibid., 253.

76. Nor are they viewed, as they should be, as the exercise of rights provided for by the Fourteenth Amendment and key Supreme Court decisions. See Bosniak, *The Citizen and the Alien*.

77. See Portes and Rumbaut, who argue that the Mexican American groups discussed in this chapter are not separatist, but instead are following the path of other minority groups in U.S. history to gain greater political status, equality, and recognition. *Immigrant America*, 2nd ed., conclusion.

78. See "States of Exception," in which Roxanne Doty reaches very similar conclusions.

79. See Smith, "Can You Imagine?"

Chapter 4

1. See Vernon M. Briggs, "The 'Albatross' of Immigration Reform: Temporary Worker Policy in the United States," in "Temporary Worker Programs: Mechanisms, Conditions,

Consequences," special issue, *International Migration Review* 20, no. 4 (Winter 1986): 995–1019, on the relatively new idea that guest-worker programs will solve the issue of unauthorized entry and the older notion that these programs are a form of aid to foreign workers.

2. Pateman, *Disorder of Women*; see also Slavoj Žižek, "Against Human Rights," *New Left Review*, July/August 2005, on the idea of pseudo-choice, the notion that we are all equal and can make choices freely, despite profoundly unfair conditions or terms.

3. Karl Marx and Friedrich Engels, "Manifesto of the Communist Party," in *The Marx-Engels Reader*, 2nd ed., ed. Robert C. Tucker (New York: Norton, 1978), 475.

4. Agamben, *Homo Sacer*, 159.

5. Saskia Sassen's oft-repeated phrase in *Globalization and Its Discontents*.

6. See Briggs, "'Albatross' of Immigration Reform."

7. To be precise, Mexico undertook at least two stages of structural adjustment policies—the first wave of these policies was implemented in the 1980s (i.e., fifteen to twenty years after the beginning of the maquila program), arguably strengthening the position of foreign capital and weakening the social safety net; the second wave was a result of the IMF-U.S. loan and peso crisis in the mid-1990s. See Cooney, "The Mexican Crisis and the Maquiladora Boom."

8. See "Human Rights Watch Welcomes U.S. Government Meat and Poultry Study," Human Rights Watch, February 2, 2005, http://www.hrw.org/en/news/2005/02/02/human-rights-watch-welcomes-us-government-meat-and-poultry-study; "Abusive Child Labor Found in U.S. Agriculture," Human Rights Watch, June 19, 2000, http://www.hrw.org/en/news/2000/06/19/abusive-child-labor-found-us-agriculture; see also "U.S. Agricultural Workers," National Catholic Rural Life Conference, January 2004, accessed February 25, 2005, http://www.ncrlc.com/AgriculturalWorkers.html; Amnesty International, "Mexico: Intolerable Killings"; Salzinger, "From High Heels to Swathed Bodies."

9. Although it is an older article, see Bacon, "INS Declares War on Labor"; see also see Vogel, "Transient Servitude," and Briggs, "'Albatross' of Immigration Reform," regarding the link between illegal work, unauthorized immigrants, and assumptions about the guest-worker program.

10. Agamben, *Homo Sacer*.

11. See Giorgio Agamben, *State of Exception*, trans. Kevin Attell (Chicago: University of Chicago Press, 2005), chaps. 1, 2.

12. On the effects of a tighter border and the creation of a mass detention system, see Dow, *American Gulag*; Kanstroom, *Deportation Nation*; see also Associated Press, "Feds Deny Protests Affected Immigration Arrests"; Krupa, "Metro Detroit Area Deportations Climb 45 Percent"; Associated Press, "Border Patrol Swells to More Than 18,000"; Ziner, "Governor's Advisory Panel to Report on Concerns of Immigrants"; Statement of Dr. Erik Camayd-Freixas (see introd., n. 15).

13. See *Life and Debt*, directed by Stephanie Black (2001; New York: New Yorker Video, 2003), DVD.

14. See Briggs, "'Albatross' of Immigration Reform."

15. Adjustments and losses can occur in a broad range of ways: structural adjustment policies, loss of tax revenues, being forced to open markets and compete with American products, brain drain when these individuals leave the country, loss of traditional economies, pollution and environmental degradation, and so on.

16. According to William Adler. As will be discussed below, there are several reasons that this program was created, some of which have been stated explicitly and others that are less obvious. Adler, *Mollie's Job*.

17. See, for example, Senator Dianne Feinstein's 2007 proposals for the guest-worker program: "Senator Dianne Feinstein on Immigration" (see introd., n. 2). It should be noted

that the combination of anti-Mexican and anti-illegal sentiment combined with a desire for cheap labor is not new—this same mixture fueled supporters of the Bracero Program in the 1950s. See Kitty Calavita, *Inside the State: The Bracero Program, Immigration, and the INS* (New York: Routledge, 1992).

18. There is, however, a considerable literature on these abuses and the exceptionality of this program in the alternative press and in more specialized academic areas. See Yeoman's *Mother Jones* article "Silence in the Fields" exposing the harsh treatment of workers, including physical danger, coupled with their political powerlessness due to heavy surveillance and lack of political rights and recourse.

19. See, for example, how Bush has broken with most conservatives on this issue: Jonathan Weisman, "Senators Back Guest Workers; Panel's Measure Sides with Bush," *Washington Post*, March 28, 2006; Buchanan, *State of Emergency*.

20. See David Bacon's photo gallery on maquilas, accessed December 20, 2010: http://search .live.com/images/results.aspx?q=maquiladora+photo&mkt=en-us#; http://dbacon.igc.org/ Mexico/border13.htm.

21. See Briggs, for example, on contracts from the Civil War period up to the early 1900s. "'Albatross' of Immigration Reform," 997.

22. Ibid., 997.

23. See Susan Sterett, "In an Indeterminate State: Calavita on the Bracero Program," *Law and Social Inquiry* 20, no. 2 (Spring 1995): 655–73. Both the INS and the Department of Labor ran the program, but the former agency exercised far more control. During this period, the INS operated outside standard bureaucratic procedures and was characterized by its "extraordinary cult of secrecy" (659n3) and the near impossibility of the group most affected by its actions—braceros—of having any impact on its rules or procedures. When workers began to organize and receive some domestic support, the program was shut down— first in the Northeast, after strikes during World War II, and later as a whole in the 1960s, as organized labor joined with workers to protest their conditions. Two seminal works on the Bracero Program are Calavita's *Inside the State*, and Ngai's historiography of the initiative in *Impossible Subjects*, chap. 4.

24. See Philip Martin, "Mexican Workers and U.S. Agriculture: The Revolving Door," *International Migration Review* 36, no. 4 (Winter 2002): 1124–42, on certification issues.

25. See Ngai, *Impossible Subjects*, among others.

26. See Martin, "Mexican Workers and U.S. Agriculture"; Briggs, "'Albatross' of Immigration Reform."

27. See, for example, Martin, "Mexican Workers and U.S. Agriculture," 1139.

28. See Calavita, *Inside the State*, 62–63, on the "freedom of contract."

29. See Martin, "Mexican Workers and U.S. Agriculture," 1128, 1129; Tom Knudson and Hector Amezcua, "The Pineros: Forest Workers Caught in Web of Exploitation," *Sacramento Bee*, November 13, 2005.

30. As Klaus Bade explains, this ideal prompted a huge number of Germans to immigrate to the United States; when they arrived, most were extremely disappointed by the actual conditions. See *Migration Past, Migration Future: Germany and the United States* (Providence: Berghahn Books, 1997).

31. See Alvaro Bedoya's discussion of the recruitment of Peruvian sheepherders in both "Captive Labor," *Dollars and Sense*, September/October 2003; and "Welcome to the First World: The Exploitation of Peruvian Sheepherders in the American West" (senior thesis, Committee on Degrees in Social Studies, Harvard University, March 2003).

32. See Shanks, *Immigration and Politics of American Sovereignty*.

33. See, for example, Parag Khanna, "Waving Goodbye to Hegemony," *New York Times Magazine*, January 27, 2008. I am not arguing that this article is wrong, but the same sort of

article proliferated from the end of the Cold War up until the end of the 1990s (or up until 9/11, depending on one's view), claiming that the United States was no longer a superpower.

34. Martin, "Mexican Workers and U.S. Agriculture," 1127, 1128.

35. There are, in fact, many more classifications for workers' visas, but these are the two broad types.

36. See Vogel's excellent chart on these proposals in "Transient Servitude," table 1.

37. See Ian Urbina, "Foreign Workers Are Caught in a Double Trap," New York Times, September 6, 2005.

38. See, for example, Bedoya, "Captive Labor"; Dan Frosch, "In Loneliness, Immigrants Tend the Flock," New York Times, February 22, 2009; braceros were also poorly housed—see Ngai, Impossible Subjects, 144.

39. Regarding all these conditions, see Bedoya, "Captive Labor"; Turnbull, "New State Import"; Yeoman, "Silence in the Fields."

40. Briggs, "'Albatross' of Immigration Reform," 1000. Because of the 60 percent provisions, employers can blacklist the remainder of workers.

41. Yeoman, "Silence in the Fields."

42. Ibid. According to Yeoman, one estimate is that 40 percent regularly escape. See Calavita on guest-worker escapes in the 1950s and 1960s (called "skips"): Inside the State, 74, 75. See also Ngai on skips: Impossible Subjects, 146–47.

43. Calavita, Inside the State, 75; see also Chang, Disposable Domestics, 104.

44. Chiaki Nishiyama and Kurt R. Leube, eds., The Essence of Hayek (Stanford, Calif.: Hoover Institution Press, 1984). But against Mae Ngai's claim that portraying guest workers' conditions as unfree and even like a concentration camp will maintain their outsider status, I want to emphasize how these conditions are precisely part of global capitalism—what was once exceptional has become the norm. See Ngai's discussion in Impossible Subjects, 161, 166.

45. See Bedoya, "Welcome to the First World," on the deaths of Peruvian sheepherders due to exposure.

46. "Abusive Child Labor Found in U.S. Agriculture" (see n. 7, above).

47. On contemporary uses of prerogative power, see Wolin, "Democracy and the Welfare State."

48. Here I am challenging the interpretation of Agamben that holds that the suspension of law creates a legal void in which politics no longer exists. To Agamben, the opposite is true: this suspension is the most political space. See Hussain, "Beyond Norm and Exception"; Rancière, "Who Is the Subject of the Rights of Man?"

49. See Arendt, Origins of Totalitarianism, chap. 9, esp. pp. 269, 297–300.

50. See Chang, "Global Trade in Filipina Workers," for example, and Chang, Disposable Domestics, 110.

51. In Arendt's words: Origins of Totalitarianism, 296.

52. See Sassen, Globalization and Its Discontents; see also Ricky Baldwin, "Free Markets and Death Squads in Haiti," in Rakocy, Reuss, and Sturr, Real World Globalization, 150–53.

53. Sassen, Globalization and Its Discontents, chap. 2.

54. Dani Rodrik, "Feasible Globalizations" (unpublished manuscript, Harvard University, July 2002), http://www.hks.harvard.edu/fs/drodrik/Research%20papers/Feasglob.pdf, 15.

55. See Friedman, The Lexus and the Olive Tree. By arguing that politics shrinks as the global economy grows, Friedman evades the problem that national sovereignty and borders are necessary to govern the flow of goods, guarantee contracts, and even use military backing or force to support trade agreements. What is lost is not sovereignty but democracy: choice, debate, discussion.

56. Rodrik, "Feasible Globalizations," 20–23.

57. Portes and Rumbaut have a similarly problematic guest-worker scheme that they offer in the conclusion to the third edition of *Immigrant America*. Their proposal splits up families in order to protect children and entails a fee that will be partially remunerated when guest workers return to their home country.

58. For a critique of the revival of the concept of embeddedness, see Leo Panitch, "The New Imperial State," *New Left Review*, March/April 2000.

59. Kirk A. Johnson and Tim Kane, "The Real Problem with Immigration . . . and the Real Solution," *Backgrounder*, March 1, 2006, 2; emphasis added.

60. Ibid., 4.

61. Ibid., 2.

62. On the indeterminate status of guest workers, see Calavita, *Inside the State*; Sterett, "In an Indeterminate State."

63. See Jones, *American Work*.

64. Edna Bonacich would call this a split market, which causes ethnic and gender antagonism, depending on which groups of workers are undercutting the workforce at the time. See "Theory of Ethnic Antagonism."

65. Cooney, "The Mexican Crisis and the Maquiladora Boom," 62.

66. See ibid.; Samuel Dillon and Julia Preston, *Opening Mexico: The Making of a Democracy* (New York: Farrar, Straus and Giroux, 2004), 468–74; Melissa Wright, *Disposable Women and Other Myths of Global Capitalism* (New York: Routledge, 2006).

67. Cooney, "The Mexican Crisis and the Maquiladora Boom," 59. Cooney further notes that a 1996 report by the United Nations Development Programme argued that 40.8 percent of Mexicans "were living in extreme poverty or indigence."

68. Interestingly, President Bill Clinton had to use his prerogative to offer the loan to Mexico. According to Cooney, he relied on an "obscure Treasury entity called the Exchange Stabilization Fund to obtain funds that did not require the approval of Congress." Ibid., 59. See also Joseph Stiglitz, who blames the U.S. Treasury, not Clinton: *Globalization and Its Discontents* (New York: Norton, 2003), 263n10.

69. See Ralph Armbruster-Sandoval, "Globalization and Transnational Labor Organizing: The Honduran Maquiladora Industry and the Kimi Campaign," *Social Science History* 27, no. 4 (Winter 2003): 551–76, regarding similar dynamics in free trade zones in Honduras.

70. On the history of unions in Mexico, see Dillon and Preston, *Opening Mexico*, chap. 16; on Han Young, see pp. 472–74.

71. Cooney, "The Mexican Crisis and the Maquiladora Boom," 64; see also Wright, *Disposable Women*.

72. See Cooney, "The Mexican Crisis and the Maquiladora Boom."

73. Wright, *Disposable Women*, chap. 3.

74. According to Cooney, women constituted about 60 percent of employees in 2000. "The Mexican Crisis and the Maquiladora Boom," 71.

75. See ibid.; Adler, *Molly's Job*; Wright, *Disposable Women*; David Bacon's photo galleries.

76. For example, see Salzinger, "From High Heels to Swathed Bodies."

77. Granted, Wright complicates the idea of a "national" division. See "*Maquiladora* Mestizas and a Feminist Border Politics."

78. Cooney, "The Mexican Crisis and the Maquiladora Boom," 64, 65; see also Wright, *Disposable Women*, chap. 3.

79. Wright, "*Maquiladora* Mestizas and a Feminist Border Politics," 119.

80. Ibid., 120.

81. See Jessica Livingston, "Murder in Juárez: Gender, Sexual Violence, and the Global Assembly Line," *Frontiers* 25, no. 1 (2004): 59–76; Pierrette Hondagneu-Sotelo, "Overcoming Patriarchal Constraints: The Reconstruction of Gender Relations Among Mexican

Immigrant Women and Men," *Gender and Society* 6, no. 3 (September 1992): 393 – 415; Sassen, *Globalization and Its Discontents*.

82. Cooney, "The Mexican Crisis and the Maquiladora Boom," 72. On similar conditions in Haitian free trade zones, see Baldwin, "Free Markets and Death Squads in Haiti"; reproductive policing is also done in China — see Wright, *Disposable Women*.

83. See Wright, "*Maquiladora* Mestizas and a Feminist Border Politics," 118; see also my discussion in chapter 2.

84. Foucault, *Discipline and Punish*.

85. Foucault, *History of Sexuality*, vol. 1. This discourse is linked, as I note in chapter 2, to the worries about anchor babies. Although Foucault emphasizes the sexualization and medicalization of women's bodies, he ties the discourse producing this hysterization to biopower in terms of controlling reproduction, public health matters, and the aims of capitalism. See pp. 104, 121.

86. Judith Butler, *Gender Trouble: Feminism and the Subversion of Identity* (New York: Routledge, 1990).

87. Cooney, "The Mexican Crisis and the Maquiladora Boom," 66 – 69.

88. See Livingston, "Murder in Juárez"; Simmons, "Remedies for the Women of Ciudad Juárez."

89. See Hondagneu-Sotelo's "Overcoming Patriarchal Constraints" and "Feminism and Migration."

90. As Sassen has suggested about other areas in *Globalization and Its Discontents*.

91. Even more have been displaced by NAFTA; see Vogel, "Transient Servitude."

92. See Livingston, "Murder in Juárez."

93. Ibid., 5. Hondagneu-Sotelo notes a similar reaction to women who leave their families in Mexico and Central America to seek work in the United States. See *Doméstica*, 25.

94. See Zebadúa-Yañez, "Killing as Performance."

95. Amnesty International, "Mexico: Intolerable Killings"; see also Wright, *Disposable Women*, chap. 4.

96. Wright, *Disposable Women*, 17–18. A similar attitude of disposability marked the beginnings of the guest-worker program in the United States, as Calavita has investigated in *Inside the State*.

97. See Amnesty International, "Mexico: Intolerable Killings"; Zebadua-Yañez, "Killing as Performance."

98. See the 2006 documentary by Vicky Funari and Sergio de la Torre, *POV: Maquilapolis (City of Factories)*, 2006; see also Adler, *Molly's Job*.

99. Regarding all these issues and workers' organization actions against these conditions, see Funari and de la Torre, *Maquilapolis*.

100. Adler, *Molly's Job*.

101. See Adler, *Molly's Job*; Cooney, "The Mexican Crisis and the Maquiladora Boom."

102. See Sassen, *Globalization and Its Discontents*, regarding the idea that what is shocking about sweatshop conditions is not that they mirror conditions of the Industrial Revolution, but that they still exist after these conditions became regulated and new norms were instituted. Today's flexible labor conditions unravel the gains of the former labor aristocracy.

103. This word is in quotes because, as Giorgio Agamben has explored, the notion of humanity has been problematic in the modern nation-state. The fact that what is human has constantly been defined and redefined has led to both innocuous and lethal results. See *Homo Sacer*.

104. See Adler, *Molly's Job*; Stiglitz, *Globalization and Its Discontents*.

105. See Cooney, "The Mexican Crisis and the Maquiladora Boom," among others.

106. Panitch, "New Imperial State."

107. See Edna Bonacich on the importance of a weak or absent sending state in lowering the standards of what is considered safe, fit, fair, just, or decent for workers (although she would not put it in such moral terms). This is also not to imply that the Mexican government has done nothing on behalf of migrant workers either. See "Theory of Ethnic Antagonism."

108. See Paul Krugman, "In Praise of Cheap Labor: Bad Jobs at Bad Wages Are Better Than No Jobs at All," *Slate*, March 21, 1997, http://www.slate.com/id/1918/.

109. Pateman, *Disorder of Women*, 83.

110. Thomas Hobbes, *Leviathan*, ed. Richard Tuck (Cambridge: Cambridge University Press, 1999), 94–99. See also John Stuart Mill, *On Liberty*, ed. Elizabeth Rapaport (Indianapolis: Hackett, 1978), 102.

111. On this ambivalence, see Walzer, "Obligation to Die for the State."

112. Pateman, *Disorder of Women*, 78.

113. Granted, one could critique both terms in Locke; see Wolin, "Democracy and the Welfare State"; Pateman, *Disorder of Women*; Stevens, *Reproducing the State*; Arnold, "Domestic War."

114. See Pateman, *Disorder of Women*, introd., chap. 4.

115. Ibid., 72.

116. See Friedrich Engels' discussion of the connection between the marriage contract and the work contract: "The Origin of the Family," in *The Feminist Papers: From Adams to de Beauvoir*, ed. Alice Rossi (1973; Boston: Northeastern University Press, 1988), 484–85, 492.

117. See Huntington's discussion of "mañana syndrome" in "Hispanic Challenge"; see also D'Souza and Herrnstein and Murray on "Hispanic" immigrants: D'Souza, *The End of Racism: Principles for a Multiracial Society* (New York: Free Press, 1995); Herrnstein and Murray, *The Bell Curve*.

118. See Agamben, *Homo Sacer*, 17.

119. On this subject, see Linklater, "Citizenship and Sovereignty in the Post-Westphalian European State," 126–28.

120. See John Stuart Mill, "On the Subjection of Women," in Rossi, *Feminist Papers*.

121. A related but alternative interpretation of the same relationships: "The Orwellian hypocrisy of a free-trade utopia cum police state, not surprisingly, favors epic corruption and transnational crime. How ironic that the Border, this now massive militarized display of bounded national identity, everywhere seems to leak sovereignty: allowing the Arellano-Felix and other drug cartels to function as shadow regional governments. In more than one way, we are recalled to Pynchon's description of 'The Zone' in *Gravity's Rainbow* and its lucrative symbiosis of warfare, nomadism, and noir capitalism." Mike Davis, foreword to Nevins, *Operation Gatekeeper*, 10.

122. Agamben, *State of Exception*, 30.

123. Ibid, 31.

124. As Sheldon Wolin has argued in *Politics and Vision: Continuity and Innovation in Western Political Thought*, exp. ed. (Princeton: Princeton University Press, 2004), for example. Nevertheless, his concerns are closely aligned with Agamben's in his analyses of prerogative power deployed domestically and regularly.

125. Agamben, *State of Exception*, 1.

126. Although this distinction must be qualified, I am using it for simplicity's sake. Agamben problematizes Carl Schmitt's claim that friend/enemy is the originary source of the political, and argues instead that bare life is the starting point for examining the foundations of both the political and sovereignty. Friend/enemy can be mapped onto this, with caveats, later in time.

127. Again, see Mae Ngai's discussion of how the Bracero Program was viewed as outside both the economy and "the national body." *Impossible Subjects*, 161, 166.

128. On a more basic level, free trade zones (or special economic zones) have clearly moved from the margins to the center as their numbers have exploded since the 1980s. See

"Free Trade Zones," *Sociologyindex*, 2009, accessed May 12, 2010, http://sociologyindex.com/free_trade_zones.htm.

129. The conditions of day laborers provide an interesting contrast.

130. Sassen, *Globalization and Its Discontents*; see also Portes and Rumbaut, *Immigrant America*, 3rd ed. This, in fact, has happened, and it occurs for a variety of reasons.

131. Up until recently, Palestinians played the same role in Israel.

132. An argument that Karl Polanyi is famous for—a so-called free market requires an incredible amount of political intervention. Karl Polanyi, *The Great Transformation* (Boston: Beacon Press, 2001).

133. See, for example, Stiglitz, *Globalization and Its Discontents*.

134. See, for example, Huntington, "Hispanic Challenge"; Auster, "Second Mexican War"; Brimelow, *Alien Nation*; the Minutemen website.

135. See Doty, "States of Exception," for a similar argument about vigilante groups in which she draws on Carl Schmitt's ideas but claims that sovereign decision making is not made only at elite levels; see also Agamben's discussion of abandonment and sovereignty: *Homo Sacer*, esp. 29.

136. See Panitch, "New Imperial State."

137. T. H. Marshall and Tom Bottomore, *Citizenship and Social Class* (London: Pluto Press, 1987).

138. For example, see Richard Heinberg, "A History of Corporate Rule and Popular Protest," *Race and History*, November 9, 2002, http://raceandhistory.com/selfnews/viewnews.cgi?newsid1036869493,49230,.shtml.

139. Sassen, *Globalization and Its Discontents*, 278. Arendt also suggests this: "Theoretically, in the sphere of international law, it had always been true that sovereignty is nowhere more absolute than in matters of 'emigration, naturalization, nationality, and expulsion.'" Arendt, *Origins of Totalitarianism*, 278.

140. As I suggest in *America's New Working Class*.

141. See Hassner, "Refugees"; Michael Hardt and Antonio Negri, *Empire* (Cambridge: Harvard University Press, 2000); Agamben, "We Refugees"; Held, "Democracy and Globalization."

142. Foucault, *History of Sexuality*, 1:95–96.

Conclusion

1. Most notably in the now defunct Proposition 187 in California, current state proposals that aim at passing elements of this proposition, and the passage of the Personal Responsibility and Work Opportunity Act in 1996.

2. As Samuel Huntington argued in "Hispanic Challenge." On the relationship between the "renationalization" of immigration policy and borders and current U.S. policy, see Sassen, "Bits of a New Immigration Reality."

3. As Saskia Sassen discusses in chapter 3 of *Globalization and Its Discontents*; see also Nevins, *Operation Gatekeeper*, 173–74.

4. Including the recent panic about swine flu in 2009.

5. Following Sassen (*Globalization and Its Discontents*), this occurs for a variety of reasons that I will summarize schematically. First, when individuals work for a foreign company, bridges or linkages are established with that country's culture and business practices. People move from rural areas to urban areas, changing the demographic makeup of a country. At the same time, traditional gender relations (i.e., the gendered division of labor) are altered and traditional economies are lost when one group moves to work. When the foreign company pulls out, workers have nothing left to lose when they migrate.

6. Sassen, *Globalization and Its Discontents*, 31.

7. Recent examples include Salvadorans and Guatemalans fleeing U.S.-initiated military conflict in the early 1980s, individuals from the Caribbean migrating to the United States as U.S. corn subsidies tank the sugar harvest in the islands, and Mexican migration as a response to the end of the Bracero Program and, more recently, NAFTA.

8. As Joseph Nevins has argued, U.S. policies have effectively created the very figure the country fears: the "illegal alien." See *Operation Gatekeeper*. See also David Bacon and Bill Ong Hing, "Rights, Not Raids," *The Nation*, May 18, 2009.

9. Symbolic because the border fence was approved by Congress but without the funding to actually complete the project.

10. If democratic countries were, by definition, democratic because they were freeing themselves from arbitrary power and hierarchy based on natural difference, it makes no sense to subordinate democratic politics today to the market to the degree this has happened under neoliberalism.

11. Sassen, *Globalization and Its Discontents*, 99; see also her broader discussion of international human rights regimes, pp. 95–97.

12. David Held, among others, has also argued that there is a clear need to foster cosmopolitan practices, activism, and institutions. Held, "Democracy and Globalization"; Mikkel Thorup and Mads P. Sørensen, "Inescapably Side by Side," Global Policy Forum, February 2004, http://www.globalpolicy.org/globaliz/define/2004/04heldinterview.htm.

13. On the limits of transnational citizenship, as well as a discussion of the rights that all receive in the United States based on legal notions of personhood (e.g., from the Fourteenth Amendment), see Bosniak, *The Citizen and the Alien*, chap. 5. This personhood is distinct from the individual recognized as a bearer of human rights based on his or her humanity; nevertheless, it could serve as a bridge to broader (though perhaps not truly universal) notions of political status.

14. For a discussion of what Arendt meant by the phrase "the right to rights," as well as its consequences for human rights implementation, see Ingram, "What Is a 'Right to Have Rights'?"

15. Arendt, *Origins of Totalitarianism*, 283.

16. Ibid., 296.

17. Ibid., 279, 288.

18. This includes setting the terms of migrant labor under "Mode 4," such that employers or contractors have nearly all the power and workers virtually none. See Vogel, "Transient Servitude."

19. "Man, it turns out, can lose all so-called Rights of Man without losing his essential quality as man, his human dignity. Only the loss of a polity itself expels him from humanity." Arendt, *Origins of Totalitarianism*, 297; see also chap. 9.

20. See Agamben, *Homo Sacer*; Hardt and Negri *Empire*; Žižek, "Against Human Rights"; Žižek, "Are We in a War? Do We Have an Enemy?," *London Review of Books*, May 23, 2002; Žižek, "Knee-Deep," *London Review of Books*, September 2, 2004; Arundhati Roy, "Do Turkeys Enjoy Thanksgiving?," CounterCurrents.org, January 19, 2004, http://www .countercurrents.org/wsf-roy190104.htm; Spivak, "Cultural Talks in the Hot Peace"; Spivak, "Righting Wrongs," *South Atlantic Quarterly* 103, nos. 2/3 (Spring/Summer 2004): 523–81.

21. Cheryl Shanks traces the historical development of this claim as it emerged at the end of the Cold War. See *Immigration and Politics of American Sovereignty*.

22. See Nicholas Xenos, "Refugees: The Modern Political Condition," *Alternatives* 18, no. 4 (Fall 1993): 419–30; Hassner, "Refugees."

23. The most notable example is the treatment of Mariel refugees from Cuba, who were immediately detained upon reaching U.S. shores. Only recently has their situation improved. See Dow, *American Gulag*.

24. There is a certain irony in the United States' refusal to recognize social and economic rights as the basis for asylum and human rights while its humanitarian aid is nearly always implemented at this same level.

25. Nirmal Trivedi, "Biopolitical Convergences: Narmada Bachao Andolan and *Homo Sacer*," *Borderlands* 5, no. 3 (December 2006), http://www.borderlands.net.au/vol5no3_2006/trivedi_biopolitical.htm.

26. Thus, Trivedi argues, "the activist develops a strategy of legal representation for those the law deems unworthy. The paradox of this advocacy, which is most often articulated through the language of human rights, is that the activist ends up appropriating bare life as the only life worth being lived." Ibid.

27. See Tirman's review of recent human rights books in which he (as well as many of the authors he reviews) analyzes why this depoliticization takes place, including focusing on how crises are treated as emergencies and are often linked to development (which, in turn, creates or exacerbates the crises). "The New Humanitarianism," *Boston Review*, December/January 2003/4.

28. See Ingram's excellent breakdown of interpretations of human rights justifications, and the consequences of these interpretations, in "What Is a 'Right to Have Rights'?"

29. Wendy Brown, "'The Most We Can Hope For . . . ': Human Rights and the Politics of Fatalism," *South Atlantic Quarterly* 103, no. 2/3 (Spring/Summer 2004): 453.

30. On the depoliticizing and dangerous aspects of moralizing human rights, see Rancière, "Who Is the Subject of the Rights of Man?"

31. Žižek, "Are We in a War?"

32. Ibid., 2.

33. See Pierre Hassner, "Refugees"; David Beetham, "Human Rights as a Model for Cosmopolitan Democracy," in Archibugi, Held, and Köhler, *Re-imagining Political Community*, 58–71.

34. Bronwyn Leebaw, "The Politics of Impartial Activism: Humanitarianism and Human Rights," *Perspectives on Politics* 5, no. 2 (June 2007): 223–39. See also Nicholas de Torrente, executive director of Doctors Without Borders, "Aid Workers and Military," letter to the editor, *New York Times*, March 11, 2007.

35. Leebaw, "The Politics of Impartial Activism," 224.

36. Ibid., 232.

37. Brown, "The Most We Can Hope For."

38. As he argues in *Homo Sacer*. See also Rancière, "Who Is the Subject of the Rights of Man?"; Hussain, "Beyond Norm and Exception."

39. Arendt, *Origins of Totalitarianism*, 296.

40. See Agamben, *Homo Sacer*, conclusion.

41. In using these two words, I am thinking of Weber's notion of charismatic political power as well as Wendy Brown's remarks about the passion evoked in political organizing. See Max Weber, "Politics as a Vocation," in *From Max Weber: Essays in Sociology*, ed. and trans. H. H. Gerth and C. Wright Mills (Oxford: Oxford University Press, 1958); Brown, "Where Is the Sex in Political Theory?," *Women and Politics* 7, no. 1 (Spring 1987): 3–24.

42. On the importance of these protests, see Ngai, "No Human Being Is Illegal."

43. See Nevins, *Operation Gatekeeper*, 180–81, for examples of unions acting internationally; see also Shah, *Dragon Ladies*, for discussions of how Asian Immigrant Women Advocates challenged the dressmaker Jessica McClintock.

44. I discuss this difficulty in Agamben in the conclusion to my book *America's New Working Class*. Unlike other critics of Agamben, I do not think he lacks a theory of agency or has a rigidly teleological notion of history, but he (like Beauvoir) seems to think that only future political movements will truly be rid of the sovereignty–bare life connection.

Agamben sees a parallel between the state of exception and the right to rebel: "The problem of the state of exception presents clear analogies to that of the right of resistance." *State of Exception*, 10–11.

45. Ingram, "What Is a 'Right to Have Rights'?," 410: "The meaning or significance (*Sinn*) of politics for her lies in creating and maintain such a space of political freedom, a realm in which people can be recognized as interlocutors, as equal partners in action and deliberation. This equality is not given from above and does not consist principally in laws or institutions but is achieved through practice." See also Honig on the "right to rights" with regard to immigrants and the stateless in *Democracy and the Foreigner*, 61–62. And see Sassen's interesting use of this phrase in analyzing the 2006 protests in major U.S. cities by controversial immigrants in "Bits of a New Immigration Reality."

46. Honig, *Democracy and the Foreigner*, 105; see also pp. 8, 104–6, 118.

47. Because it has not been (fully) realized.

48. Agamben, "We Refugees."

49. Linklater, "Citizenship and Sovereignty in the Post-Westphalian European State."

50. Ibid., 116.

51. I am referring to Sheldon Wolin's notion of "fugitive democracy." See *Politics and Vision*, 601–6.

52. I also address this in the conclusion to *America's New Working Class*.

53. See J. Oloka-Onyago and Deepika Udagama, "Globalization and Its Impact on the Full Enjoyment of Human Rights" (United Nations Economic and Social Council, New York, June 15, 2000).

54. Stiglitz, *Globalization and Its Discontents*.

55. See, for example, Oloka-Onyago and Udagama, "Globalization and Its Impact on the Full Enjoyment of Human Rights."

56. On the invaluable role of civilian participation in "independent humanitarian organizations," see Torrente, "Aid Workers and Military

57. See Beetham, "Human Rights as a Model for Cosmopolitan Democracy"; see also Jacques Derrida, "The Last of the Rogue States: The 'Democracy to Come' Opening in Two Turns," *South Atlantic Quarterly* 103, no. 2/3 (Spring/Summer 2004): 332–33.

58. See Hassner, "Refugees," 277, 283.

59. As Hardt and Negri have argued for in *Empire*; see their introduction.

60. See Daniele Archibugi, "Principles of Cosmopolitan Democracy," and Derk Bienen, Volker Rittberger, and Wolfgang Wagner, "Democracy in the United Nations System: Cosmopolitan and Communitarian Principles," both in Archibugi, Held, and Köhler, *Re-imagining Political Community*, 198–228, 287–308; see also Hassner, "Refugees."

61. Bienen, Rittberger, and Wagner proposed this in "Democracy in the United Nations System."

62. Giorgio Agamben, *Means Without Ends: Notes on Politics*, trans. Vincenzo Binetti and Cesare Casarino (Minneapolis: University of Minnesota Press, 2000), 16.6.

63. On this greater inclusivity (and therefore also exclusivity), see Rogers Brubaker, *Citizenship and Nationhood in France and Germany* (Cambridge: Harvard University Press, 1998). On the history of the U.S. border, see Nevins, *Operation Gatekeeper*. It is unclear if Agamben would agree with my time line; most of his interpreters wrongly believe he contends that these dynamics have been present and explicit throughout history.

64. Arendt, *Origins of Totalitarianism*, 277.

65. See Shah, *Dragon Ladies*; Wright, *Disposable Women*, chap. 7.

66. Sassen, *Globalization and Its Discontents*, 99.

67. This is exemplified in the United Nations Commission on Human Rights's focus on abuses of women for "cultural reasons." See Smith, "Can You Imagine?," 30.

68. Rancière criticizes Arendt and Agamben for formulating statelessness and the exercise of human rights as purely meaningless; I disagree with this interpretation. Again, they both argue (Agamben perhaps more than Arendt) that statelessness is devoid not of politics but rather democracy and the possibility of autonomous political action. "Who Is the Subject of the Rights of Man?," 307.

69. On the critique of rights as the "answer" to human rights issues, see Brown, "The Most We Can Hope For."

70. See Xenos, "Refugees," and Hassner on the danger of individualizing human rights in "Refugees." See also Michael Ignatieff on the value of individual rights in "Introduction: American Exceptionalism and Human Rights," in *American Exceptionalism and Human Rights*, ed. Michael Ignatieff (Princeton: Princeton University Press, 2005), 1–26.

71. In this regard, it is important to note that a significant number of refugees are *internally* displaced. Thus even the definition of statelessness must be interpreted more broadly than it is conventionally used. See Hassner, "Refugees"; Jack Donnelly, *International Human Rights*, 2nd ed. (Boulder, Colo.: Westview Press, 1998).

72. Xenos, "A Patria to Die For."

73. See "Truth and Power" in Michel Foucault, *The Foucault Reader*, ed. Paul Rabinow (New York: Pantheon, 1984), 51–75.

74. Miriam Ching Louie, "Breaking the Cycle: Women Workers Confront Corporate Greed Globally," in Shah, *Dragon Ladies*, 121–31. But one should note Gayatri Spivak's trenchant critiques of UN forums, particularly those that emphasize sororal bonding: see "Cultural Talks in the Hot Peace," and "Righting Wrongs," for example.

75. His example is an indigenous Guatemalan refugee group that represented themselves at United Nations mediation talks with the Guatemalan government. Smith, "Can You Imagine?," 25–26; see also his discussion of a meeting of the Coalition for Immigrant and Refugee Rights and Services with Mujeres Unidas y Activas (a grassroots organization of Latina immigrant women), p. 30.

76. Which I discuss in terms of the homeless in *Homelessness, Citizenship, and Identity: The Uncanniness of Late Modernity* (Albany: SUNY Press, 2004), and in terms of free speech zones and other uses of administrative and judicial power to limit protest in *America's New Working Class* (especially the conclusion).

77. Such as in New York and San Antonio.

78. As Sassen has discussed in terms of the economy; see *Globalization and Its Discontents*, 154.

79. See Honig for a similar critique: *Democracy and the Foreigner*, 106–9.

80. Benhabib, *Another Cosmopolitanism*, 56–58, 67–69.

81. Ibid., 67.

82. Soysal, *Limits of Citizenship*; Keaton, "Arrogant Assimilationism."

83. Keaton, "Arrogant Assimilationism."

84. As Keaton notes in "Arrogant Assimilationism." See also Rancière, "Who Is the Subject of the Rights of Man?"; Bonnie Honig, "Another Cosmopolitanism: Law and Politics in the New Europe," in Benhabib, *Another Cosmopolitanism*, 102–27.

85. See Agamben's implicit critique of discourse ethics in *Remnants of Auschwitz: The Witness and the Archive*, trans. Daniel Heller-Roazen (New York: Zone Books, 1999).

86. See Tirman's critique of human rights as the temporary fix for crises and emergencies: New Humanitarianism."

87. Arendt, *Origins of Totalitarianism*, 269.

88. More specifically, nation-states are vehicles for distributing rights, but human rights norms structure how these rights are legislated and implemented. Soysal, *Limits of Citizenship*, chap. 8.

89. See Seyla Benhabib's analysis of the German case in *Another Cosmopolitanism*. Soysal's earlier analysis is more complex and accounts for Turkish workers in Germany, a group that is still operating outside the bounds of the nation-state. German policy has yet to resolve this and many other issues. See *Limits of Citizenship*.

90. See Brubaker, *Citizenship and Nationhood in France and Germany*, 178. On another note, Soysal's analysis of the French model of immigrant integration is interesting in that this country has some of the highest levels of political mobilization by migrants as well as important instances of democratic "taking." See Soysal, *Limits of Citizenship*, 104–7. In contrast, because countries like Sweden meet nearly every need, there is little mobilization on the ground. See p. 99.

91. See Soysal's analysis of France, as well as her conclusions, in chapter 6 of *Limits of Citizenship*. See also Keaton's "Arrogant Assimilationism" on Muslim girls in the Paris suburbs who consider their identities hybrid.

92. Soysal, *Limits of Citizenship*, 30; see also chap. 3.

93. Even more extreme, it has been argued that these programs were overly tolerant and thus responsible for allowing terrorist cells to form while governments (like Germany) actually funded them. But two of the main countries harboring the 9/11 terrorists were the United States and Britain, and each provides little to no official assistance for immigrant integration.

94. This is not to idealize the treatment of European guest workers, but to note that there have been significant differences in how they are treated as compared to those in the United States.

95. On the legal dynamics of noncitizens' rights (and lack thereof), see Bosniak's analysis in *The Citizen and the Alien*; see also Mark Dow's examination of the war on terror in *American Gulag*, which began before 9/11 and has led to the internment of individuals based on legal status. On the same topic, see Kanstroom, *Deportation Nation*; Tom Barry, "A Death in Texas," *Boston Review*, November/December 2009. See also the language used in Lisaius, "Border Patrol Unveils Military-Style Off Road Vehicle." Finally, the Obama administration has taken advantage of the broadening of presidential powers in important respects. See Editorial, "Mr. Obama and the Rule of Law" (see chap. 2, n. 45); Savage, "Obama's Embrace of Bush Tactic Criticized by Lawmakers."

96. Something that is implied by Robert Post in the introduction to Benhabib, *Another Cosmopolitanism*.

97. See Bauman, *Globalization*.

98. See Hardt and Negri, *Empire*.

99. See Fukuyama, "Immigrants and Family Values"; Fukuyama, "Identity Crisis"; Huntington, "Hispanic Challenge."

100. Alternatively, see Smith's discussion of Mixtecs in "Can You Imagine?," 27–28.

101. Anzaldúa, "How to Tame a Wild Tongue."

102. Anzaldúa, *Borderlands*, 25.

103. Ibid., 26.

104. Ibid., 33.

105. Ibid., 26.

106. Ibid., 34.

107. Agamben, "We Refugees."

108. See Charles Lee, "Bodies in Motion: The Liberal Gaze of Suspicion and Making-Do of the Travel Agents" (paper presented at the Western Political Science Association Meeting, Portland, Ore., March 2004); Nevins, *Operation Gatekeeper*, 180.

109. Bade, *Migration Past, Migration Future*, 29–31.

Index

3m

18289588R00111

Made in the USA
Lexington, KY
26 October 2012